International Marketing

D1591893

BRAD KLEINDL

SOUTH-WESTERN
CENGAGE Learning

Australia • Brazil • Japan • Korea • Mexico • Singapore • Spain • United Kingdom • United States

SOUTH-WESTERN
CENGAGE Learning

International Marketing

Brad Kleindl

VP/Editorial Director
Jack W. Calhoun

VP/Editor-in-Chief
Karen Schmohe

Executive Editor
Eve Lewis

Project Manager
Enid Nagel

Sr. Marketing Manager
Nancy Long

Marketing Coordinator
Angela A. Glassmeyer

Production Manager
Patricia Matthews Boies

Senior Production Project Manager
Kim Kusnerak

Technology Project Manager
Scott Hamilton

Manufacturing Coordinator
Kevin Kluck

Editorial Assistant
Linda Watkins

Art Director
Tippy McIntosh

Cover and Internal Designer
Ann Small, a small design studio

Cover Photo Source
Alamy Images, Corbis, PhotoDisc

Production House
Lachina Publishing Services

Printer
Courier Kendallville, Inc.
Kendallville, IN

For more information about our products, contact us at:

South-Western
5191 Natorp Boulevard
Mason, Ohio 45040
USA

REVIEWERS

ABOUT THE AUTHOR

Brad Kleindl is Dean of the School of Business at Missouri Southern State University. His publications include articles in the *Journal of Developmental Entrepreneurship, Research at the Marketing/Entrepreneurship Interface, Journal of Strategic Marketing, Cross Cultural Management, Management Research News,* and others. Dr. Kleindl has written three books and a chapter on the Internet Value Chain for the Internet Encyclopedia. He has presented papers and has spoken at both academic and industry conferences in the U.S. and around the world. Dr. Kleindl has negotiated business relationships in the U.S., Europe, Asia, South America, and Africa. He was a Senior Fulbright Scholar in South Africa lecturing on Internet marketing, e-business, and e-commerce.

International Marketing
Contents

Destination: Marketing Success

International Marketing is a brand new package that brings excitement and relevance to your marketing course. By presenting key marketing concepts using real examples from the global economy, learning becomes easier and more permanent. DECA Prep activities in every chapter allow users to participate in competitive events in a non-threatening environment, while building presentation skills, marketing competencies, and confidence. Icons in the text visually identify the marketing concepts covered, linking theory to practice.

Instructors save time and improve planning using the wealth of resources in the Multimedia Module. The variety of review and assessment activities integrated throughout the text and supplements streamlines assessment and provides lots of opportunities for reinforcement. Minimize prep time and maximize learning by using these multimedia instructional materials: Annotated Instructor's Edition, Video, ExamView electronic testing CD, and Instructor's Resource CD.

Manage the Course with Multimedia

- **Multimedia Module**   Keep interest levels high and instruction relevant with the wealth of resources included in the Multimedia Module: Video, Instructor's Resource CD, Annotated Instructor's Edition, and ExamView CD

- **Annotated Instructor's Edition***   Teaching suggestions, lesson plans, answers to text activities, and additional resources at point of use make planning, teaching, and assessment easier

- **Instructor's Resource CD***   Lesson Plans, PowerPoint presentations, and video discussion guide questions are portable and easily accessible

- **ExamView CD***   Test creation, delivery, and grading are quick and easy with this complete test bank and electronic assessment tool

- **Video***   Video clips and related discussion questions present real-world examples of chapter content and generate discussion about international marketing

* Included in the Multimedia Module

National Marketing Standards— We've Got You Covered

Your planning and teaching just got a little easier. You can cover national marketing standards using an industry that brings relevance to learners. *International Marketing* follows the **Marketing Education Resource Center®** core standards for the marketing curriculum, described as follows:

Distribution Understands the concepts and processes needed to move, store, locate, and/ or transfer ownership of goods and services

Marketing-Information Management Understands the concepts, systems, and tools needed to gather, access, synthesize, evaluate, and disseminate information for use in making business decisions

Pricing Understands concepts and strategies utilized in determining and adjusting prices to maximize return and meet customers' perceptions of value

Product/Service Management Understands the concepts and processes needed to obtain, develop, maintain, and improve a product or service mix in response to market opportunities

Promotion Understands the concepts and strategies needed to communicate information about products, services, images, and/or ideas to achieve a desired outcome

Selling Understands the concepts and actions needed to determine client needs and wants and respond through planned, personalized communication that influences purchase decisions and enhances future business opportunities

To the Student

WELCOME TO *INTERNATIONAL MARKETING*!

The field of international marketing is rapidly growing. Many universities, colleges, and high schools now offer specializations in international marketing. The general principles of marketing that are presented throughout this book are intended to be a guide in taking your first career step into the exciting world of international marketing. Begin your journey by learning how to plan and market products and services.

The core standards of marketing are visually identified by icons throughout the text.

MARKETING CORE STANDARDS

In addition to the six core standards, the text also covers the important topic of **financing**.

Winning Strategies presents successful, real-world strategies used in international marketing.

Tech Zone investigates the impact of technology and the Internet on international marketing.

Going Global begins each lesson and encourages you to explore the material in the upcoming lesson. Going Global also gives you opportunities to work with other students in your class.

Ethics Around the World examines ethical issues in international marketing.

Marketing Myths explores questionable international marketing strategies or other marketing-related assumptions.

Marketing Myths

Checkpoint provides you with an opportunity to assess your comprehension at key points in each lesson. Ongoing review and assessment helps you understand the material.

Time Out introduces you to interesting facts and statistics about international marketing.

intlmarket.swlearning.com includes Internet activities and crossword puzzles for every chapter.

▶ ▶ ▶ ▶ intlmarket.swlearning.com

Put Marketing on the Map provides you with an ongoing project to develop your own marketing plan.

World Stars acquaints you with people who have succeeded in international marketing.

World Stars

Passport provides end-of-lesson review and critical thinking questions for ongoing assessment.

Passport

DECA Prep prepares you for competitive events with a Case Study and Event Prep in every chapter.

Introduction to International Marketing

CHAPTER 1 · CHAPTER 1 · CHAPTER 1 · CHAPTER 1 · CHAPTER 1

1

© GETTY IMAGES/PHOTODISC

Point Your Browser

▶ ▶ ▶ ▶ ▶ intlmarket.swlearning.com

A Tale of Two Planes

The world is shrinking. Today, global travelers cross the world in jets that fly as far as from New York to Beijing, China. Two major manufacturers are building jets to meet this increased demand. U.S.-based Boeing and Europe's Airbus have adopted two different strategies to meet the world's need for travel.

Airbus started in 1970 as a partnership between the French and German governments. Later, Airbus was joined by a Spanish company and by British Aerospace. Owned primarily by European governments, Airbus is building the world's largest jetliner, the A380. With a wingspan as wide as a football field, the two-story A380 can hold as many as 880 passengers and can fly as far as 8,000 miles without refueling—the distance from London to Sydney, Australia.

Boeing started in California in 1916. Its first orders were from the U.S. military in World War I. Boeing builds airplanes for both the U.S. military and for commercial airlines. Boeing is building a 787 Dreamliner, which will hold about 260 passengers and will be able to fly as far as 8,500 miles without refueling.

These two companies are on the verge of setting off a global trade war. Boeing complains that Airbus receives European government subsidies. A subsidy is financial assistance granted by the government. Airbus claims that Boeing has received more than $5 billion in U.S. government subsidies to pay for the 787's research and development. This trade war could block sales of these jets and other products.

International marketing is often complicated by national interests. Marketers must be concerned with building products to meet customers' needs and also must take into consideration the political, legal, and cultural differences that exist around the world.

Think Critically

1. Discuss the differences between the Airbus A380 and Boeing 787 Dreamliner strategies and the benefits of both.

2. Why do you think governments would subsidize airplane manufacturers?

International Marketing Basics

Goals

- Describe what drives the need for international marketing.
- Explain the core standards for marketing.

Terms

- international marketing
- distribution
- marketing-information management
- pricing
- product/service management
- promotion
- selling
- financing

Going Global

The United States was a winner in more than military terms at the end of World War II. U.S. factories were undamaged, and the economy was growing strongly. The GI Bill made it possible for a record number of people to receive college degrees. The United States was well positioned to win a global business and marketing race and to become a dominant global business power.

Over the last 60 years, countries around the world have recovered economically. The fall of the Iron Curtain in the Soviet Union and the opening of China for trade are allowing for a truly global marketplace. Many countries now have modern factories, skilled labor, financial resources, and strong marketing programs. Countries are competing with high-quality products and low prices. This global development opens an opportunity for new markets. It is creating intense competition, forcing all companies to operate in a globally competitive environment.

Work with a partner and discuss how global competition would change the way in which a U.S.-based company would need to compete.

MARKETING FOUNDATIONS

A series of activities that creates an exchange that satisfies the individual customer across national borders is known as **international marketing**. As with domestic marketing, this process begins with identifying the customer's needs and then planning to meet those needs. International marketing is more complicated because the goods or services customers desire can be different across cultures. In addition, marketing activities may need to be adjusted because of geographic, competitive, cultural, or legal differences.

Companies use a variety of strategies to engage in international marketing. This could vary from engaging in importing and exporting to issuing licensing agreements giving foreign companies the right to sell a company's product for a fee. Other strategies may include participating in joint ventures with companies in other countries or using a wholly owned subsidiary, which is an independent company owned by a parent company. Wal-Mart is the world's largest retailer. It started in the United States and has expanded into new markets. In 1991, Wal-Mart entered Mexico as a wholly owned subsidiary without a Mexican partner. In 1998, Wal-Mart entered Germany by purchasing an existing business. In 2002, Wal-Mart entered Japan in partnership with another company. Including the United States, Wal-Mart is in eleven countries around the world. Wal-Mart has attempted to use the same retailing strategy in each of the countries it has entered.

Global Drivers of International Marketing

International marketing is growing in importance for a number of reasons. The world is getting smaller, not only because of jet travel but also because of advances in technology. The Internet now connects customers to businesses around the world. New transportation systems make shipping fast and efficient. New market opportunities exist due to the fall of the Iron Curtain, the opening of trade in China, and the economic development of new markets such as South America, Africa, and Southeast Asia.

Communication technology has shrunk the world more than any other factor. Individuals around the world are seeing the same movies, television shows, and Internet content. Companies can use these media to send the same message around the globe.

Transportation systems are delivering products much faster and cheaper than in the past. Containerized shipping allows companies to package their products in sealed containers for ocean shipping. These ships use satellite technology to avoid bad weather. They can cross the Pacific Ocean from Asia to the United States in ten days. Smaller shipments can be sent almost anywhere in the world by shipping companies such as UPS, FedEx, and DHL.

The strongest driver of international marketing is the opening of new markets around the world. As trade barriers have been dropping, personal income has been increasing worldwide. According to World Bank data, the United States ranks 18th in the world in personal income. Companies look to these new markets for growth opportunities. If U.S.-based companies do not enter these new markets early, they may not have the opportunity later.

Ethics Around the World

Star Wars: Episode III Revenge of the Sith was attacked by pirates within hours of its release in movie theaters. Within one day of its release, copies of the movie were available online and from street vendors. Movie piracy is a multibillion-dollar worldwide business. U.S. Immigration and Customs Enforcement agencies attempt to limit distribution of these movies, but they can control only U.S. borders.

China is considered to be the center of movie piracy. In Beijing, the *Star Wars* premiere was attended by top American studio executives to help stress to the Chinese government that it should attempt to end movie piracy. Movie theater attendance for *Xishi de Fanji* (the Chinese name for the *Star Wars* movie) was very light in China.

THINK CRITICALLY

1. What impact do you think the sale of pirated movies has on the movie industry as a whole?
2. Should American movie executives consider releasing their films only in countries that have anti-piracy laws? Why or why not?

The United States accounts for only $3.8 trillion of the $7 trillion in worldwide annual retail sales.

Planning for International Marketing

Pursuing global market opportunities can be riskier than selling in a local market. This increases the need for developing an international marketing plan. To engage in marketing, all businesses need to create, communicate, and deliver value to customers and manage customer relationships in ways that benefit the organization and its stakeholders. Profit-oriented businesses must be able to create a *profit*, which is the amount of money from sales and services remaining after all costs have been paid.

Businesses that engage in international marketing must understand how marketing activities differ in the cultures they are entering. In addition, businesses must understand how customers' needs differ and how not to offend in advertising or sales. Legal and political environments also are different. Companies must be sure that they will be paid for the products they sell. Even though international marketing can increase risk, global markets are too large and too important to ignore.

International Professional Development

Careers related to international marketing require a range of skills and educational levels, from a high school diploma to a college degree. The ability to communicate in a foreign language often is required, but a strong competency in English is a necessity. You should develop a cultural understanding of the country in which you will work. Technology skills are also important because various technologies may be used to conduct business globally. It would be beneficial to have some international experience either from traveling or living abroad. Student exchange programs offer excellent ways to learn about another country.

Checkpoint

List three of the major drivers of international marketing.

_____

_____

MARKETING CORE STANDARDS

The six core standards of marketing identified in the National Standards for Marketing Management, Entrepreneurship, and Business Administration include distribution, marketing-information management, pricing, product/service management, promotion, and selling. The six core standards of marketing are involved in every transfer of goods and services to the consumer. Businesses provide many of these. Consumers often are responsible for one or more when they make purchases.

DISTRIBUTION

Distribution involves determining the best methods and procedures to allow customers to locate, obtain, and use the products and services of an organization. Careful shipping, handling, and storing of products are needed for effective distribution.

Marketing-information management is obtaining, managing, and using market information to improve business decision making and the performance of marketing activities. This includes marketing research and the development of databases with information about products, customers, and competitors.

Pricing means establishing the price of the products and services. A business must price the products and services low enough that customers are willing to buy but high enough that the business can make a profit. Pricing can mean the difference between making a sale and losing it.

Product/service management is designing, developing, maintaining, improving, and acquiring products and services to meet consumer needs. Producers and manufacturers develop products, but other businesses are involved in product/service management when they obtain the products for resale.

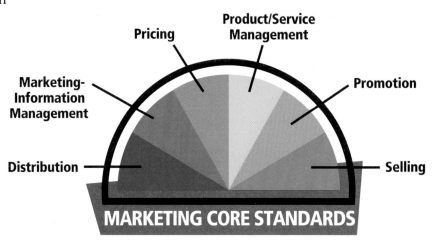

MARKETING CORE STANDARDS

Pricing · Product/Service Management · Marketing-Information Management · Promotion · Distribution · Selling

Promotion is communicating to potential customers about a company's products and services. This can be done using a variety of methods such as advertising, publicity, public relations, and personal selling.

Selling is communicating directly with prospective customers to assess and satisfy their needs. Selling can be face to face, such as when a customer visits a business or when a salesperson goes to the home or business of a prospective customer. Selling also can be performed using a telephone or other technology, including Internet tools such as instant messaging or videoconferencing.

In addition to these six core standards, this text will also cover the important topic of financing. **Financing** is budgeting for marketing activities, obtaining the necessary funds needed for operations, and helping customers purchase the business's products and services. Good financing strategies help ensure that a company stays in business.

Name the six core standards of marketing.

Checkpoint

Passport

Understand Marketing Concepts

Circle the best answer for each of the following questions.

1. International marketing is
   a. getting people to buy things
   b. understanding business motive
   c. creating satisfying exchange relationships across national borders
   d. none of the above

2. Four of the six core standards of marketing are
   a. selling, distribution, promotion, and pricing
   b. exchanges, distribution, pricing, and promotion
   c. purchasing, planning, advertising, and distribution
   d. planning, distribution, pricing, and advertising

Think Critically

Answer the following questions as completely as possible. If necessary, use a separate sheet of paper.

3. Explain some of the factors that must be considered when planning to engage in international marketing.

_____

_____

_____

_____

_____

_____

_____

4. **Communication** China is considered to be the center of movie piracy. If you were a top movie executive, how would you communicate to Chinese officials the need to stop movie piracy?

_____

_____

_____

_____

_____

_____

_____

International Marketing Foundations

Goals
- Explain the importance of international marketing.
- Describe the positive and negative arguments for free trade.

Terms
- gross domestic product (GDP)
- free trade
- mercantilism
- fair trade

Going Global

In the 1950s, Japan exported toy cars made from discarded tin cans to the United States. In the 1970s, Japan exported compact cars to the United States. In the 1990s, Japanese car companies were major car manufacturers in the United States. Today, "Made in China" is commonly associated with low quality and cheap products. The United States exports raw materials such as cotton and steel to China and receives back t-shirts and finished steel products. These are higher value-added products.

The United States has a *balance of trade* (the difference between exports and imports) deficit with China of more than $125 billion annually. This means that the

United States imports more products from China than it exports to China. Why does this matter if consumers in the United States get the benefit of cheaper products? Trade deficits can have an impact on currency exchange rates and inflation. These are concerns that consumers don't see but that governments worry about. China may be sending toys today, but it plans to send cars soon.

Work with a partner and compile a list of reasons why a trade deficit could cause problems for the United States.

THE ROLE OF INTERNATIONAL MARKETING

International trade does more than just bring cheap products to consumers. International trade improves the world's economy. Countries that trade together are much less likely to go to war. They have shared interests and economic ties. One of the factors given as a cause of the 1930s worldwide depression was the closing of international trade to protect home markets.

The United States has a tradition of focusing on its internal market. The U.S. economy is the largest in the world, with a gross domestic product of more than $10 trillion. The **gross domestic product (GDP)** is the total value of all goods and services produced in an economic region. Western Europe is the second largest economy with a GDP of more than $8 trillion. Japan has a GDP of close to $5 trillion, and China and India combined have a GDP of close to $1.6 trillion. These regions represent a

considerable marketing opportunity for companies in the United States. The problem is that the United States can be seen as one market while each of the countries in Europe and in Asia needs to be seen as unique markets. This situation makes exporting products to the United States easier than devising separate international marketing strategies for each of the other markets in other countries.

A Short History of International Marketing

DISTRIBUTION

International trade is not new. Archeologists have found Stone Age trading objects that were carried over long distances. International traders were often the first explorers, discovering new lands and new objects to trade. One of the oldest continuous trading routes is the Silk Road. This is a series of trails and sea routes that allowed trade between China and the Middle East. This trade route was so important that the Romans developed a series of forts along part of its 4,000-mile length.

Most large cities in the ancient world acted as international trading centers. Products from around the world would find their way to these central market locations where they would be traded. North America was discovered and explored by individuals and by companies, such as the Hudson Bay Company, seeking new products and markets.

Marketing scholars differ on whether or not these traders engaged in marketing as it is currently defined. However, traders could not sell a product that did not meet their customers' needs.

The Movement Toward Free Trade

Totally free trade between countries is not the norm. **Free trade** allows for unhindered trade of legal goods and services between countries. Free trade allows products to be sold in markets at whatever price the seller is willing to accept. Free trade provides an incentive for a low-cost producer to sell products in new markets, which can put a local producer at a disadvantage. Many countries have developed policies to limit free trade in order to protect local businesses.

An extreme example of limiting free trade is a mercantilist approach. **Mercantilism** is a strategy in which a nation promotes exports but limits imports. This strategy is based on the idea that a country benefits when it is able to pull in the wealth from another country by having a positive trade balance. This idea was popular when payments were made in gold or silver bullion. When mercantilism is practiced today, it can cause the exporting country's currency to become overvalued, leading to economic problems.

Today, the most widely held belief is that free trade is good for all economies. While free trade may create problems in the short term, it should lead to economic development over the long term. Countries try to balance the desire for open markets with the concerns of locally based companies that want to protect their markets and their businesses.

Define gross domestic product (GDP).

Checkpoint

Time Out

If Wal-Mart were its own country, its economy would be 23rd in the world, with a GDP right behind Austria. More than 70 percent of the products sold at Wal-Mart are made in China.

ARGUMENTS FOR AND AGAINST FREE TRADE

Adam Smith argued against mercantilism in his book *An Inquiry into the Nature and Causes of the Wealth of Nations*, published in 1776. Smith's arguments against mercantilism were based on the economic idea that free trade increases the total number of goods and services produced by having individuals specialize in areas where they have an advantage. For example, a country may have abundant farmland and good, year-round weather conditions, giving it the advantage over other countries of growing and exporting produce. Allowing free trade also is seen as a way for exporting countries to import more products. Exporters should be able to increase their wealth, allowing them to purchase more imported products from other countries.

Another argument for free trade is that it lowers the chance of war. Taiwan and China have had a tense relationship since the communist takeover of mainland China in the 1950s. Today, the chance of an armed conflict seems unlikely as the Taiwanese and Chinese economies are strongly linked with more than $25 billion in trade. Likewise, the economic union in Europe has resulted in more than 50 years of peace after centuries of conflict.

Free trade is seen as a means of increasing the quality of life by introducing new products and services to individuals.

© GETTY IMAGES/PHOTODISC

Information flows through the Internet across the globe. High bandwidth connections allow for richer content, such as video, to be sent to individuals' homes. The United States is behind many other countries in high bandwidth connections. The world leaders in high bandwidth connections in homes are found in Singapore, South Korea, Sweden, and Hong Kong.

THINK CRITICALLY

List the advantages that a high-speed Internet connection offers to a user. Specify how these high-speed Internet connections can allow these countries to gain a competitive advantage in learning how to market over the Internet.

Open markets increase a customer's choice of products. This includes products from television shows to food items and cars. Free trade also forces competitors to become more efficient, improving quality and lowering costs and prices.

Free trade also is a means of lowering poverty. Low-wage countries have an advantage because they can produce products at a lower cost. Increased demand for their labor should lead to higher salaries, job training, and higher standards of living.

There are a number of arguments against free trade. These include the idea that free trade often benefits more advanced countries. For example, countries that sell raw materials may become locked into selling only those products because they have limited resources to produce and sell other goods. Some countries may only outsource parts of the production process, which may not create more total products. Free trade also can be seen as being socially disruptive. Culturally dominant countries, such as the United States, may be viewed as exporting their culture (clothing, food, and so on) around the world. Another argument is that there is no such thing as pure free trade. Instead, countries always try to protect some aspect of their economies by restricting trade.

Many people argue for fair trade. **Fair trade** is a commitment to buy products at a fair price and with labeling that identifies the source of the products. The idea is to allow sellers in developing markets to be recognized and rewarded for their production. For example, Starbucks sells fair-trade coffee. This allows Starbucks to develop relationships with impoverished coffee growers instead of the large coffee wholesalers. The coffee growers receive premium prices, have access to credit, set socially desirable work standards, conserve farmland, and receive aid through social development programs. Starbucks uses the fair-trade labeling on its coffee to promote its socially responsible image.

Checkpoint

Name three arguments against free trade.

_____

_____

_____

Understand Marketing Concepts

Circle the best answer for each of the following questions.

1. Which of the following is *not* an argument in favor of free trade?
   a. an increased quality of life
   b. a means of lowering poverty
   c. benefits for more advanced countries
   d. none of the above

2. Mercantilism is
   a. a strategy that promotes exports but limits imports
   b. a means of marketing a product all over the world
   c. a commitment to buy products at a fair price
   d. a way to limit exports while increasing imports

Think Critically

Answer the following questions as completely as possible. If necessary, use a separate sheet of paper.

3. Briefly describe the concept of fair trade and the benefits of this type of practice.

_____

_____

_____

_____

_____

_____

_____

_____

4. Communication Write a letter to the leader of a small developing country that has implemented a mercantilism strategy explaining why that country would benefit from free trade.

_____

_____

_____

_____

_____

_____

_____

_____

_____

International Marketing Strategies

- Describe the various levels of commitment to international marketing.
- Explain the steps in developing an international marketing plan.

- no active international marketing strategy
- surplus driven international marketing

- international marketing strategy
- global marketing strategy

Going Global

McDonald's is a global marketing company. It has restaurants in more than 120 countries around the world. Each McDonald's has the same look and feel. You can see the logo and the colors from the outside. You enter the doors to see the order counter and open kitchen area. The tables and chairs look the same. Differences are found once you order.

While most of the food items are similar, changes are made to meet taste in individual countries. For example, in Asia, rice is often a side order. In Taiwan, a burger can be served between two rice cakes. In Europe, beer is often offered on the menu. McDonald's has a global strategy with individual cultural variations.

In a group, visit the McDonald's web site. Choose a foreign country from the site's list. Click on the links to explore the site and compare this McDonald's to a U.S. site. Discuss the similarities and differences.

LEVELS OF COMMITMENT

MARKETING–INFORMATION MANAGEMENT

Companies engaging in international marketing have two major strategic considerations. The first is their level of commitment. The second is how much they are willing to change their marketing strategies for new markets.

Companies commit to international marketing at varying levels. The first level is to have **no active international marketing strategy**. This does not mean that these companies will not sell in international markets. They may receive and respond to an order, but they do not actively seek out international sales.

Surplus driven international marketing occurs when a company has excess inventory that it cannot sell in its home market. This can lead to infrequent efforts to sell its products overseas. The company is not devoting any resources to develop and maintain international sales.

With an **international marketing strategy**, a company commits and plans to sell to international markets. This strategy can occur at two levels. At the lowest level, a company focuses its marketing strategy on a single international market. With a more committed strategy, a company plans and develops strategies for multiple markets around the world.

The highest level of commitment is a **global marketing strategy**. With a global marketing strategy, a company treats the entire world, including its home country, as potential markets. These companies focus on global market segments, not individual countries. Companies that follow this strategy develop products to serve global markets. For example, the Coca-Cola Company follows a global marketing strategy. It focuses on using its marketing strategy to serve similar markets around the world. As another example, the chairman of Honda once said that he didn't care where Honda had its global headquarters. Today, Honda has more production plants and sales in the United States than in Japan.

Companies that commit to international marketing at lower levels may be unwilling to change their product strategies for foreign markets. Failing to do so, however, could increase their costs in those markets. As companies increase their level of commitment, they are more likely to develop a marketing strategy that is unique for the new markets. Companies with global marketing strategies look to develop products that can be sold around the world with variations in strategy to meet unique market demands.

Time Out

McDonald's worldwide sales actually reduce economic risk for the company. In 2004, U.S.-based stores gained sales. Although European sales were flat, sales in Asia, the Middle East, and Africa increased.

Checkpoint

List the four levels of commitment to international marketing.

DEVELOPING AN INTERNATIONAL MARKETING PLAN

MARKETING-INFORMATION MANAGEMENT

Entering international markets requires a new understanding and a well-thought-out plan to reduce risk. An international marketing plan requires investigating a country's culture and its economy, conducting a competitive analysis, and then developing a plan. The plan must set marketing activities so that a company can enter a market by meeting customer needs.

A cultural analysis is an important first step in developing a marketing plan. Evaluating a culture allows a company to understand the nature of customer needs and the meanings behind behaviors. For example, karaoke started in Japan in the 1980s. Karaoke is a Japanese compound word consisting of "kara," which comes from "karappo," meaning empty, and "oke," which is an abbreviation of "okesutura," meaning orchestra. When you put them together, you have "empty orchestra." In the United States, people sing karaoke for fun. In Asia, businessmen often use karaoke. It is a way for Asians, who often do not like to openly express emotion, to show their emotions through their singing.

© GETTY IMAGES/PHOTODISC

An economic analysis of a country should include more than just raw data. This part of the plan should look at population characteristics such as distribution of age and income. It also should consider factors such as national GDP and wealth distribution. At the same time, an economic analysis should include the nature of the current marketing system such as retail stores, wholesalers, transportation systems, and media.

A competitive analysis should analyze who the competitors are, what competitive products are sold, and how well the needs of the market are being served. This analysis can help a company determine how to design its product offerings to gain an advantage over its competitors.

The marketer must implement the core standards of marketing to fit the unique nature of the international market. The core standards of marketing must connect to the information discovered about the country's culture, its economic conditions, and competing products.

Checkpoint

What four steps are parts of an international marketing plan?

World Stars | HERBERT HAINER

In 1987, Herbert Hainer went to work for Adidas, the number two sportswear company in the world, second only to Nike. Hainer started as a sales director for Adidas products before becoming the CEO in 2001. He now oversees Adidas's global operations and is often credited as the driving force behind Adidas's comeback in the sporting goods market.

Hainer is a marketing professional who realizes that markets differ around the world. For example, in Europe, customers buy fewer than two pairs of sports shoes per year while Americans buy between six and seven pairs each year. In search of other growing markets, Adidas and Hainer have turned their attention to China. Adidas has 1,500 stores in China, and it opens another 40 stores each month. Under Hainer's leadership, Adidas has been selected as the official outfitter of the National Olympic Committee in China for 2008.

Despite Adidas's marketing successes, Hainer still faces challenges in the marketplace, such as the counterfeiting problem in China. Chinese authorities confiscate between 4 million and 6 million pieces of counterfeit apparel each year. Hainer continues to help Adidas retain its market leadership by developing new product technologies and using innovative marketing strategies. In 2005, Adidas and Hainer were working on a deal to purchase a major competitor, Reebok International Ltd., to gain an even bigger share of the international market.

THINK CRITICALLY

Explain why Herbert Hainer needs to have a strong understanding of the different markets where Adidas sells.

Understand Marketing Concepts

Circle the best answer for each of the following questions.

1. An international marketing strategy is
   a. selling excess inventory to a foreign country
   b. investigating a country's culture and economy
   c. treating the entire world as a market
   d. committing and planning to sell internationally

2. Which of the following is *not* a step in developing an international marketing plan?
   a. selling various products first to see which ones will be bought
   b. conducting a competitive analysis
   c. investigating a country's culture
   d. examining the economy of a country

Think Critically

Answer the following questions as completely as possible. If necessary, use a separate sheet of paper.

3. Briefly describe the four commitment levels of international marketing and give one advantage for each.

_____

_____

_____

_____

_____

_____

4. What factors need to be considered when doing an economic analysis of a country?

_____

_____

_____

_____

_____

_____

Review Marketing Concepts

Write the letter of the term that matches each definition. Some terms may not be used.

_____ 1. Total value of all goods and services produced in an economic region

_____ 2. A commitment to buy products at a fair price

_____ 3. A strategy where a company responds to international orders but does not actively seek them

_____ 4. A series of activities that creates an exchange that satisfies the individual customer across national borders

_____ 5. Strategy in which a nation promotes exports but limits imports

_____ 6. Communicating directly with prospective customers to assess and satisfy their needs

_____ 7. Selling inventory internationally when it cannot be sold in home markets

_____ 8. Designing, developing, maintaining, improving, and acquiring products and services to meet consumer needs

_____ 9. Communicating to potential customers about a company's products and services

_____ 10. Budgeting for marketing activities, obtaining funds needed for operations, and helping customers purchase your products and services

a. distribution
b. fair trade
c. financing
d. free trade
e. global marketing strategy
f. gross domestic product (GDP)
g. international marketing
h. international marketing strategy
i. marketing-information management
j. mercantilism
k. no active international marketing strategy
l. pricing
m. product/service management
n. promotion
o. selling
p. surplus driven international marketing

Circle the best answer.

11. International marketing is
    a. focused on only large countries
    b. selling goods to a company's home country
    c. driven by changes in technology, transportation systems, and new markets
    d. done only by companies with an existing foreign presence

12. What was the Hudson Bay Company searching for in the United States?
    a. religious freedom
    b. new products and markets
    c. land to colonize
    d. gold

Think Critically

13. Explain some of the factors that must be considered when planning to conduct international marketing.

_____

_____

_____

_____

14. Name the two marketing core standards that you recognize most often. Why do you think those are the most recognizable?

_____

_____

_____

_____

15. What are the advantages and disadvantages of having a global marketing strategy?

_____

_____

_____

_____

16. Think about some of the products you use on a daily basis. Identify where some of those products were produced. Explain the role of international marketing in your purchase and use of those products.

_____

_____

_____

_____

_____

17. On the Internet, research the North American Free Trade Agreement (NAFTA). What do you see as the benefits of this agreement? What are the downfalls?

_____

_____

_____

_____

_____

Make Connections

18. **Geography** Use the Internet to find the population of India. Why would it be important for a U.S.-based company to consider exporting to India?

_____

_____

_____

_____

19. **History** Use the Internet and other resources to learn about the Silk Road. Why was it developed and what was its purpose?

_____

_____

_____

_____

20. **Research** Your company is considering marketing your product to China. Use the Internet to find the population of China and the purchasing power per capita (per person). If your product sells for $2,000, should you market it to China? Explain your answer.

_____

_____

_____

_____

21. **Marketing Math** Mexico has approximately 100 million people who each have an estimated $10,000 in purchasing power. If McDonald's were to market to Mexico and capture one percent of the purchasing power for one-tenth of the population, how much revenue would that generate?

_____

_____

_____

_____

22. **Research** Using the Internet, search for information comparing the export statistics for the United States and two other countries. Determine the total export dollars, exports per capita, and exports by GDP. Describe the importance of exports to the United States versus the other two countries you chose. (*Hint:* The NationMaster web site is one good source for this data.)

_____

_____

_____

_____

23. **Geography** Look at a map of Europe. Count the number of countries. Assume that at least one unique language is spoken in each country. Explain why a company would find it easier to enter the U.S. market than the European market.

_____

_____

_____

_____

PUT MARKETING ON THE MAP

International Marketing Plan Project

An international marketing plan is built around a company's desire to sell a product in an international market. Your plan will need to be built around a product idea.

Work with a group and complete the following activities.

1. Identify a product that you think you would like to sell internationally. It can be a new or existing product. Write a description of the product.
2. Specify the characteristics of the market segment to which you want to sell.
3. Identify a country where you would like to sell your product.
4. Explain the reasons you think the product would or would not need to be changed for this international market.
5. Create a short PowerPoint presentation about the history and current economic status of the country you have chosen. Include reasons why this would be a good country in which to sell your product.

Case Study

INTERNATIONAL FLORAL INDUSTRY

Cut flowers recently comprised almost half of total U.S. imports of floral and nursery products. Live plants, trees, and cuttings are the second-largest import group. U.S. floral and nursery exports (mostly live plants, trees, and foliage) represented less than a quarter of imports. Sales of domestic cut flowers were down and sales of domestic flowering plants were flat.

Colombia, Ecuador, the European Union, and Mexico provide most of the cut-flower imports. The most popular include fresh roses (about 36 percent), carnations (13 percent), and chrysanthemums (11 percent). Lower production costs in Colombia, Ecuador, and Mexico are driving forces behind the business. A strong U.S. dollar that has boosted the purchasing power of U.S. consumers has led to stronger sales of imported flowers.

In the 1990s, the United States began seeing an increase in imports of flowering plants, predominantly from Canada. Taiwan, The Netherlands, Costa Rica, Thailand, and China are other major suppliers of flowering plants. The North American Free Trade Agreement (NAFTA) helped open the market, and exports of horticulture crops to the United States have dramatically expanded. A thriving U.S. housing market has increased the need for landscaping materials.

The weak Canadian dollar has helped keep prices low for exported flowering and bedding plants. Mexico is able to keep export costs low because it has lower transport costs compared to other cut flower exporters such as Colombia and Ecuador.

Production of major cut flowers—roses, carnations, and chrysanthemums—has shifted from U.S. to South and Central American growers who have year-round production, lower labor costs, and little or no energy costs. U.S. growers have focused on growing higher-value specialty cut flowers (orchids, irises, lilies, and tulips). U.S. sales of cut specialty flowers equal 25 percent of total U.S. cut-flower sales.

Canada purchases almost 80 percent of U.S. floral exports. Large floral trade between the countries can be attributed to the long-standing absence of major U.S. and Canadian restrictions on plant imports with soil attached. Other countries are now allowed to export plants in various forms to the United States.

THINK CRITICALLY

1. Why has the cut-flower market become so competitive?
2. What factors have caused the price of cut flowers to go down for consumers?
3. What special concerns may be raised when conducting business with Central and South America?
4. What advantage does Mexico have in the cut-flower industry?

You have been hired by a major supermarket chain to design an in-store promotion to build a loyal customer base for its new full-service floral department. The floral department in this supermarket chain will be able to offer a wide variety of cut flowers throughout the year because it imports from warm climate countries. Cut flowers are guaranteed to last for seven days after purchase. If the flowers perish before that time, customers will receive a refund. All employees working in the floral department have certification in floral design. These professionals will give guidance on flowers for weddings, funerals, and other important events. Free delivery will be made locally for purchases of $25 or more.

A lot of competition exists in the local floral industry. The supermarket that has hired you can sell flowers for up to 50 percent less than other florists due to the large quantity purchased by the supermarket chain. Since the supermarket chain regularly purchases so many floral imports, it can order and receive special shipments on short notice. The supermarket is located in an area where agriculture and regional flower growers are predominant. Because of this, the supermarket must also be sensitive to the local nursery and flower growers.

You must design a local in-store promotion to generate business for the supermarket floral department.

Performance Indicators Evaluated

- Understand the challenge and opportunity facing the local supermarket.
- Emphasize the advantages of buying flowers from a supermarket.
- Highlight the professional service available at the supermarket floral department.
- Design an in-store promotional strategy that will attract repeat customers.

Go to the DECA web site for more detailed information.

THINK CRITICALLY

1. Why is a promotion necessary to introduce a new department in an existing business?
2. Why should the new floral department create a relationship with the local flower growers?
3. What special services offered by this floral department make it unique compared to its numerous competitors?
4. Can you think of other ways the supermarket can increase sales in its floral department, such as selling other products that complement the sale of flowers or sponsoring special community events?

www.deca.org

Environment of International Marketing

© BRAND X PICTURES

Point Your Browser

► ► ► ► intlmarket.swlearning.com

A Rice Culture

Rice is the main food in Japan, just as bread is the main food in many Western cultures. For the Japanese, rice is more than rice. The Japanese word for cooked rice, *gohan*, is also the word for meal. Rice straw, or *wara*, has been used for thousands of years to make clothing, mats, and household items. Rice planting is a cultural and religious event.

The United States is very efficient in producing food, including rice. U.S. rice farms often cover many square miles. They use highly mechanized planting and harvesting methods. Japanese rice farms are small. They average only 1.5 acres. Countries such as Thailand and Vietnam have low labor costs. They are major exporters of rice.

Japanese consumers pay up to seven times as much for rice as U.S. consumers do. Japanese consumers pay such a high price because of Japanese government policies. Japan pays almost $2 billion a year to support rice farmers. In addition, Japan imposes a 700 percent tariff (tax on imported goods) to increase imported rice prices to the same level as domestic rice prices. Japanese rice growers claim that Japanese rice is superior to all imported rice. The farmers' lobby in Japan is very powerful in Japanese politics. It is difficult for foreign rice growers to market their products in Japan. Japan views foreign rice as being inferior, and foreign rice cannot be sold at prices that reflect its true cost of production.

Economic theory shows that countries gain from free trade. However, governments try to justify their reasons for limiting free trade between countries. International agreements have been put in place over time to limit trade restrictions. These agreements allow companies to engage in international marketing to develop, promote, and sell their products based on their competitive advantages. A competitive advantage is something a company does better, faster, or cheaper than other companies do.

Think Critically

1. Discuss what would happen if Japan were to remove all tariffs on rice imports.

2. Explain why Japanese consumers continue to purchase domestically grown rice.

International Trade Basics

Goals

- Describe the concept of comparative advantage.
- Define factors of production and identify some examples.

Terms

- absolute advantage
- comparative advantage
- production possibility curve
- opportunity cost
- commodity
- factors of production

Going Global

In the early 1800s, the United States was an infant economy. It had only a 1.8 percent share of global GDP. By the eve of World War I in 1913, it was the world's leading economy with 18.9 percent of global GDP. The United States was helped by a wealth of natural resources and a hard-working population. Open world markets allowed inventions and products to move around the world without much governmental interference. After World War I, global free trade slowed due to political instability and high tariffs.

Since the early 1980s, a different infant economy is on the verge of becoming the largest economy in the world. China had 3.2 percent of global GDP in 1980. In 2004, it had 13 percent. By 2015, it may be the global leader with 20.3 percent. This growth is possible because world markets are now more open to free trade. China has been able to take advantage of being a low-wage producer. China also is educating its people and investing in new plants and equipment. The United States is facing a global challenger in the world's economic race.

Working with a partner, discuss how the rise of China can help the world's economy. Consider what the United States will need to do to remain competitive.

THEORY OF COMPARATIVE ADVANTAGE

PRODUCT/SERVICE MANAGEMENT

International marketers must understand the basics of international trade. They must know trade theories. They must be aware of the types of barriers that are erected to limit trade. They also must know the institutions that exist to help marketers sell products globally. International marketers must become advocates of lowering trade barriers and using trade organizations for support.

Economists propose theories to explain how economic systems operate. One theory includes the concepts of absolute advantage and comparative advantage. **Absolute advantage** means that a country can produce more units of a product at a lower cost using fewer resources than other countries. For example, the United States has an absolute advantage over Japan in rice and cotton production. This means that the United States can produce much more rice and cotton at a lower cost per unit than Japan. These absolute advantages do not mean that the United States should be the sole producer of both products. Japan can have a comparative advantage in production for one of the products. The law of **comparative advantage** states that a country should specialize in the production of a product that it can produce relatively better, or more efficiently, than other countries. For example, rice production makes better use of Japan's resources than cotton production. Cotton production makes better use of the United States' resources than rice production. Thus, Japan is relatively more efficient than the United States is in producing rice, and the United States is relatively more efficient than Japan is in producing cotton.

© GETTY IMAGES/PHOTODISC

These concepts are illustrated in the following graphs. Graph A shows production possibility curves for rice and cotton production. A **production possibility curve** shows the tradeoff in production between two products. Each country can produce both cotton and rice, but producing more of one product reduces production of the other. Each country's production possibility curve has a different tradeoff slope. This tradeoff slope represents an opportunity cost.

An **opportunity cost** is the value of what is given up in producing one product when another product is produced. The United States can produce both more cotton and more rice than Japan, but it has a different opportunity cost tradeoff. For example, Japan is more efficient in producing rice over cotton. As Japan gives up units of cotton production, it moves to the right along the dashed line. In doing so, it can produce more units of rice than the number of units of cotton it has given up. As the United States gives up rice production, it moves to the left along the solid line. In doing so, it can produce more units of cotton than the number of units of rice it has given up.

Graph A
Production Possibility Curves

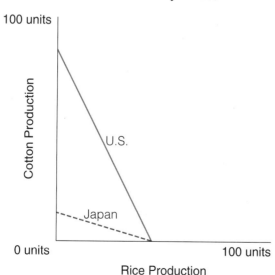

Japan and the United States want to use both cotton and rice. They could try to produce both products for themselves, but this would mean a limited supply of one of the products. By focusing on their areas of comparative advantage, both countries could meet their internal needs. They could use the excess production to trade for the other product.

Graph B shows the total production capacity of both countries when they focus on areas where they have a comparative advantage. If the United States focused on cotton production and traded to Japan for rice, both countries would be better off. The total amount of both products would be greater.

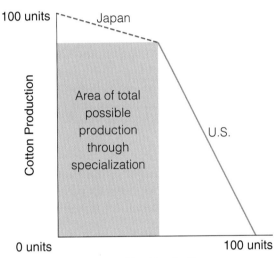

Graph B
Total Production Capacities

Why then don't countries focus on one product? Some countries do focus on producing commodities. A **commodity** is a raw material or agricultural product. Therefore a commodity may be the same regardless of who produces it. For example, many consumers consider rice to be of the same quality no matter where it is produced. Given this, consumers will purchase rice that is exported from most any country. Surprisingly, Thailand is the world's leading exporter of rice, not Japan. Most countries do not want to rely upon other nations to provide all of their products, so they attempt to maintain production in key areas such as food. Countries also try to make their production processes more efficient. By doing this, they increase their comparative advantages over other countries.

Checkpoint

Explain the difference between absolute advantage and comparative advantage.

_____

_____

_____

GLOBAL FACTORS OF PRODUCTION

PRODUCT/SERVICE MANAGEMENT

A country's comparative advantage comes from its factors of production. **Factors of production** are items that are used to produce products. They include the following:

- **natural resources** such as land, forests, minerals, oil, and bodies of water

- **human resources** (or labor) such as workers, management, and entrepreneurs

- **capital resources** (or manmade items) such as buildings, machinery, and funds

Countries use these factors of production to produce goods and services that meet the needs and wants of consumers worldwide. A country can utilize its factors of production in different ways to help it gain a comparative advantage. Developed countries, such as the United States, have a comparative advantage in a highly skilled workforce. This comparative advantage has allowed developed countries to create higher-value products. These products include complicated machinery and software. Less developed countries have maintained a lower-paid, unskilled workforce. They traditionally have focused on more labor-intensive work.

Some countries, such as the United States, have available resources in all factors of production. They have lots of land, skilled labor, and capital. The United States has large areas of farmland, fresh water, and minerals. It currently has the most educated workforce in the world. It also has a highly entrepreneurial culture and a good capital market. These factors of production are being developed by other countries around the world. The educational level of many countries is increasing. Capital flows freely across borders, allowing companies to obtain financing to start businesses. Management talent also crosses borders. Entrepreneurship training is taking place in other countries to help grow the global economy. Countries around the world are improving their human factors of production to compete internationally.

© DIGITAL VISION

Time Out

China and India each graduate more students from colleges and universities each year than the United States does.

MARKETING - INFORMATION MANAGEMENT

Comparative Advantage of Nations

Economists have looked at how countries gain competitive advantages. One economist, Michael Porter, stated that a country's industries develop competitive advantages through strong internal competition. As domestic

Ethics Around the World

Is it ethics or just good business sense? Many U.S. companies have decided that global warming is a serious issue. They are beginning to take action. Companies such as General Electric (GE) are developing technologies to limit greenhouse gases, such as carbon dioxide. GE has announced that it is going "green" by developing environmentally friendly technology.

Are GE and other U.S.-based companies going green because they believe that it is an ethically sound decision? Global companies must consider global reactions. GE sells in global markets. Many nations require that companies use clean technologies. Investors are worried that companies may be hurt financially in the long term if they don't act now to limit greenhouse gases. Also, technology companies that don't invest in green technology now may not be able to meet environmental standards in the future. This could prevent them from being able to sell their products.

THINK CRITICALLY

1. Do you think GE is more concerned about protecting the environment or about protecting future profits? Explain your answer.

2. Why do you think investing in green technology makes good business sense?

companies compete, only the strongest and the best producers survive. As a result, higher-quality products are produced and exported.

Companies in Japan have had a comparative advantage in producing small home electronic devices. These devices, such as televisions and cameras, are exported around the world. This advantage comes in part from Japan's factors of production such as a skilled manufacturing workforce and suppliers of component products. This advantage can also be attributed to internal competition heightened by a consumer market that demands quality. Japan's highly competitive home electronics industry has forced Japanese producers to manufacture some of the world's best electronic devices.

The personal computer industry started in the United States. A highly competitive industry has forced U.S. producers to manufacture some of the best hardware and software in the world. U.S. farmers also are very competitive. They export high-quality products at low prices. The United States also has a very competitive entertainment industry. It exports movies and television shows. The Disney Corporation is exporting its theme park management skills. It is developing new parks in Tokyo, Beijing, and Hong Kong.

Checkpoint List some of the factors of production that have allowed the United States to gain comparative advantages.

Understand Marketing Concepts

Circle the best answer for each of the following questions.

1. An absolute advantage is
    a. the ability to produce more units of a product than another country
    b. the ability to produce a product relatively better than another country
    c. owning the rights to produce and sell all of one product
    d. being the only country in the world that can produce a certain product

2. Opportunity cost is
    a. the price of purchasing a product
    b. the total cost of producing a product
    c. the value given up when one product is produced instead of another product
    d. the price of a competitor's product

Think Critically

Answer the following questions as completely as possible. If necessary, use a separate sheet of paper.

3. Explain why it is important to gain a comparative advantage over another country in producing a product.

    _____

    _____

    _____

    _____

    _____

4. **Communication** The benefits of focusing on the production of cotton and rice by the United States and Japan were discussed in this lesson. Explain how you would communicate to Japanese officials the benefits of specialization and trade of cotton and rice within countries.

    _____

    _____

    _____

    _____

    _____

    _____

Barriers to International Trade

Goals

- Explain why nations develop trade barriers.
- Discuss how nations use their commercial policies to control trade.
- Identify export support activities in which governments engage.

Terms

- infant industry argument
- national security argument
- commercial policies
- tariff
- import quotas
- embargo
- non-tariff barriers
- dumping
- export subsidies

Going Global

How much is that sweater? The U.S. government agreed to a deadline to eliminate a system that imposed import restrictions on the textile trade. However, less than five months later, it imposed limits on the import of some textile products from China. It said that it had a commitment to America's textile manufacturers and their employees.

The Chinese government disagreed. It argued that the U.S. textile industry has been the most protected industry in the country. Even so, it still lost about one million jobs over the last decade. The U.S.

textile industry did little to prepare for international competition. Instead, it called for protection from competition by using government-imposed restrictions.

U.S. consumers pay more due to protectionist policies on textiles. A sweater made in China has a production cost of $26. It has additional costs of $6 in tariffs and $12 in other import fees. U.S. consumers could save up to $24.4 billion each year if U.S. trade restrictions on textiles were removed.

Working with a partner, debate the U.S. and Chinese arguments relating to the textile trade. Be prepared to discuss your arguments with the class.

TRADE BARRIERS

Nations have many reasons for limiting international trade. Often these limitations are designed to protect special interests or selective industries. They also may be designed to help reach national goals. International marketers must understand the nature of trade barriers. They also must understand the reasons countries set barriers and how nations negotiate to lower barriers.

One of the arguments for setting barriers to free trade is the **infant industry argument**. This argument is based on the idea that a developing industry in a country needs time to become globally competitive. Setting protections allows companies to compete without pressure from international competitors. A question that arises is how long the protection should be kept in place. Without competition, it is unlikely that the industry could be globally competitive.

A **national security argument** also is used as a reason for barriers. This argument is based on the idea that a country does not want to become dependent upon other countries for products. For example, Japan could allow foreign rice to enter its market at low global prices, but it would drive Japanese farmers out of business. Although the land could most likely be used for more economically productive uses, this plan could make Japan dependent on other countries for its main food source, rice.

Another argument for trade barriers is based on the idea that free trade favors rich countries. Large, developed countries often have comparative advantages in many areas. These countries can use their advantages to control markets. For example, Canadians have expressed a fear that the United States could dominate the Canadian media market. The United States has a large media industry, and Canadians can access U.S. programming using the Internet and satellite technology.

Barriers also are raised to protect a country's culture. Japan protects its rice farming in part because of rice's role in a 2,000-year-old cultural heritage.

Name three arguments in favor of setting trade barriers.

COMMERCIAL POLICY

DISTRIBUTION

International marketers must understand the commercial policies of their home country and every country in which they do business. **Commercial policies** are the regulations and restrictions that countries use to control international trade.

© GETTY IMAGES/PHOTODISC

Marketing Myths

There is a widely held belief that countries with low-cost labor specialize only in manufacturing. The belief is that product innovation occurs only in developed countries because they have a comparative advantage in research and development. In reality, research and development also is moving "offshore." Sixty-five percent of notebook PCs are designed in Taiwan. Seventy percent of PDAs are designed in Asia. India is heavily involved in the research and development of software products.

This shift in research and development reflects a change in comparative advantages. Educational levels, especially in the sciences and engineering, have been increasing in Asia. Any country that wishes to maintain competitiveness must train its human resources to compete in a global marketplace.

THINK CRITICALLY

1. What should the United States do to maintain the comparative advantage it has held in the educational level of its workforce?
2. What industries and careers will be most directly affected by a shift of technology expertise from the United States to countries in Asia?

Tariff One of the most common tools used to control trade is a tariff. A **tariff** is a tax placed on imported or exported products. It also is called a *custom's duty*. *Import tariffs* are taxes placed on goods coming into a country. *Export tariffs* are taxes placed on goods going out of a country. Tariffs directly raise a product's price. Countries use tariffs as a means of income. Tariffs also help ensure that imported products are not sold for less than local, or domestic, products. Japan's rice tariff keeps imported rice from selling for less than domestic rice.

Quota **Import quotas** are restrictions on the amount of a product that can be imported into a country. Quotas are set for a number of products that are traded internationally. The purpose of a quota is to protect domestic products by limiting competition. However, quotas may not always work as expected. Instead of developing plans to become more competitive, companies often rely on quotas to limit competition. This also allows companies to increase prices.

In 1981, Japan agreed to voluntarily limit exports on cars shipped to the United States. This agreement was to give U.S. manufacturers time to retool for production of fuel-efficient cars. Instead of retooling, U.S. auto manufacturers raised prices to increase profits. The increased prices reduced the need to cut costs. The auto companies used their profits for unrelated ventures, which proved to be unwise. Although the quotas had set a limit on the number of cars imported from Japan, they did not set a limit on their dollar value. This made it possible for the Japanese manufacturers to export larger, more profitable cars. They then used the profits to build car plants in the United States. As a result, Japan captured more market share, and Americans now pay about $3,000 more per car.

Another country is making a move in the car manufacturing business. At the beginning of 2005, China agreed to abolish its car import quota system. It also said that it would continue to lower car import tariffs to 25 percent. Chinese demand for cars is growing rapidly. At the same time, China is producing more cars for its home market and for export. In 2003, China was the world's fourth largest car manufacturer. Only the United States, Japan, and Germany produced more cars. China is using its growing experience to develop cars for export to the United States, meaning more competition.

Embargo A country or group can refuse to take part in trade with another country or group for various reasons. An **embargo** is the ban of commerce and trade with a certain country. The United States has imposed embargoes of trade with countries, businesses, and individuals. These embargoes are designed to limit trade with terrorists, drug dealers, or politically undesirable countries. For example, U.S.-based companies are not allowed to do business with Cuba.

Perhaps the most famous embargo is the 1973 oil embargo by the Organization of Arab Petroleum Exporting Countries (OPEC). OPEC countries refused to sell crude oil to Europe and the United States. They also raised the price of a barrel of oil by 400 percent. Gasoline prices in the United States increased from 38.5 cents per gallon to more than 55 cents per gallon. The New York Stock Exchange lost $97 billion dollars in value.

A *boycott* is a type of embargo. Participants in a boycott usually believe that the boycotted organization or country has done something morally wrong. In the 1970s, consumer groups in the United States and Europe imposed a boycott on Nestlé. The company was marketing its infant formulas in developing countries. These consumer groups believed that Nestle was targeting poverty-stricken consumers with products they did not need or know how to use.

Non-Tariff Barriers

Countries use a variety of barriers that are classified as **non-tariff barriers**. These barriers often are based on legislative rules and regulations related to a product. For example, many countries have imposed import restrictions on genetically modified (GM) plants. Europe has required that GM food products be labeled as "genetically modified." Countries such as the United States that export GM products view this requirement as an attempt by Europe to limit the import of U.S. farm products.

When countries engage in trade negotiations, they often set *voluntary export restraints*. These restraints limit the total amount of products exported. For example, Japan voluntarily limited the total number of cars exported to the United States. China has voluntarily limited the total amount of textiles exported to the United States. In both cases, U.S. firms have used these restraints to raise prices rather than to prepare to meet competition.

Countries are said to be **dumping** products when they sell products for less than the cost of production. Dumping is a type of predatory pricing. *Predatory pricing* is the lowering of a price to gain market share. Countries use anti-dumping penalties to counteract this tactic. Anti-dumping penalties include imposing tariffs and setting quotas or limits on imports. Anti-dumping claims have been made on a large number of products. These products include steel, textiles, televisions, computer hardware, farm crops, and many others. China has been a primary target for anti-dumping complaints.

Time Out

In 1946, the average U.S. import tariff was 26 percent. By 2001, the average import tariff dropped to 5.4 percent.

List and define three types of commercial policies used to regulate trade.

Checkpoint

EXPORT SUPPORT SYSTEMS

Countries have an interest in supporting exports. Because of this, countries have developed export support systems. International marketers can use these support systems to help market their products in other countries.

Export Support Activities

PRICING

Governments undertake *indirect support activities* to support the sales of products. These activities include promoting export product sales through special trade fairs and *consulates*. Consulates are government appointed officials from one country that reside in another country to represent the business interests of the appointing country's citizens. Government workers also may invite foreign buyers to visit the exporting country's producers.

Export subsidies are payments made by governments to support the export of products. Export subsidies can be direct or indirect. Direct export subsidies clearly support exporting by lowering the price of an

© BRAND X PICTURES

exported product. Direct export subsidies could include payments made directly to the exporter by the government or through other types of export support programs, such as low-interest loans to support sales. Direct export subsidies are heavily used by European governments to support their farm exports. The United States also uses direct export subsidies to lower the price of their exported farm products.

Indirect export subsidies support exporting in a roundabout way. For example, aircraft manufacturers Boeing and Airbus have received indirect export subsidies. Both companies have received help from their government in the research and development of their planes. This lowers Boeing's and Airbus's internal research and development costs and, in turn, helps both companies keep the cost of their planes lower for their customers. By aiding in the research and development processes, the governments have indirectly helped these two companies compete globally.

Checkpoint

Briefly describe how countries attempt to support exports.

Understand Marketing Concepts

Circle the best answer for each of the following questions.

1. Which of the following is *not* an argument in favor of setting trade barriers?
   a. a developing industry needs time to grow before facing competition
   b. trade barriers allow domestic products to be sold at a lower price
   c. a country does not want to become dependent on another country
   d. rich countries benefit more from having no trade barriers

2. An import tariff is
   a. a tax placed on products going out of a country
   b. a restriction on the amount of a product that can be imported
   c. a tax placed on products coming into a country
   d. a ban of commerce and trade with a certain country

Think Critically

Answer the following questions as completely as possible. If necessary, use a separate sheet of paper.

3. Briefly describe what tariffs are. Explain the effect they have on the price of products imported to the United States.

_____

_____

_____

_____

_____

_____

4. What purpose do export subsidies serve and why are they needed?

_____

_____

_____

_____

_____

_____

Lesson 2.3

International Trade Institutions

Goals

- List and describe types of U.S. federal and state support for international marketing.
- Describe the roles of international trade organizations.

Terms

- General Agreement on Tariffs and Trade (GATT)
- World Trade Organization (WTO)

Going Global

Exporting sugar is a sticky business. Many of the developed countries around the world are producers of sugar. However, they often are not importers. The United States and Europe both use price support loan programs, tariffs, and quotas to support the domestic price of sugar and to ensure that there is an adequate supply of sugar for consumers and producers.

Even so, U.S. consumers pay twice the world price for sugar due to trade protections.

A General Agreement on Tariffs and Trade (GATT) panel found U.S. actions regarding price supports, tariffs, and quotas to be illegal under GATT agreements. North American Free Trade Agreement (NAFTA) negotiations attempted to open trade between the United States and Mexico. U.S. producers were afraid that high-fructose corn syrup would be sent to Mexico where soft-drink makers would use the syrup as a sweetener. This action would free up raw sugar that Mexico could then export to the United States.

Developing countries could have a comparative advantage in producing raw sugar. They have complained to the World Trade Organization (WTO) that developed countries use unfair practices to limit their exports.

Working with a partner, list the advantages and disadvantages to both the United States and Mexico of lifting the tariffs and quotas on sugar imports.

U.S. FEDERAL AND STATE EXPORT SUPPORT

MARKETING-INFORMATION MANAGEMENT

When marketers design international marketing plans, they often look to governmental agencies, both federal and state, for support. Governments are interested in promoting exports. Exports improve their *balance of trade*, which is the difference between the dollar value of exports sold and the dollar value of imports purchased. Exports also ensure employment.

In the United States, federal international trade support is the responsibility of the Department of Commerce. The Department of Commerce has many roles in international trade. It tries to make sure that foreign nations obey trade agreements. It also acts as a promoter of U.S. products. The Department of Commerce offers the following support services:

- **U.S. Commercial Service** A service to help businesses export goods and services to markets worldwide. This service provides access to a global listing of trade events and international market research. It also provides tools to help with the export process.

- **Export.gov** A web site that provides links to export-related programs and services. It also contains market research information from 19 federal agencies.

- **Manufacturing and Services** A service that helps small businesses increase their export potential.

- *Export America* **Magazine** A federal source for global business news.

- **Central and Eastern Europe Business Information Center** A program for U.S. firms interested in expanding their business into central and eastern Europe.

- **Business Information Services for the Newly Independent States** A market information center for U.S. companies exploring business opportunities in Russia and other newly independent states.

- **Platinum Key Service** A service that offers customized U.S. commercial service assistance.

Individual states also offer help to their businesses. Most states offer services to link businesses with companies and opportunities in foreign markets. States may have support offices in foreign countries. These offices maintain contacts with governments, local chambers of commerce, and business communities.

Export Assistance Centers

The U.S. Department of Commerce runs *Export Assistance Centers* (EACs) to help businesses with all aspects of exporting. Services include finding sales prospects, developing export strategies, and promoting products. EACs organize trade shows in countries around the world. Companies can display products with or without sending a representative. EACs counsel clients and train individuals on export details. They provide international marketing research and help firms win overseas contracts. Many countries around the world provide similar services for their own companies.

List seven services provided by the Department of Commerce that support exports.

Checkpoint

Arguments for free international trade surfaced in the early 1800s. However, it is only recently that worldwide agreements have been put in place to allow for expanded free trade. At the end of World War II, Europe and Asia were devastated. In addition, the world had divided into two major political blocs. The United States believed that international trade was a key factor to revive economies around the world.

In 1948, the charter for the International Trade Organization (ITO) called for the creation of the United Nations, a General Agreement on Tariffs and Trade to reduce tariffs, a World Bank, and an International Monetary Fund. Even though these institutions were developed, a set of international commercial policies was not fully approved. Countries were concerned about giving up too much power. Today, a number of international institutions govern international trade.

The World Trade Organization

The **General Agreement on Tariffs and Trade (GATT)** was a treaty agreement that developed a set of rules allowing countries to grant a *Most Favored Nation* status. This agreement lowered tariffs between member countries. Prior to the GATT, countries reached individual agreements with other countries. These agreements allowed special pacts that could block out other nations. In 1995, GATT became part of the **World Trade Organization (WTO)**. The WTO governs international trade rules and trade agreements. It has expanded international trade agreements. These agreements cover services, agriculture, intellectual property, and other trade issues. The WTO also allows for a means to settle trade disputes. Each member of the WTO must grant *Most Favored Nation* status to all other members.

All members of the WTO have equal rights. Trade disputes are heard by panels. This process allows even small countries to take action against larger countries. The WTO does not have the ability to impose sanctions. Instead, countries are authorized to impose their own sanctions.

World Financial Institutions

Two institutions are involved in helping countries develop economically. They try to provide economic stability to markets. The *International Monetary Fund (IMF)* is an organization of 184 countries. It supports global monetary cooperation

Tech Zone

How do you impose tariffs on e-commerce? The Internet allows digital products to move across borders with little control. The United States has comparative advantages in producing digital content. It would like to sell these products around the world. Member countries of the WTO have agreed not to impose customs duties on electronic transmissions. Developing countries are not as interested in allowing their citizens to purchase tariff-free online. These countries want to protect their electronic markets from control by developed countries.

THINK CRITICALLY

1. List the factors of production that could give the United States a comparative advantage in producing digital content.
2. Explain why developed countries would be interested in minimizing tariffs on digital content.

and secures financial stability. It also helps in regulating international currency exchange rates. The IMF works to promote high employment and sustain economic growth. It observes economic activity within and between countries. Its purpose is to spot problems before they can lead to financial instability. For example, some countries' debts could affect the stability of their currency. This instability can lead to devaluation, resulting in a loss of jobs and other financial crises. The IMF can grant loans on the condition that a country adopts a sound set of economic policies.

The mission of the *World Bank* is to fight poverty and improve the living standards of people in developing countries. The World Bank provides loans to low- and middle-income countries. It also provides policy advice, technical help, and knowledge-sharing services. The World Bank promotes economic growth to create jobs and to allow the poorest countries to take advantage of economic opportunities.

Protests Against World Organizations

Countries, groups, and individuals have protested against world organizations for many reasons. The WTO has often been a target of protests. Some individuals believe the WTO's agreements threaten human rights. They think that it promotes trade liberalization in less developed countries. They believe that the WTO's agreements put workers in these countries at a disadvantage. In November 1999, 50,000 people protested at a WTO meeting in Seattle, Washington. They demanded a more democratic, socially just, and environmentally sustainable global economy.

Nations may resist world organizations because they do not want to give up control over their international trade and laws. For example, a WTO ruling found that the U.S. cotton program violates international trade rules. To comply with the WTO, the U.S. Department of Agriculture changed its export programs to reduce subsidies. To further comply, the United States government would need to rewrite farm policy, lift market prices, and stop agricultural dumping.

A number of other individuals and groups accuse world organizations of imposing standards, such as controlling wages or working environments. For example, groups in developed countries may call for changes to labor laws in less developed countries.

The World Bank also has come under criticism. It has been accused of sponsoring projects that have little economic value. Rulers in many developing countries have been accused of stealing money from economic development funds that were intended for the good of their country.

Views of Global Free Trade

Economists agree that global free trade is leading to economic development around the world. Thus, free trade may not be as problematic as protesters see it. Many economic problems may actually stem from the changes caused by a shifting global economy. Production often will shift to countries with comparative advantages. This shift can result in job losses in other countries. For example, many U.S. production jobs have recently shifted to Mexico and China. These two countries can produce products more efficiently due to an abundant supply of low-wage human resources.

Countries must be careful in the approach they take to meet the challenges brought on by global free trade. Countries may believe that they can lower the risks of free trade by setting up trade barriers. However, trade barriers are often used to increase profits instead of industry competitiveness, as previously described in the auto industry example. Without global competition, companies may not strive to produce the highest-quality products and could become outdated. In the meantime, consumers could suffer from limited supplies, low-quality products, and high prices.

Central and Eastern Europe offer a good example of a shift in the global economy. They were previously under communist control, which prevented outside competition. After the fall of the communist governments in 1989, they discovered their industries were out of date and were forced to close them. As a result, a large percentage of the population became unemployed. Global free markets require that countries develop high-quality factors of production in order to compete in a global marketplace.

Checkpoint

Describe the role of the World Trade Organization (WTO).

_____

_____

World Stars | CARLOS M. GUTIERREZ

Carlos Gutierrez was sworn into office as the U.S. Secretary of Commerce on February 7, 2005. He is the former chief executive officer of Kellogg Company. Kellogg is the largest packaged-food manufacturer in the United States.

Gutierrez has come a long way since his early days in Cuba. In 1960, shortly after Fidel Castro came to power in Cuba, Gutierrez and his family fled to the United States. Gutierrez began working for Kellogg selling cereal out of his van in Mexico in the 1970s. In 1999, at age 43, he became the youngest CEO in the company's history. When Gutierrez took over Kellogg's operations, the company was in a slow decline of sales and profits. Gutierrez arranged the purchase of Keebler Foods. This purchase proved to be very profitable. Because of Gutierrez's leadership, Kellogg continues to be a global leader in its industry.

As the U.S. Secretary of Commerce, one of Gutierrez's top priorities is to open international markets to U.S. companies to create jobs and build a stronger America. "We have the best people; we have the training; we have the culture," Gutierrez says. "I believe the 21st century is really and truly the American century."

THINK CRITICALLY

Explain how Carlos Gutierrez's background has contributed to his success in business. How will it help him in his current office?

Understand Marketing Concepts

Circle the best answer for each of the following questions.

1. Which of the following is *not* a service provided by the U.S. Department of Commerce?
   a. U.S. Commercial Service
   b. General Agreement on Tariffs and Trade
   c. *Export America* Magazine
   d. Export Assistance Centers

2. Which of the following international organizations oversees international trade agreements?
   a. World Trade Organization
   b. World Bank
   c. U.S. Department of Commerce
   d. International Monetary Fund

Think Critically

Answer the following questions as completely as possible. If necessary, use a separate sheet of paper.

3. Briefly describe three of the services provided by Export Assistance Centers.

   _____

   _____

   _____

   _____

   _____

   _____

   _____

4. Explain the mission of the World Bank. List the services it provides to low- and middle-income countries.

   _____

   _____

   _____

   _____

   _____

   _____

   _____

   _____

Chapter Assessment

Review Marketing Concepts

Write the letter of the term that matches each definition. Some terms will not be used.

_____ 1. Items that are used to produce products

_____ 2. A country specializes in the production of a product that it can produce relatively better than other countries

_____ 3. A country can produce more units of a product at a lower cost using fewer resources

_____ 4. An argument based on the idea that a developing industry in a country needs time to become globally competitive

_____ 5. A tax placed on imported or exported products

_____ 6. Restrictions on the amount of a product that can be imported into a country

_____ 7. The regulations and restrictions that countries use to control international trade

_____ 8. The ban of commerce and trade with a certain country

_____ 9. When products are sold for less than the cost of production

_____ 10. Payments made by governments to support the export of products

a. absolute advantage
b. commodity
c. commercial policies
d. comparative advantage
e. dumping
f. embargo
g. export subsidies
h. factors of production
i. GATT
j. import quotas
k. infant industry argument
l. national security argument
m. non-tariff barriers
n. opportunity cost
o. production possibility curve
p. tariff
q. WTO

Circle the best answer.

11. The General Agreement on Tariffs and Trade
    a. offers loans to developing countries
    b. sets a limit on the amount of trade in which countries can engage
    c. is a set of rules allowing countries to grant a *Most Favored Nation* status
    d. is a branch of the Department of Commerce

12. The World Trade Organization
    a. is part of the world government
    b. is an institution that coordinates international trade issues
    c. is a part of the U.S. government that regulates trade
    d. helps in regulating international exchange rates

Think Critically

13. Explain the meaning of opportunity cost and provide an example.

_____

_____

_____

_____

_____

14. Choose two products. Draw a production possibility curve on a graph showing the trade-off in production between these products. Explain how opportunity costs exist as you move along this line.

_____

_____

_____

_____

_____

15. List and define the factors of production.

_____

_____

_____

_____

_____

16. Identify the factors of production for which you think your country has an advantage. Justify why you believe that your country has these advantages over other countries.

_____

_____

_____

_____

_____

17. Explain how countries are able to gain competitive advantages for export products. Give an example.

_____

_____

_____

_____

_____

Make Connections

18. Geography Use the Internet to find three major producing countries for three farm products. Explain how the countries' geography could give those countries comparative advantages in producing those products.

_____

_____

_____

_____

19. History Use the Internet and other resources to learn about the change in the number of college students graduating from China and India. Explain how this could affect your career goals.

_____

_____

_____

_____

_____

20. Research Select two of the factors of production. Use the Internet to conduct research on a country in Europe and a country in Asia. Describe how the two countries compare in the two selected factors of production.

_____

_____

_____

_____

_____

21. Marketing Math Assume a country earns $3,250,000 on exported products and pays $2,775,000 for imported products. What is the balance of trade for this country? If this country increases the amount earned on exports by 15 percent, what is the new total of exports?

_____

_____

_____

_____

_____

22. **Communication** You have been chosen to represent your school at a local educational meeting. Use the concepts in this chapter and write a one-page paper. Argue for an increase in educational support to enhance students' abilities to compete in a world marketplace.

_____

_____

_____

_____

_____

_____

_____

_____

_____

_____

_____

PUT MARKETING ON THE MAP

International Marketing Plan Project

Your product must have a comparative advantage to be successful in a global marketplace. In addition, you will need to take advantage of federal and state support to market your product around the world.

Work with a group and complete the following activities.

1. List the factors of production that are needed to produce your product. Compare your factors of production to other countries around the world. Describe where you think you have a comparative advantage in producing your product.

2. Describe the types of barriers you are likely to find as you attempt to sell your product in international marketplaces. Devise a strategy to deal with these barriers.

3. Use the Internet to learn whether there are any commercial policies related to your product in the countries in which you want to sell your product. Determine whether your target countries are members of the WTO. Decide whether you need to look at some other countries as alternative places to sell.

4. Use the Internet to identify how your federal and state governments can help you in marketing your product internationally.

WHERE'S THE BEEF?

Beef has become an increasingly popular food choice in the United States and around the world. Successful beef campaigns encourage people to eat beef for dinner. The USDA indicated that total U.S. beef consumption was 27 billion pounds in 2003 and 27.6 billion pounds in 2004.

Just when the U.S. beef industry seemed to be at its prime, it suffered a serious blow—Bovine Spongiform Encephalopathy (BSE), or Mad Cow Disease. BSE is a slowly progressive, degenerative, fatal disease affecting the central nervous system of adult cattle. Creutzfeldt-Jakob Disease is believed to occur in people who consume BSE-contaminated beef.

When Mad Cow disease was discovered in Canada on May 2, 2003, the United States shut down imports of Canadian cattle. Closing down beef imports might appear to be beneficial to the U.S. beef industry. However, U.S. meat packers that rely on Canadian imports were hit hard, and 5,000 people lost their jobs. Employment in the U.S. cattle industry is heavily dependent upon international trade. Seven months later a case of Mad Cow Disease discovered in the state of Washington led to the loss of most U.S. beef export markets. These events confirmed that the global economy greatly depends on international trade. An open-trade environment best serves the beef industry. Open trade allowed the U.S. to annually import $3.7 billion and export $5.7 billion in cattle, beef, and by-products.

The ban on beef has been a detriment to producers and consumers in the United States and Canada even though there has been no evidence of public health risk. Two North American cases of BSE posed no noticeable health threat to humans and even less threat to the health of cattle herds. If the trade border between Canada and the United States remains closed too long, both countries will have to adapt permanently, resulting in higher costs from duplicated facilities once shared by the two countries. The United States continues to guard against contaminated meat with the 1997 feed ban, import controls, BSE surveillance program, and proactive health response plans.

THINK CRITICALLY

1. How can consumer panic impact an entire industry?
2. What is the advantage of shutting down imports from a country with a serious food problem?
3. What is meant by "increasing costs of production by duplicating processing efforts"?
4. Are consumers more likely to believe statistics that show low risk for a fatal disease or a news report that shows the disastrous results?

PUBLIC RELATIONS PROJECT

The purpose of the Public Relations Project is to provide an opportunity for students to demonstrate the skills needed in planning, organizing, implementing, and evaluating a single public relations campaign conducted by the DECA chapter.

The American Cattle Growers Association has hired your team to develop a promotional campaign for beef. The recent Mad Cow Disease scare has negatively affected the sales of beef. Your public relations campaign must stress the nutritional value of beef, the high-quality product offered in the United States, and the truth about Mad Cow Disease and the American food supply.

The project consists of two major parts: the written document and an oral presentation. The written document will account for 70 points, and the oral presentation will be worth 30 points. One to three students may participate in the oral presentation. The body of the written entry must be limited to 30 numbered pages, including the appendix.

The format of the written document should include an executive summary, campaign theme or focus, local media and other promotional possibilities, campaign organization and implementation, evaluation and recommendations, bibliography, and appendix.

Students will have ten minutes to present their plan to judges. Note cards will not be allowed during the presentation, and no materials may be passed to the judge.

Performance Indicators Evaluated

- Understand the importance of public relations for the beef industry.
- Identify the theme for a public relations campaign.
- Plan, organize, and implement a public relations campaign for the beef industry.
- Evaluate the planning and implementation of the public relations project.

Go to the DECA web site for more detailed information.

THINK CRITICALLY

1. Why is public relations essential for the beef industry after Mad Cow Disease?
2. List two major concepts that the public relations campaign for the beef industry should emphasize.
3. What are two of the most effective means for getting the message to the intended audience?

www.deca.org

Cultural Environment of International Marketing

3

© GETTY IMAGES/PHOTODISC

Point Your Browser

▶ ▶ ▶ ▶ intlmarket.swlearning.com

Coca-Cola and McDonald's Take on the World Market

Perhaps no two companies represent America more than Coca-Cola and McDonald's. At the same time, these two brands are successful global businesses. Coke is the leading world brand. Coke is sold in almost twice as many countries as McDonald's. Coke has always entered new markets early. It uses its global expertise to help McDonald's expand overseas. When the Soviet Union broke up, Coke entered the market with the slogan "Always Coca-Cola." Coke introduced a new cola called C2 in Japan before it took the product to America. C2 contains half the sugar, carbohydrates, and calories of regular colas.

Coca-Cola has had several CEOs with global experience. Coke's past CEO, Roberto Goizueta, was Cuban. He had worked as a chemist for Coca-Cola in Havana. Douglas Daft, another past CEO, is Australian. The current CEO, Neville Isdell, is from Ireland. He has helped take Coca-Cola into new overseas markets.

McDonald's CEO Jim Cantalupo was previously the company's head of international operations. McDonald's is targeting a new generation of children in China. China has a one-child-per-family policy. McDonald's is nurturing these only children, or "little emperors." McDonald's records names and birth dates in a *Book of Little Honorary Guests*. The children are then sent a card just before their birthday. Asian McDonald's restaurants are places for young people to hang out. McDonald's menu is limited, lessening the danger of customers "losing face" because someone else orders a more expensive meal. McDonald's adapts its restaurants to local cultures. In some countries, McDonald's customers do not even realize that the restaurant is American.

Think Critically

1. Discuss the advantages to Coke and McDonald's of having CEOs with international experience.

2. Which brand do you think would be easier to expand into new markets—Coke or McDonald's? Explain your answer.

Lesson 3.1

The Elements of Culture

Goals

- Define culture and explain how cultures are developed.
- Explain how cultural influences affect international marketing.
- Describe how an international marketer can communicate effectively.

Terms

- culture
- enculturation
- context

- geography
- belief system
- religion

- back translation
- non-verbal communication

Going Global

The Coca-Cola Company does a good job of marketing its products around the world. Coke has found a strong link between a country's demographics and culture and its Coke consumption. Coke is consumed more in wealthier countries. There also is a stronger link between Coke drinking and a country's general quality of life. The quality of life is measured by wealth, education, health, and literacy. The more developed a country is, the more Coke its population consumes. Also, the more political freedom a country has, the more Coke its population drinks.

Coca-Cola is experiencing loss of share in some markets. As the United States loses popularity around the world, products from other countries have a chance to enter the market. Many Muslim entrepreneurs are developing colas for their own markets. Their colas also are popular in Muslim communities in Western countries.

Working with a partner, discuss why more Coke would be consumed in developed countries. Explain why some consumers might not drink Coke if they knew it was an American product.

CULTURE

The United Nation's Educational, Scientific, and Cultural Organization (UNESCO) works to preserve the world's cultural heritage. UNESCO defines culture as "a set of distinctive spiritual, material, intellectual, and emotional features of society or a social group that encompasses art, literature, lifestyles, ways of living together, value systems, traditions, and beliefs." Essentially, **culture** is a system of shared beliefs, values, customs, and behaviors that define how a group of people lives.

International marketers must understand the culture where they sell. For Americans, Coca-Cola is one of several soft drinks. U.S. customers may purchase Coke because of its flavor. But in many foreign markets, Coke may be viewed as an American product. People may want to drink it because it is part of a Western culture, even if there is a cheaper local product. On the other hand, they may actively avoid Coke because it is an American product.

Cultural Learning

MARKETING-INFORMATION MANAGEMENT

From the first day you are able to learn, you begin an enculturation process. **Enculturation** is a process that helps people learn about their culture. For example, in many Western cultures, babies are taken out into the world almost as soon as they are born. In Ghana, mothers spend the first weeks alone with their babies.

Early on, children begin to learn the sounds and patterns of their family's language. They learn favorite foods and drinks. As children grow, they also learn about the world around them. They learn how they fit into that world. Children learn about each of the elements of culture. Those elements include language, belief systems, values, attitudes, manners, and customs. Children are also introduced to material goods and social institutions such as families and educational systems. This learning process structures children's brains as they learn to adapt to their environment.

Humans determine meaning within a cultural context. **Context** refers to the background or surrounding circumstances of an event. Context can be interpreted through the communication process. For example, in a business meeting, the context can be conveyed through all acts of communication in the meeting. This could include the discussions held by the participants as well as their facial expressions or gestures.

Cultures range from high-context cultures to low-context cultures. In a *high-context culture*, interpersonal relationships are important. People in a high-context culture are guided more by intuitions and feelings than by logic or facts. Decisions are made by groups rather than by individuals. Communication is more indirect and vague. Context is more important than words. Examples of high-context cultures include Japan, China, and France.

In a *low-context culture*, people value individualism. These people base decisions on facts. Communication is concise, structured, and direct. The focus is placed on the words used and their meanings rather than on context. Personal relationships are less important than getting the task done. Examples of low-context cultures include the United States, Germany, and Switzerland.

Problems can occur when high-context cultures work together with low-context cultures. What one person says and does must be determined within the larger cultural context. For example, the simple statement "I agree" can mean different things in these two types of cultures. In Japan, it may mean only that I understand what you are saying. In Switzerland, it means that there is an actual agreement. International marketers must understand the cultural context of communication. If you are not able to interpret cultural context, you may misunderstand behaviors and messages.

Time Out

The Chinese language is complex. Children must learn the different meanings for each of the four tones that can be used for a single word. There also are more than 40,000 Chinese characters. Reading a newspaper requires knowledge of 2,000 to 3,000 different Chinese characters.

Checkpoint

List at least six elements of culture.

_____

_____

_____

CULTURAL INFLUENCES

MARKETING– INFORMATION MANAGEMENT

Cultures develop from a number of influences, including a group's history, the geography of a region, and the type of belief systems held by members of a culture. Cultures can change over time, but they also can resist change. An international marketer must understand the history, geography, and belief system of a cultural group. These factors provide an understanding of how a consumer will likely react to products. They also help international marketers understand how to create a promotional campaign and how to distribute products efficiently.

History and Geography

Americans have a short view of history. The settlement of the Americas is only a little over 500 years old. As settlers moved across North America, they built individual homesteads and towns that acted as commercial hubs. Most homes in the United States were built after 1900. In both Europe and Asia, towns are much older. They were the center of cultural life. Towns offered protection from wars and bandits. Homes and cultural traditions in these towns were passed down from generation to generation. Individuals in these towns have a different sense of community than Americans.

Most Americans cannot trace back any part of their consumer culture more than a few decades. Americans are willing to let go of their past. They embrace new ideas, products, and practices. Many other cultures around the world can trace their cultural heritage back thousands of years. The Japanese rice culture is 2,000 years old. International marketers have found it difficult to overcome the Japanese preference for domestically grown rice. Many countries around the world have a tradition of open-air markets. These markets have been providing food and other products for thousands of years. Consumers who shop for food in these markets often prefer to deal with local farmers who can ensure freshness.

International marketers must understand how consumers currently meet their needs. If there is a strong historical pattern, it may be difficult to get customers to change their habits. For example, traditional French bread becomes stale quickly because it contains no fat. French shoppers often shop daily at the local *boulangerie*, or hot bread shop, where bread is handmade. To protect these shops, the French government passed a law to ensure that a bakery could only be called a boulangerie if it made, kneaded, and cooked bread entirely from scratch on the premises.

Geography is the study of the differences that exist in physical, biological, and cultural features of the earth. Cultures develop under unique geographic conditions such as temperature and weather conditions, population density, and the nature of neighboring cultures. These conditions affect how food is produced or gathered. Cultures formed in hot coastal areas with plenty of land and seafood have developed differently from cultures in colder climates where annual farming has been the primary means of survival.

International marketers also should consider the city size where they are selling. There can be major wealth and cultural differences between rural and urban areas. These differences are greater in developing countries.

Belief Systems

A **belief system** allows individuals to understand their place in the larger universe. A belief system plays a number of roles. It can set rules of conduct and ethics. These rules can include how one should interact with others. They tell people how they should live their lives. A belief system can answer questions about the nature of reality. For example, before the rise of science, religion answered questions about all natural events from the creation of life to the nature of the stars. **Religion** is a belief system that answers spiritual questions. There are a number of religious belief systems. With over 2 billion followers, Christianity currently is the largest religion in the world. Other major world religions include Islam, with 1.3 billion followers, and Hinduism, with 900 million followers. Three major religious belief systems also can be found in Asia. These belief systems are Buddhism, which has more than 350 million followers, Confucianism, and Shinto.

Non-religious belief systems do not answer spiritual questions, but they do set rules of conduct and ethics. They tell people how they should interact with others and live their lives. A culture's history also acts as a guide for setting rules of conduct. In the twentieth century, leaders in communist countries tried to impose belief systems on their citizens regardless of their history or religion. For the most part, they were only partially successful.

An international marketer must be able to identify and understand how these belief systems will affect product design, sales practices, and business negotiations. In many countries, violations of belief systems can be violations of law.

Explain why international marketers should be familiar with the belief system of a culture.

Checkpoint

COMMUNICATION

MARKETING-
INFORMATION
MANAGEMENT

Fortunately for Americans, the world's business language is English. Students in other countries master English in addition to their own language. Unfortunately, this is not always true of U.S. students. International marketers will be most successful if they know the language of the culture where they work. Marketers must be able to collect information and work with others. They need to be able to make decisions and communicate those decisions. If marketing managers do not understand the local language, they will need to rely upon others to perform these parts of their job. Many international marketers visit countries for only a limited period of time, so it is difficult to learn the local language. As a sign of respect, international marketers should learn the basics of the languages in the countries they visit. These basics include local greetings and other common phrases.

Marketing Myths

What is an urban leg end? "No va" means "it doesn't go" in Spanish. Could this explain why the Chevy Nova automobile might not sell well in Latin America?

While this makes a nice story, it is an urban legend. For Spanish speakers, "nova" and "no va" are not pronounced the same, just as "legend" and "leg end" are pronounced differently in English. A Spanish speaker would not use "no va" to describe a car that doesn't go. They are more likely to say "no funciona."

In fact, the Chevrolet Nova sold well in Latin America. So how do these stories get started? Often non-native speakers look at the words used and translate word-for-word rather than conveying the real meaning behind the words. So what is an urban leg end? A foot!

THINK CRITICALLY

1. Explain how the urban legend of Nova's lack of sales in Spanish-speaking countries may have gotten started.
2. How can a company be sure that it doesn't use a name that could cause problems?

Verbal

There are many different languages spoken around the world. Languages exist within families. For example, in Europe there are a number of *language families*. These language families include Germanic, Romance, Slavic, Celtic, and Greek. Language families can include many individual languages. French, Spanish, and Italian are all Romance languages. Languages can shift radically at borders. A German can cross a border and go from a Germanic to a Romance or Slavic language area. Some cultures actively protect their languages. In both France and Quebec, there are laws to protect the French language. These laws even limit the ability to add new non-French words to the official language.

Even within a language there are many differences. English is one of the official languages in a number of countries. These countries include the United States, Canada, Australia, Great Britain, South Africa, and India. Within these countries, pronunciation, spelling, and word meanings differ. George Bernard Shaw, a famous early-twentieth-century playwright and political figure, stated that "England and America are two countries separated by the same language." For example, an Englishman is likely to use a lift to get to the second storey. "Lift" is British for elevator, and "storey" is British for floor.

Language differences make translating a difficult process. Marketers recommend that translations go through a **back translation** process. Using this process, a native speaker translates material to his or her own language. This translation is then translated by another native speaker back to the original language. This process helps to ensure that words and meanings are translated correctly. Often, when non-native speakers translate, the meaning may come across, but the words can be wrong.

Non-Verbal

Non-verbal communication is what people communicate with their bodies. Non-verbal communication can include facial expressions, eye contact, hand gestures, bowing, and showing emotions. Understanding non-verbal communication can be as important to an international marketer as understanding the verbal language. Even if an American is speaking in English, non-verbal communication is interpreted within the cultural context. For example, handshaking is common throughout the world, but it varies within cultures. In France, as in many other countries, individuals shake hands every time they meet. In the United States and Northern Europe, individuals may not shake hands once they know each other. In Japan, individuals may bow to each other when they shake hands. The person with lower status will bow lower. In Colombia, individuals may take a long time before they shake hands because they feel it conveys respect. In many countries around the world, you would never shake hands or eat food with your left hand. This hand is reserved for "unclean" tasks.

Individuals communicate at different *interpersonal distances*. In Southern Europe and much of South America, individuals move very close to others when they talk. In North America and Northern Europe, interpersonal distances are much greater. In high-context cultures, non-verbal communication can be very important.

Americans are often viewed as highly aggressive when they communicate. They often speak loudly and appear argumentative. They may use excessive hand gestures without regard to local hand gesturing customs. Marketing managers should be sure to understand both verbal and non-verbal communication standards before they attempt to do business in another culture.

List five types of non-verbal communication.

Understand Marketing Concepts

Circle the best answer for each of the following questions.

1. Which of the following is *not* included in defining a culture?
   a. art
   b. television
   c. literature
   d. lifestyles

2. Non-verbal communication includes
   a. writing
   b. radio
   c. hand gestures
   d. newspapers

Think Critically

Answer the following questions as completely as possible. If necessary, use a separate sheet of paper.

3. Explain the difference between a high-context culture and a low-context culture. Give an example of how communication works in both types of cultures.

_____

_____

_____

_____

_____

_____

4. Research Search the Internet to find a map of world languages. Explain the relationships that may exist between the shared languages used and other cultural similarities.

_____

_____

_____

_____

_____

_____

_____

Cultural Dynamics

Goals

- List and describe Hofstede's measures of cultural differences.
- Explain how cultures change over time.

Terms

- expatriate
- self-reference criteria
- diffusion of innovations
- cultural hegemony

Going Global

"Art de Vivre à la francaise" means the "Art of Living" French style. The French are proud of their culture. French culture has developed from its past aristocratic and bourgeois (middle) classes. The art of living means that the French seek pleasures in food, drink, and life. The French will take time to drink coffee at a café. They will spend hours cooking and eating. They believe that individuals should enjoy all that life can bring. Perhaps this belief is why more tourists visit France than any other country in the world.

At the same time, France is reluctant to change. This may be one reason France has a high unemployment rate. France has passed laws to ensure the purity of the French language. France also voted down the European constitution. France has a tradition of protecting its independence in Europe. This tradition can be a problem for companies that want to sell products in France and greater Europe.

Working with a partner, discuss the advantages and disadvantages to a marketer who is trying to sell to a country that strongly holds on to its traditional culture.

CULTURAL DIVERSITY

One of the most interesting aspects of working in international marketing is the chance to experience the cultural diversity of the world. A key way for international marketers to learn about other cultures is through traveling or working overseas. An **expatriate** is an individual who lives or works in a foreign culture. Working as an expatriate helps you gain the knowledge needed to be a successful international marketer.

Defining Cultures

MARKETING-
INFORMATION
MANAGEMENT

In order to understand foreign cultures, international marketers must overcome any *xenophobia*, which is the fear of anything foreign. They also must avoid *ethnocentrism*, the belief that one group is better than another group. International marketers must not fall victim to

© GETTY IMAGES/PHOTODISC

the use of **self-reference criteria**, which lead marketers to view the world through their own cultural beliefs.

Many studies have been completed on how the workplace is influenced by culture. One of the most comprehensive studies was conducted by Geert Hofstede, who identified a number of factors that can be measured and used to understand cultural differences. International marketers must understand each of these factors before they develop a marketing plan.

- **Power Distance** A measure of power inequity between superiors and subordinates is *power distance*. In cultures with a high score in this category, power and social standing come from an individual's position or from inheritance or family connections. Countries with a low power distance score expect more equality. They distrust the use of power. Countries with a high power distance include Mexico, India, and the Arab countries. Countries with a low power distance include Germany, The Netherlands, Great Britain, and the United States.

- **Individualism/Collectivism** A measure related to an "I" (individualism) versus "we" (collectivism) view is *individualism/collectivism*. Cultures with high individualism believe that individuals should look out for themselves. These countries include the United States, The Netherlands, and Great Britain. Cultures with high collectivism view individuals as belonging to a strong cohesive group for their entire lifetime. High collectivism can be found in West Africa, South America, and China.

- **Uncertainty Avoidance** How threatened people feel by uncertain circumstances is measured by *uncertainty avoidance*. It also measures how much they have developed cultural barriers to uncertainty. Cultures with high uncertainty avoidance scores resist new ideas and change. These cultures prefer to stay with past patterns of behavior. High uncertainty avoidance countries include Greece, Japan, and France. Low-scoring cultures are more willing to take risks. These countries include Singapore, Great Britain, and the United States.

- **Masculinity** A measure of the dominant values in a society is *masculinity*. These values relate to material success versus caring for others and the quality of life. Japan scores high because it values material success. The Netherlands scores low because its dominant value is caring for others. The United States, Great Britain, and Germany rate in the middle of this measure.

Once marketers have identified these factors, they can develop strategies. For example, the United States has low power distance, high individualism, low uncertainty avoidance, and medium masculinity. So, marketers may want to use individualism, success and achievement, and newness as ways of marketing their products.

Time Out

The stronger a country's individualism score, the higher its GNP is. The higher a country's masculinity score, the more it spends on defense and the less it spends on overseas aid.

Checkpoint

List each of Hofstede's measures for identifying cultural differences.

_____

_____

_____

CULTURAL CHANGE

On July 8, 1853, the ships of U.S. Commodore Matthew Perry arrived off the coast of Edo (Tokyo), Japan. They were there to force Japan to open to the world as a trading country. Japan had been a closed state for 250 years. Within 20 years of Perry's arrival, Japan opened to Western ideas. It opened bakeries, photo shops, and cinemas. It began offering telephone service, daily newspapers, and public restroom access. At the same time, some 150 years later, Japan still holds on to many of its traditions.

Cultures are naturally slow to change. A culture acts as a framework. It tells people how they should live their lives and how they should interact with others. Cultural change implies a change in this framework for the people within a culture. The United States often is seen as a cultural melting pot. Individuals from many cultures came to the United States. They brought with them cultural traditions that have blended into the larger American culture. The American culture is known for constantly reinventing itself.

Diffusion of Innovations

The **diffusion of innovations** is a theory that explains what influences cultural change. The rate at which a culture changes depends on the type of change and on the number of people who are able and willing to try new things. It also depends on the culture's uncertainty avoidance score and on the communication and marketing systems that are available.

The diffusion process often starts with marketers who are willing to bring new products or ideas to a market. The product or idea does not have to be totally new to the world. For example, Starbucks has taken its coffee shop idea around the world. Starbucks was innovative in how it standardized and marketed its coffee to customers. Starbucks has been successful worldwide. Its success has encouraged a number of imitators that have created logos with a similar appearance to Starbucks' logo. Innovators often are *change agents* who start the change process.

Individuals within a culture must be willing to accept the new product or idea.

These individuals are early adopters. Early adopters most often are willing to adopt products that fit closely to what they already recognize. A typical situation exists in restaurants. Some restaurants in China serve fresh fish as well as jellyfish, sea cucumbers, and snails. Most Americans are not familiar with these types of foods. Chinese restaurants in the United States often use ingredients familiar to their U.S. customers. At the same time, they bring part of the Chinese culture to the United States.

Cultural norms or religions can hinder a person's willingness to accept innovations. However, change can occur even in high uncertainty avoidance countries such as Japan and France. In these countries, change may be slower, or new ideas may need to be adapted to the local market.

Communication About Innovations

Often marketers use media and communication to teach new markets about new products. When Russia opened to international commerce, Western companies entered the market with products that were new to Russian customers. One of these new products was toothpaste. Russians traditionally had used tooth powders. Western marketers used mobile vans to take toothpaste around Russia to demonstrate this new product.

Japanese have consumed both hot and iced coffees for many decades. Starbucks in Japan recently introduced its blended variation of iced coffee called Frappuccino®. This new product was supported by information on the Internet and brochures in the coffee shops explaining the benefits of the product. Product variations also were made for the local Japanese markets by making green tea Frappuccinos®.

Today, communication about new products or ideas can easily spread across the globe. The Internet, satellite television, and other media have made crossing borders easy. More than 1.5 billion people have access to the Internet. These media currently are dominated by the English language and U.S.-based media. This situation has led to charges of cultural hegemony. **Cultural hegemony** is the idea that a culture can be dominated by another group's culture. What is perceived as the "American culture" is dominant in television and movies. Many cultures see U.S. cultural hegemony as a direct threat to their traditional lifestyles.

The media have had the greatest impact on young people around the world. The *MTV generation* is a name given to the global youth market. This generation has been influenced by the same television shows, Internet content, games, stores, and products. In many parts of the world, young people have a stronger shared cultural background with their age group worldwide than they do with their own families. This shared cultural background allows marketers to view the MTV generation as one global market.

Checkpoint

What factors influence the rate of change within a culture?

_____

_____

Understand Marketing Concepts

Circle the best answer for each of the following questions.

1. Which of the following leads marketers to view the world through their own cultural beliefs?
   a. ethnocentrism
   b. self-reference criteria
   c. xenophobia
   d. power distance

2. Which of Hofstede's measures looks at the power inequity between superiors and subordinates?
   a. power distance
   b. uncertainty avoidance
   c. individualism
   d. masculinity

Think Critically

Answer the following questions as completely as possible. If necessary, use a separate sheet of paper.

3. Briefly describe each of Hofstede's measures of culture. Describe how these measures could affect an international marketing strategy.

_____

_____

_____

_____

_____

_____

_____

4. Explain how a marketer can influence the acceptance of innovations in a culture.

_____

_____

_____

_____

_____

_____

Business Customs in International Marketing

Goals

- Explain the importance of understanding the values of other cultures.
- Describe what a negotiator must consider in international meetings.

Terms

- face
- values
- customs
- bribe

Going Global

What does it mean to save face? Most Americans love competition. Even more, they love to win. Americans begin competing in sports at an early age. Most players learn to lose as part of the sport. Americans tend to carry this competitive spirit into the international negotiation process.

One U.S. executive was at a business meeting. He engaged in a political discussion with his Japanese counterpart. The U.S. executive used his debate training to show that the Japanese executive was incorrect. The U.S. executive felt good that he won the debate. Then the Japanese executive's face fell, and he walked off to a corner. All conversation and negotiations stopped at that point.

Working with a partner, explain the mistake the U.S. executive made. What should the executive have done to prepare for the meeting and gain an understanding of the Japanese executive's culture?

THE IMPORTANCE OF BUSINESS CULTURE

The idea of **face** is related to your self-image. In most cultures around the world, business negotiators try to avoid losing face. They also try not to create embarrassing or uncomfortable situations that would cause others to lose face. Often this requires the negotiator to allow someone else to *save face* or to get out of a situation without harming his or her dignity. In many cultures, allowing people to save face is seen as a sign of having high ethics and manners.

MARKETING-INFORMATION MANAGEMENT

To be an effective negotiator, international marketers need to understand the business customs and traditions of the people with whom they negotiate. International business is a two-way street. Both sides will likely have to make compromises. However, businesspeople in the United States will not always bend to the needs of foreign partners just as foreigners will not completely change their behaviors to meet the expectations of Americans.

Living in a foreign culture is one of the best ways to understand cultural differences. If international marketers do not have this opportunity, they should learn as much as possible about how negotiations are conducted in these foreign markets.

Values and Customs

Values are the shared beliefs held by members of a culture that help define what is right and wrong or good and bad. Values can be related to Hofstede's measures. U.S. executives operate under a number of basic assumptions. They believe that innovation, strong competition, and free markets are a social good. They also believe that they will personally benefit if they negotiate a positive business outcome for their company. Cultures that are more collectivist may hold different values. Individuals from these cultures may believe that they are negotiating only for the good of their country or their business. They may view their individual success as less important.

International marketers must understand the customs and manners in the cultures they encounter. **Customs** are common practices among a group of people passed from one generation to the next. Customs and manners may include knowing acceptable topics of conversation. They also may include using local table manners when dining and understanding how to interact with people of the opposite gender. For example, in Arab countries, it is considered an insult to show someone the bottom of your feet. In Japan and many Scandinavian countries, it is customary to take your shoes off when you enter a home.

Gifts

Gift giving is expected in some cultures. It helps reinforce business relations. Some countries consider gifts a sign of respect. International marketers must be aware of proper gift-giving etiquette. For example, in Europe, flowers are a customary gift when visiting a home, but make sure you do not bring flowers that are used for funerals in that culture. In other countries, flowers are not considered a good gift.

It is important to conduct research to ensure that appropriate gifts are given for each culture visited. For example, there are many gift giving guidelines to follow in China. Gifts for Chinese individuals should be small and personal. Gifts between businesses should not be given until after negotiations are finished. Gifts should not include products made in Taiwan. They also should not be anything expensive that could be viewed as a bribe. Even the color of the wrapping paper is important. Gifts should be wrapped in red but not in black.

International marketers must be careful that gifts are not viewed as bribes. A **bribe** is money or something of value that is given in order to persuade someone else to violate ethics or laws. In some countries, bribery is considered to be illegal if it is conducted inside or outside of the national

Time Out

Some countries pay bribes to encourage export sales. Countries rated as the highest bribe payers include China, South Korea, Taiwan, and Italy. Countries least likely to bribe are Sweden, Australia, and Canada. The United States is the seventh country that is least likely to bribe.

borders. With the passage of the Foreign Corrupt Practices Act in 1977, the United States made it illegal for U.S. companies to bribe foreign governments. Bribery in other countries, especially underdeveloped countries, is common. In some European countries, bribes are a standard way of doing business. Some countries have structured their civil employment system around the concept of paying for services rendered. Because civil employees may be underpaid, they are expected to supplement their income through other types of payments.

Checkpoint

What is the difference between a gift and a bribe?

INTERNATIONAL MARKETING MEETINGS

International marketers must be prepared to participate in meetings with individuals from other cultures. Cultures will vary on many aspects related to meetings, including the arrival and starting time and the language used. The proper greeting and the exchange of business cards are other considerations. It also is important to recognize who has the authority to make decisions in these meetings.

Tech Zone

Economic espionage is a problem for most developed countries. Economic spies try to steal corporate information, product processes, and new product ideas. Many of the tools they use are high tech. One tool being used to collect information on companies is the Internet. The Internet also is used to attack company and government data networks through computer hacking and the spread of viruses. Companies must ensure that they do not allow secret information to be posted on their Internet sites. They also must have strong firewalls to prevent unauthorized access and to protect their data.

THINK CRITICALLY

List the problems companies face by having their computer networks connected to the Internet. What policies should a company follow to reduce the chance of an online espionage attack?

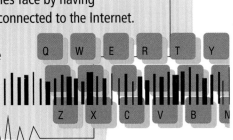

Meeting Basics

Cultures vary on the issue of time. An appointment set for 11:00 A.M. may mean that everyone should be ready to start exactly at that time. In other cultures, it may mean that the meeting will take place sometime around the noon meal. The Chinese, Americans, and many northern Europeans like meetings to start on time. Many warmer-climate countries do not hold the same tight schedule for starting times.

The language used in the negotiation process is often a practical matter. The global business language is English. At the same time, it is often a good idea for the business host to arrange for a translator. Business decisions should not be made on the basis of an incorrect translation. Even for individuals who do not speak the foreign language, it is still important to know a few key phrases.

Different customs are involved in greetings. In many Arab and Muslim cultures, women should be greeted only verbally. Men should not kiss women on the cheeks or shake their hands unless their hands are offered. In France, kissing a French woman on the cheeks may be expected.

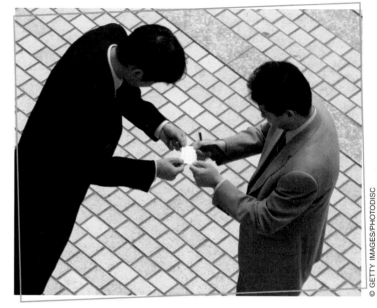

Business cards are almost always exchanged at meetings. It is a good idea to have business cards printed on both sides. One side should be in English. The other side should be in the language of the negotiation partner. In Asian cultures, a business card should be handed over with two hands. It also should be turned so that the person receiving the card can read it. Cards should be studied for a few moments as a sign of respect to the other person. In China, the cards may be lined up on the negotiation table, so all names can be recognized.

Often business negotiations are conducted over a meal. It is important to understand and observe meal customs. In Japan, noodles should be eaten with a loud slurping sound. In China, it is important to try each item brought to the table buffet. Eating everything at the buffet may be a signal to bring more food. If traveling to Asia, a marketer should learn how to use chopsticks. In Europe, meals can be based on regional foods and drink. It is always a good idea to study the region and its foods in order to be able to talk about the meal.

Negotiations

SELLING

Culture has an impact on business negotiations. All sides of the negotiation process will try to make the most of their position. At the same time, negotiators and businesses must be able to trust each other. Some countries have strong contract laws. These countries include the United States, Canada, and the European Union. In these countries, agreed-upon negotiations are backed by the threat of legal action. In other countries, people distrust contracts and believe they signify a lack of trust. In countries with weak contract laws or weak enforcement of contract laws, trust becomes very important. The negotiations process may start by developing trusted relationships. Then business negotiations follow.

Negotiation is an art. Many cultures practice negotiation every day. They may even negotiate prices at a local market. Each culture may employ negotiation tactics based on how they view the other party. For example, Japanese negotiators view Americans as being impatient. They may remain silent in order to pressure Americans into making compromises. In high power distance cultures, the real authority may reside with a top manager. In Japan, this is likely to be the oldest person on the negotiating team. It is important to identify where the real negotiating power lies. To be successful, negotiators should study the cultures and tactics used in the cultures where they are negotiating.

Checkpoint Describe one way an international negotiator should prepare for a meeting.

_____

_____

_____

_____

World Stars | MEG WHITMAN

Meg Whitman is a multibillionaire and one of the richest CEOs in the world. She is President and CEO of eBay Inc. Whitman has made eBay the world's most valuable Internet brand and the number one consumer e-commerce web site. EBay's official slogan calls it the World's Online Marketplace®. Whitman started her career with Procter & Gamble where she gained experience in brand management. She then worked for a number of companies, including Disney and Stride Rite, the maker of Keds. Whitman has considerable experience in international business. She was president and CEO of FTD, the world's largest floral products company. She also was general manager of Hasbro Inc.'s Preschool Division, where she was responsible for global management and marketing of Playskool brands and Mr. Potato Head. Whitman has a Bachelor of Economics from Princeton University and a Master of Business Administration from Harvard Business School.

Whitman wants eBay to become a strong global player. She hopes that international revenue will increase from 10 percent to 50 percent within the next few years. Whitman expects China to represent the largest part of eBay's business in ten years. She is so confident of China's growing role in the world's economy that she persuaded her son to spend his senior year of high school with a Beijing family to learn about its culture.

Whitman must be able to negotiate in every country where eBay has a division. This includes negotiating with business partners and governments. Her knowledge of international cultures is vital to her job as CEO of the world's online marketplace.

THINK CRITICALLY

Explain the types of skills that Meg Whitman needs in order to be an effective global CEO. Explain how she has gained these skills.

Understand Marketing Concepts

Circle the best answer for each of the following questions.

1. A negotiator has caused someone else to be embarrassed. The embarrassed person has
   a. saved face
   b. lost face
   c. no face
   d. the right to sue

2. What is given that encourages someone else to violate ethics or laws?
   a. a gift
   b. a negotiation
   c. a bribe
   d. a value

Think Critically

Answer the following questions as completely as possible. If necessary, use a separate sheet of paper.

3. What impact do you think bribery has on international business?

_____

_____

_____

_____

_____

_____

_____

_____

4. Explain why an international negotiator should study other cultures before engaging in international negotiations.

_____

_____

_____

_____

_____

_____

_____

Review Marketing Concepts

Write the letter of the term that matches each definition. Some terms
will not be used.

_____ 1. A system of shared beliefs, values, customs, and behaviors that
defines how a group of people lives

_____ 2. An individual who lives or works in a foreign culture

_____ 3. Allows individuals to understand their place in the larger universe

_____ 4. A process that helps people learn about their culture

_____ 5. A theory that explains what influences cultural change

_____ 6. The idea that a culture can be dominated by another group's culture

_____ 7. What people communicate with their bodies

_____ 8. Leads marketers to view the world through their own cultural beliefs

_____ 9. The study of differences existing in physical, biological, and cultural features of the earth

_____ 10. Money or something of value that is given in order to persuade someone else to violate ethics or laws

a. back translation
b. belief system
c. bribe
d. context
e. cultural hegemony
f. culture
g. customs
h. diffusion of innovations
i. enculturation
j. expatriate
k. face
l. geography
m. non-verbal communication
n. religion
o. self-reference criteria
p. values

Circle the best answer.

11. The largest religion in the world is
    a. Christianity
    b. Islam
    c. Hinduism
    d. Shinto

12. The shared beliefs that help define right and wrong
    a. hegemony
    b. culture
    c. values
    d. face

13. Cultural influences include all of the following except
    a. geography
    b. belief systems
    c. history
    d. uncertainty avoidance

Think Critically

14. Define culture and explain how it is developed.

_____

_____

_____

_____

_____

15. Explain how history and geography can have an influence on the development of a culture.

_____

_____

_____

_____

_____

16. Using the diffusion of innovations theory, develop a plan to introduce a new product into a foreign market.

_____

_____

_____

_____

_____

17. Explain the concept of "face." Describe what a negotiator needs to do to be sure that a foreign partner does not "lose face."

_____

_____

_____

_____

_____

18. Explain why international marketers view young people around the world as one global market? Why are they called "the MTV generation"?

_____

_____

_____

_____

19. Geography Locate a map of world languages on the Internet. Use it to explain why the language patterns often match climatic conditions.

_____

_____

_____

_____

_____

_____

_____

20. History Use the Internet to learn about the history of a country other than the United States. Identify how this country's history has influenced its present culture.

_____

_____

_____

_____

_____

_____

_____

21. Communication Write a one-page report on the importance of proper verbal and non-verbal communication for international marketers.

_____

_____

_____

_____

_____

_____

_____

22. Marketing Math Assume that the population of the world is 6.5 billion. Determine the percentages of the world population for each of the major world religions as described in Lesson 3.1.

_____

_____

_____

_____

_____

23. Problem Solving Assume that you have been put in charge of translating your company's promotional material. Explain how you will ensure that you have a correct translation.

_____

_____

_____

_____

_____

24. Research Use the Internet to learn about gift giving customs in another country. Describe what kinds of gifts would be appropriate and inappropriate to give a businessperson from this country.

_____

_____

_____

_____

_____

_____

PUT MARKETING ON THE MAP

International Marketing Plan Project

You will need to undertake a cultural assessment of your target country before you engage in product development, sales, or negotiations.

Work with a group and complete the following activities.

1. Research your target country's history and geography. Indicate how these factors have influenced this country's culture.
2. Research your target country's major religion. Indicate how this religion could influence the business practices in this country. Give specific examples.
3. Use the Internet to find the major languages spoken in this country. Identify any types of non-verbal communication that should be avoided.
4. Use the Internet to research Hofstede's cultural measures for this country. Specify how these measures will impact your marketing plan.
5. Use the Internet to develop a plan for engaging in negotiations in this country's culture. Include in this plan how you will organize and run the meeting.

Case Study

A CHANGING CULTURAL TREND

Television and other media recognize and reward human beauty. High value is placed on a youthful, beautiful appearance. Television commercials market products that claim to help you stay younger looking and fit. The cosmetics industry has always heavily depended on women to purchase its wide array of products ranging from makeup to beauty creams. Now men are paying greater attention to how they look, driving up sales of men's skin care products.

There are many motives behind men's spending on vanity products. Some men think that a youthful appearance is helpful in business. They think it will help them gain business or increase their chances of a promotion. Men are spending more time in the gym and paying attention to diets to stay trim because they think it gives them a competitive advantage. Men now try to obtain a youthful appearance by adding new products, such as hair color and skin wrinkle creams, to their daily grooming habits.

The cosmetics industry has seized the opportunity of a growing men's market. New lines of men's cosmetics have entered the marketplace. Marketing strategies are planned around the newfound vanity of men. Sales of men's skin care products sold in department stores increased 13 percent in 2004, more than twice the total growth for women's skincare markets. High-end department store products are not the only benefactors.

Sales at mass-market retailers increased 68.6 percent compared to 6 percent for women's products. Shampoo and conditioner sales for men rose 17 percent while the market was flat for women's hair products.

Major cosmetic manufacturers, such as Estee Lauder, Clinique, Avon, Gillette, and L'Oreal, have developed new brands for men. The drugstore chain CVS Corporation is introducing an exclusive line of men's skin care products. The company has quadrupled shelf space for men's grooming products last year, and sales are up over 20 percent this year.

An increasing number of U.S. men are concerned about their looks and willing to pay high prices for beauty products. A shift in cultural attitudes has made it more acceptable for men to spend time looking good. Cosmetic companies hope that the trend for men's cosmetic products will spread to other parts of the world.

THINK CRITICALLY

1. Why are males purchasing more cosmetic products?

2. How might the current cosmetic trends become targets for deceptive trade practices?

3. How has the cosmetic industry successfully entered a market that previously held a macho image?

4. How has society influenced the cosmetic industry for men?

CREATIVE MARKETING PROJECT

The Creative Marketing Project will help you develop an awareness of the analytical and creative approach to the marketing process. It actively engages you in the marketing activities of your community. It also provides you an opportunity to work with experienced executives that have guided and assisted in developing the marketing, management, and entrepreneurship leaders of tomorrow.

One to three students are allowed to work together to complete this project. One part of this project includes the written document, which is worth 70 points. Another part of the project is the oral presentation, which is worth 30 points. The written document must not exceed 30 pages and should include the following sections: Executive Summary, Introduction, Proceedings and Research Methods Used, Findings and Conclusions, Recommendations, Bibliography, and Appendix. Students will have ten minutes to present their project to the judges, and judges will have five additional minutes to ask questions about the project.

A local drugstore in your community plans to expand its line of men's skincare products. It has asked you to devise a marketing strategy that will gain the attention of the male target market and result in increased sales of its men's skincare products.

Performance Indicators Evaluated

- Understand the local target market and its projected response to the product.
- Analyze the market potential.
- Develop a plan to take advantage of market opportunities.
- Demonstrate a teamwork approach to this project.
- Demonstrate critical thinking and problem-solving skills.
- Communicate the plan effectively to appropriate stakeholders.

Go to the DECA web site for more detailed information.

THINK CRITICALLY

1. Why is it challenging to market men's skincare products?
2. What theme could you use in your promotions to grab the attention of the target market and persuade them to purchase the new men's skincare products?
3. What techniques would you suggest that the drugstore use to capture the interest of the target market?

www.deca.org

The International Political Economy

© GETTY IMAGES/PHOTODISC

CHAPTER • CHAPTER 4 • CHAPTER 4 • CHAPTER 4 •

4

Vote Here

Point Your Browser

▶ ▶ ▶ ▶ intlmarket.swlearning.com

From Conflict to Unity

Europe is built upon a history of warfare and conflict between countries and cultures. The second half of the 20th century is one of the longest periods of peace that Europe has ever seen. One of the keys to this lasting peace has been the development of economic and political unity in Europe. This unity started in 1950 with a proposal to combine the coal and steel industries of Western Europe. The six countries that formed the initial alliance went on to sign the Treaties of Rome. This alliance created the European Economic Community (EEC). The EEC was later called the European Community (EC). This common market allowed member states to remove trade barriers.

The original six countries were Belgium, Germany, France, Italy, Luxembourg, and The Netherlands. In 1973, they were joined by Denmark, Ireland, and the United Kingdom. Greece joined in 1981, and Spain and Portugal joined in 1986. Austria, Finland, and Sweden joined in 1995. In 2004, ten new countries joined.

The current European Union (EU) is a group of democratic European countries that use treaties to work together economically and politically. Member countries must abide by trade agreements and some political control over economic policies. The European Union has helped ensure peace and economic development. It has raised living standards and created a Europe-wide market. It also has developed a single European currency, the euro. It has given Europe a stronger political voice.

In 2005, two of the original EU countries, France and The Netherlands, voted down a new European constitution. That constitution would have further integrated Europe politically. This vote was seen by some to be a rejection of turning Europe into a United States of Europe. This, in part, is due to differing economic and political philosophies within Europe. Some countries are in favor of strong free market policies. Others want to maintain more state control and strong social policies.

Think Critically

1. Explain why political and economic integration in Europe would lead to 50 years of peace.

2. Why do you think both France and The Netherlands would reject the EU constitution?

National Demographics

- Explain the importance of demographics to international marketing.
- Describe the effect of population and class on international marketing.

- developed countries
- newly industrialized countries
- developing countries

- Lorenz curve
- population pyramid
- social class

Going Global

Africa's largest retailer is the Shoprite group. This company started in South Africa in 1979, and it began to expand in 1994. Shoprite has a number of businesses that serve grocery and home shopping needs for countries in Africa and around the Indian Ocean. Shoprite's stores serve different income levels in these developing countries. Shoprite has found customers with disposable income that will buy in these low-income countries.

The Indian government recently allowed Shoprite into the Indian market. Its store in Mumbai is India's largest store. Shoprite has competition from South African grocer Pick 'n Pay, which also is expanding into new markets. Both of these stores cater to local markets to meet their inventory needs. They also have strong social responsibility policies to help economic development and to maintain sustainability of resources.

Working in groups, discuss why these two grocery stores would choose to expand in less-developed countries.

IMPORTANCE OF DEMOGRAPHICS

MARKETING-INFORMATION MANAGEMENT

A company must take three steps when considering whether an international market is right for a product. First, the company must determine whether there is a need for the product. Then it must decide whether the potential market can pay for the product. Finally, the company must find out if the market is large enough. The last two steps require an analysis of the potential market's demographics. *Demographic factors* include things like income, age, social status, and education. They draw a picture of the population in a market.

Traditionally, countries have been grouped into three development categories. The first category includes **developed countries**, sometimes called *first world countries*. These countries have a high per capita, or per-person, income. They have a high standard of living and a strong diversified economy. Developed countries include the United States, Canada, most of Western Europe, Australia, New Zealand, and Japan. The second classification is **newly industrialized countries**, sometimes called *second world countries.* These countries have high levels of industrialization. However, they may not have the high personal incomes or the infrastructure (modes of communication and transportation) of developed countries. Countries in this category include Turkey, Thailand, Malaysia, Mexico, and South Africa. The third classification is **developing countries**, sometimes called *third world countries.* These countries have low personal incomes. They also have low levels of industrialization and poor infrastructure.

Some countries, such as China and India, are harder to classify. These countries are developing, but development and income vary widely across the country. Urban centers could be considered to be newly industrialized while rural areas may be considered to be developing.

Income Distribution

MARKETING–
INFORMATION
MANAGEMENT

Marketers must find customers who are able to pay for their products. The United States and Western Europe have the highest incomes, but other countries should not be ignored. Using data such as an average *per capita income* of a country can be misleading. National income is not distributed evenly among populations. National income is often evaluated based on the Lorenz curve. The **Lorenz curve** looks at the distribution of income in a population by *quintiles,* or fifths. The *line of absolute equality* means that income is spread evenly across the population. The *line of absolute inequality* means that a small percentage of the population has all of the national income. The farther the Lorenz curve is to the lower right, the less equally a nation's income is distributed.

Lorenz Curves

A graph titled "Lorenz Curves" with the y-axis labeled "Percent of Total Income" ranging from 0% to 100% and the x-axis labeled "Percent of Total Population" ranging from 0% to 100%. The legend shows: Sweden, United States, South Africa, Line of absolute equality, Line of absolute inequality.

The Lorenz curves for Sweden, the United States, and South Africa are shown in the above graph. Sweden shows the most equality of income. South Africa shows the most inequality. This distribution of income has implications for market segmentation within a country. A company should not ignore a country because of low average incomes. South Africa's average

The percentage of national income that goes to the wealthiest top 10 percent of a population varies. European countries and Canada have the least variation. Less than 24 percent of income goes to the top 10 percent. Less-developed and developing countries often have the highest variation with over 40 percent. The United States is between China and India at 30 percent.

income is only $2,780, but it has considerable income inequality. The majority of its population has a very low income. The top 20 percent have almost 65 percent of the national income and have a lifestyle comparable to that in the United States.

Education

One of the strongest links to higher income is the educational level of a country. Most developed countries have high levels of mandatory education. Most countries require twelve years, but some countries require thirteen years. Less-developed countries require only seven to nine years. For marketers, the educational level of a country suggests two things.

First, an educated workforce makes it easier for an international company to expand into a market. A country with an educated workforce and educated managers can design, build, and sell products. Higher educational levels in India and China have resulted in economic booms. India graduates two million English speakers from universities every year. These individuals go to work in businesses that compete in the world marketplace. They work in call centers, software firms, engineering companies, and other businesses.

Second, individuals with higher educational levels are more likely to purchase the same types of products. For example, medical doctors need the same types of supplies, tools, medicines, and training. Managers in companies also have similar needs across borders. These individuals also are likely to have the same lifestyles. They will purchase the same products for their homes. These products include computers, technology equipment, and transportation. Educational level can be a strong market segmentation tool.

Checkpoint

List the three levels of country development.

_____

_____

POPULATION

MARKETING-INFORMATION MANAGEMENT

The current world population is over 6.5 billion people, and it increases by one percent each year. Even if this growth rate drops below its current one percent increase every year, there will be over 9 billion people by the year 2050. Most of this growth is occurring in developing countries. Populations in many developed countries actually are declining. As countries develop economically, family size often shrinks. This reduction in family size is due to less infant mortality, dual-income families, and the desire for higher living standards.

Europe's population may shrink from 331 million to 243 million over the next 50 years. In turn, Europe's share of the GDP could shrink from 22 percent to 12 percent. Japan's population also has been decreasing for the last 22 years.

This population reduction has its own set of problems. The average age in these countries is increasing. Europe and Japan both have strong social safety nets for their older populations. These social programs increase the tax burden on the younger population. The increased tax burden decreases the ability to purchase products.

Developing countries, on the other hand, have a much larger population of younger people. With shrinking family sizes, these younger people have higher disposable incomes. This market has huge potential for international marketers.

A **population pyramid** shows the number of males and females in different age groups in the population. Age groups make up layers of the pyramid. The age increases as you move up the pyramid. A wide base with a narrow top represents a high birth rate and a high death rate. A wider top with a narrow bottom indicates a lower birth rate and a lower death rate. Less-developed countries often have a wide base and narrow top, which indicates there are a large number of young people. Some developed countries, such as Japan and Germany, will have an upside-down pyramid by 2050. This means that the number of elderly citizens will surpass the number of children.

Ethics Around the World

China has historically had a number of cultural reasons to increase the total number of children for each family. High infant mortality rates claimed a number of lives. The more males a family had the greater the chances for keeping the family name and heritage alive to pass along to later generations. In addition, after the communist takeover in 1949, there was a policy to increase the total population of China. In that year, China's population was 600 million. By the 1970s, the population was close to 900 million. China faced a population crisis.

In 1979 China implemented a one-child policy. In practice, families in urban areas were allowed one child. In rural areas, where cultural traditions were more important, the family was allowed a second child if the first child was female. Ethnic minorities were exempt from the one-child policy.

Many claims have been made about China's one-child policy. These claims include female infanticide (the intentional killing of baby girls), sex selection, and a disproportional number of males over females. Demographic studies have shown that China has close to the same male/female ratio as Korea, Taiwan, and India.

THINK CRITICALLY

1. China currently has 1.3 billion people. Estimate what would have happened to China's population if it did not have a one-child policy.
2. Argue for or against China's one-child policy. Consider the results, both pro and con, of this policy.

Social Class

International markets are often segmented based on social class standing. A **social class** is a group that is distinguished from others in a society based on criteria such as income, net worth, education, family history, political power, or lifestyles. Social classes in the United States often are based on income. They are divided into lower, lower-middle, middle, upper-middle, and upper classes. The importance of social class differs among cultures.

Great Britain has traditionally had three classes. The upper class includes people with inherited wealth and families that are titled aristocrats. The middle class includes the majority of industrialists, professionals, businesspeople, and shop owners. The working class includes laborers, such as agricultural, mine, and factory workers. Social class differences in Britain are reinforced by the education individuals receive. They also are reinforced by spoken accents, interests, and even the type of food eaten.

India's class structure is based on a 3,000-year-old view that four groups sprang from body parts of a prehistoric man created from clay by the God Brahma. These four groups included Brahmans, the highest class that provided for intellectual and spiritual needs. The Kshatriya class was to rule and to protect others. The Vaishyas were businessmen and merchants. The Shudras were farmers and manual laborers. A fifth class was the Untouchables, who worked only in menial jobs related to bodily decay and dirt. These classes were part of the Hindu religion. One could only move to another class through the cycle of rebirth, or reincarnation.

International marketers often find that the individuals from top social classes around the world have shared interests and purchasing behaviors. Lower social classes may be more traditional in their purchasing behavior. They have less experience and contact with other cultures and media.

Class Mobility

When analyzing social class, marketers must look at opportunities for *class mobility,* or the ability of individuals to change social classes. Typically, individuals want to move up to higher social classes. In much of the developed world, this movement is achieved through education and increased income. In some culturally bound countries, there is less social class mobility. For example, in India, although it is against the constitution to discriminate on the basis of social class, social class structure still exists.

Social class mobility is important because marketers sell products that allow individuals to appear to belong to higher social classes. Individuals who purchase a luxury car may be seen as belonging to a higher social class. In cultures where individuals are unlikely to move to higher social classes, they may not purchase products related to higher classes.

Define social class and class mobility.

_____

_____

_____

Understand Marketing Concepts

Circle the best answer for each of the following questions.

1. A country with a high per capita income, a high standard of living, and a strong diversified economy is called a
   a. developed country
   b. newly industrialized country
   c. developing country
   d. none of the above

2. A(n) _____ looks at the distribution of income in a population by quintiles, or fifths.
   a. income curve
   b. population pyramid
   c. Lorenz curve
   d. demographic

Think Critically

Answer the following questions as completely as possible. If necessary, use a separate sheet of paper.

3. List and describe four demographic factors used to understand markets.

   _____

   _____

   _____

   _____

   _____

   _____

4. **Research** Use the Internet to find a population pyramid for a country. Discuss the implications of the age distribution on marketing strategies for this country. (*Hint:* The U.S. Census Bureau web site creates population pyramids for every country.)

   _____

   _____

   _____

   _____

   _____

   _____

Economic Environment

- Describe the four types of economic systems.
- Explain the effects of economic integration on international marketing.

- economic system
- market economy
- mixed economy

- planned economy
- traditional economy
- free trade area

Going Global

Wal-Mart has always had a unique marketing strategy. When Wal-Mart started, it avoided bigger competitors in larger, wealthier markets. Instead, it chose to locate in smaller, lower-income, rural areas. Wal-Mart proved that there were huge profits to be made in these ignored markets. But Wal-Mart's growth has hurt smaller retailers. City governments have put restrictions on Wal-Mart's ability to expand in the United States. Wal-Mart has continued this strategy in its global expansion. Trade agreements allowed Wal-Mart to expand into Mexico. Changes in the Chinese economy have allowed Wal-Mart to open new stores in China without local partners. Chinese consumers are not concerned about the loss of smaller businesses. They see Wal-Mart as providing the quality and prices they want in products. Wal-Mart sees the potential in the Chinese market in 100 cities with populations over one million each. There are more than 150 million urban families with incomes over $10,000 per year. China also has retail sales of over $6 trillion dollars. The rate of sales is growing at 15 percent per year.

Working with a partner, list reasons why Wal-Mart would want to expand outside of the United States. Explain why China would be a good choice for Wal-Mart.

THE POLITICAL ECONOMY

MARKETING-INFORMATION MANAGEMENT

The term *political economy* refers to the idea that international business is influenced by the economic and political/legal environments of countries. For example, the United States has a *mixed economy* where the government sets rules and regulations on both production and trade. It also has a *republic* where a democratic process elects representatives to govern the country. China, on the other hand, has one political party with no real democracy. At the same time, it has been opening its economy to operate as a strong free market system, often with little regulation for workers' safety or for environmental concerns.

International marketers must understand the economic environment and political/legal environment in the countries where they want to sell products. The political economy will have a direct impact on all of the core standards of marketing.

Economic Systems

A country's **economic system** governs how it controls the production, distribution, and consumption of goods and services. Several types of economic systems are used around the world.

- **Market economy** In this economic system, the free market determines which products are produced. It also decides how they are marketed and priced. Private property and entrepreneurship are characteristics of a market economy. Pure free markets have little government interference.

- **Mixed economy** This system combines market economy characteristics with varying levels of government control. Most developed countries have mixed economies. In most cases, government control is used to protect consumers and laborers. It also ensures that businesses compete fairly. *Socialism* is a strong form of a mixed economy. Socialism sets strong rules and regulations to control business practices. It aims to protect all citizens.

- **Planned economy** The government acts as the central planner in a planned or *command* economy. This system plans the types of products produced. It also determines where they can be sold and the prices to be charged. The former Soviet planned economies in Central and Eastern Europe collapsed. China has moved some products from a planned economy toward a market-based economy. Large industries such as electrical utilities are still controlled by the state. Only a few countries in the world, such as North Korea and Cuba, still operate as planned economies.

- **Traditional economy** In traditional economic systems, customs, religious beliefs, and historical patterns determine how economic questions are answered.

International marketers will need to develop different sales strategies based on the type of economic system in which they are operating. For example, many companies are cautious about selling in the Chinese market. Weak government control over patents and competitive practices allows Chinese companies to steal product designs and packaging. Chinese companies also do not have to contend with rules and regulations

---

Marketing Myths

The Chinese have a planned economy. The United States is a free market. In fact, these statements are only partially true. In the 1990s, China reformed its economic system following the principle of *"zhua da fang xiao."* This statement means "grasp the large and let go of the small." In China, the state retains ownership and control over large businesses. But it allows small businesses to survive or fail on their own in a free market. For many companies, it is compete at all costs or die.

The United States operates as a mixed economy. The federal government owns very little of the factors of production. The United States does impose a large set of rules and regulations on how businesses compete. It attempts to ensure the quality and purity of products. It regulates the working environment. It also sets rules to limit environmental damage.

These two philosophies have caused trade friction. U.S. companies have accused Chinese companies of having unfair advantages because they operate in a less-regulated environment.

THINK CRITICALLY

1. Why do you think China would allow only some free markets?

2. Explain why China's free market approach could be considered as an unfair advantage.

regarding workers' safety or the environment. This situation allows them to produce at a lower cost than developed countries. An international marketer will need to learn how to sell to a country in which the government handles the planning for large products, such as electrical utilities or telecommunication systems.

Over the last 15 years, the general trend in the world has been toward market-based or mixed economic systems. The international marketer becomes a key tool in helping an economic system meet the needs of a country. The marketer helps to develop and promote products and identify where and how they are sold. The marketer also helps set the sales price. Under the guidance of marketers, stores such as Shoprite and Wal-Mart are bringing high-quality, low-cost products to millions of the world's lower classes.

Checkpoint   List the four types of economic systems.

_____

_____

_____

ECONOMIC INTEGRATION

PRODUCT/SERVICE MANAGEMENT

Global economic integration refers to the development of trading partnerships through the elimination of restrictions on trade. Elimination of restrictions increases trade and makes for more efficient use of each country's resources. The more integrated countries are, the more likely factors of production will shift between countries, enabling them to produce the highest return. For example, a worker in Europe can move his or her labor resources to other countries to make more money. The goal of economic integration is to improve all countries' economic welfare.

The European Union moved through a number of stages of economic integration. The least restrictive economic integration is called a free trade area. In a **free trade area**, all barriers to free trade are removed. A *customs union* is a free trade area with a common trade policy to non-members. A *common market* is a customs union that allows for labor, capital, and technology to move between members. Europe's current *economic union* coordinates economic policies between member countries.

There are a wide variety of regional trade agreements around the world. These include free trade areas, customs unions, and common market agreements. Examples are the Association of Southeast Asian Nations (ASEAN) and the Common Market for East and Southern Africa

(COMESA). Other examples are the Central America Common Market (CACM) and Caribbean Community and Common Market (CARICOM).

Free trade areas allow companies to locate in a single country instead of multiple countries. For example, Ireland has experienced tremendous growth from the European Union agreements. Many international companies located in Ireland because it has an educated workforce that speaks English. The entire European Union can be served from that one location. In addition, the more integrated the region, the fewer variances needed in product development. A standardized set of rules and regulations brings down the cost of product development and sales.

The Americas

In 1989, the United States signed a free trade agreement with Canada. In 1992, this agreement was expanded into a set of treaties called the *North American Free Trade Agreement* (NAFTA). NAFTA created a free trade zone linking Canada, the United States, and Mexico. NAFTA went into effect in 1994. It eliminated duties on half of all U.S. goods shipped to Mexico. It also set agreements to phase out other tariffs over the next 14 years. The treaty also protects patents, copyrights, and trademarks. It makes it easier to invest among the three countries. NAFTA also has rules related to worker and environmental protections.

NAFTA has had an impact on the economies of North America. Trade in products between the United States and Canada grew twice as fast as it did before 1994. Trade between the United States and Mexico expanded three times as fast. U.S. direct foreign investment in Mexico grew at twice the rate of the U.S. investment in the rest of the world. NAFTA's impact on the reduction in tariffs, the free movement of capital, and more unified laws has helped marketers sell products throughout North America.

NAFTA has drawn some criticism. There have been numerous debates about whether NAFTA has resulted in job losses in the United States. NAFTA was a trade agreement between two developed countries and one developing nation. Some data shows that jobs have moved to Mexico because of its lower labor costs.

A new trade pact called the *Central America Free Trade Agreement* (*CAFTA*) was passed in July 2005. This agreement will link the United States with Costa Rica, El Salvador, Guatemala, Honduras, Nicaragua, and the Dominican Republic. It will make 80 percent of U.S. exports duty-free, with the remaining tariffs phased out in ten years. It could increase U.S. exports by $3 billion annually. Most of these countries are considered to be less-developed, low-wage countries. An even larger *Free Trade Area of the Americas* (*FTAA*) has been proposed. This agreement would partner all countries in the Americas except Cuba into a free trade zone.

Time Out

In 2001, China joined the World Trade Organization. As part of its trade agreement, China agreed to eliminate trade barriers and lower tariffs. By 2005, the tariffs on U.S. agricultural exports and industrial products were projected to be reduced by at least 16 percent.

Checkpoint

Name two types of free trade areas.

Understand Marketing Concepts

Circle the best answer for each of the following questions.

1. An economic system where the free market determines which products are produced, how they are marketed, and how they are priced is called a
   a. market economy
   b. mixed economy
   c. planned economy
   d. traditional economy

2. An economic integration where all barriers to free trade are removed is a(n)
   a. economic union
   b. customs union
   c. common market
   d. free trade area

Think Critically

Answer the following questions as completely as possible. If necessary, use a separate sheet of paper.

3. Explain why international marketers need to develop different sales strategies for each type of economic system in which they are operating.

_____

_____

_____

_____

_____

_____

4. Explain what NAFTA is and how it has affected trade.

_____

_____

_____

_____

_____

_____

Political and Legal Environments

Goals

- Describe the different types of political systems.
- Describe the different types of legal systems.

Terms

- political system
- democracy
- republic
- one-party state
- theocracy
- political risk
- legal system
- contract
- sustainability

Going Global

Russia has over 140 million people and stretches across 11 time zones. It is the largest land mass of any country in the world. It has a highly educated workforce and vast natural resources. Yet, Russia has never been able to reach the same level of economic development as other countries. This lack of development is largely due to Russia's history of having a one-party political system.

Russia was ruled by czars from its early history until 1917. These one-party kings were overthrown in the Russian Revolution. Vladimir Lenin's Bolshevik Communist Party took control. It formed a one-party state known as the Union of Soviet Socialist Republics (USSR). After World War II, Soviet Russia gained control of much of Central and Eastern Europe. In 1991, Soviet Russia collapsed back into 15 independent republics and the country of Russia. Russia attempted to develop a democratic political system and market economy. But it has been plagued by internal corruption and weak legal systems. By 2005, Russia's President Putin was accused of returning Russia to a one-party state.

For Russia to move toward economic development, it must first put into place political and legal systems that allow for stability, enforcement of contract laws, and an end to corruption. Russia must decide if it can do this better under a democracy or under a one-party leader.

Working in small groups, explain why Russia has not been able to become a developed country. Outline a plan for Russia to move toward economic development.

POLITICAL SYSTEMS

A **political system** sets the laws under which businesses operate. International marketers need to develop strategies that will work in a variety of political and legal systems.

Most countries consider themselves to be *sovereign states,* free from external control. A few countries are *protectorates,* which are under partial control of a larger country. For the majority of the world's history, governments were run by kings, czars, emperors, or dictators. Just as there has been a worldwide movement toward free markets, in the last few

decades, there has been a strong movement toward democracy around the world. Unlike one-party states, democracies must respond to the will of their citizens.

Types of Political Systems

MARKETING-INFORMATION MANAGEMENT

There are several types of political systems used around the world. They range from pure democracies to one-party states.

A **democracy** allows for direct elections by a country's citizens. Democracy was practiced in ancient Athens in the 5th century B.C., but it only allowed for direct voting by a small percentage of the population. Democracies must have both fair and free elections. Some countries hold elections, but the government controls the election process. Therefore, they are not free or fair.

A **republic** is a form of government in which citizens elect representatives who, in turn, vote on laws. The Roman Empire was the first republican form of government. Most often these systems have a chief executive, such as a president or prime minister. Most democracies operate under a republican form of government. Republics are most often just called democracies. Today, more than 62 percent of the world's countries have democracies. Most of these countries use a republican form of democracy.

One-party states allow for only one political party. Very few countries today have kings with actual political power. *Communism* is a one-party political system in which all property belongs to the state. This form of government rose and declined in the 20th century. Today there are still a few communist countries, such as Cuba, North Korea, and Vietnam. China is a communist country, but it allows for the ownership of personal property. Some countries with supposedly democratic or republican forms of government do not have free or fair elections. These countries are run

by one-party leaderships that control the election process. Mexico was a one-party state for almost 70 years. The Institutional Revolutionary Party (PRI) held control in Mexico until after elections in 2003. Since then, Mexico has moved toward a multi-party democratic system.

Theocracy is a special form of government where religion or faith plays a dominant role. In most theocracies, religious leaders play a direct role in controlling government actions. Iran is a theocracy. In 2005, Iran held an election. A group of religious leaders first chose the candidates who could run for election. They then endorsed one of the candidates. The endorsed candidate won the election.

Political Risk

MARKETING-INFORMATION MANAGEMENT

Understanding political and legal systems allows a business to engage in long-term planning. Businesses face increased **political risk** when there is uncertainty about the stability of a political or legal system. Political risk is considered to be very troubling for international marketers. Change in political or legal systems can result in general uncertainty. It also can result in the voiding of contracts and the nationalization of property, which occurs when the government takes ownership of property.

Multi-party democracies have proven to be a highly stable form of government. Most developed countries are democracies. One-party states and theocracies can see businesses and business activity as a threat to their power. Chances for corruption increase in one-party states. Leaders in one-party states are often concerned only about their own welfare. They are not necessarily concerned about the welfare of their citizens. The relationship between a business and political leaders is more important when international marketers do business with one-party states.

International marketers deal with political risk by increasing the amount of information they collect on a country and its leaders. They must develop contingency plans in case there is political change. Businesses should act as good corporate citizens by following the laws and customs of a country. Businesses also can purchase political risk insurance to protect assets or profits.

Political Economy Movement

The political economy of a country does not necessarily remain stable over time. The general shift of countries has been toward democratic mixed economies. After 1990, two countries started in this direction. Russia attempted to undertake a political and economic reform. It tried to move from a communistic command economy to a democratic mixed economy. The results were not good. Corruption resulted in a few people obtaining tremendous wealth while most citizens' lives did not improve. These citizens often voted to return to a more command economy. The diagram below shows the path (orange) that Russia has taken.

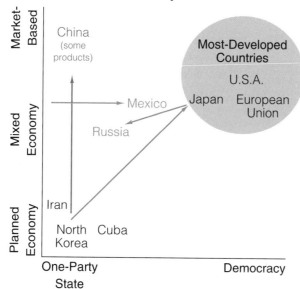

Political Economy Movement

China is taking another path (blue). China has maintained its one-party state control, but it has allowed for economic reform. This move has resulted in high economic growth and some limited political freedom. The diagram shows the path that China has taken. There has not yet been any indication from China that it is moving toward a true democracy.

International marketers play an important role in providing goods at a reasonable price to the citizens of a country. Marketers try to avoid one-party states that develop planned economies or create political risk. This limits a country's ability to move toward economic development.

Not all countries see democratic mixed economies as an ideal system. Many developing countries are in danger of moving from democracies to one-party states under planned economies. Leaders in some theocracies have stated that democracy and free markets are Western ideas and should not be followed.

Countries in Latin America have some of the most unequal income distributions in the world. This inequality has created political problems. These countries are democracies, and the voting poor have elected candidates who are willing to move away from free-market economies. This situation could lead to political instability and economic uncertainty. It could increase political risk. In 2005, President Chávez of Venezuela threatened to nationalize the oil industry. This action would give the Venezuelan government more control over international oil companies' assets and oil distribution.

Checkpoint   Name the four types of political systems.

_____

_____

_____

LEGAL SYSTEMS

MARKETING–
INFORMATION
MANAGEMENT

A **legal system** creates, interprets, and enforces the laws of a country. International marketers have two concerns. The first concern is the nature of the laws and legal system of the country. The second concern is how well those laws are enforced. For example, China has historically had weak contract laws. New legislation was put into place to allow businesses in China to develop contracts. Western companies have found it difficult to enforce these contracts. Even if they win in court, there may be no means for enforcing the contract or collecting damages.

There are two major types of legal systems used around the world. One is based on statutory law. The other is based on case law. *Statutory law* systems attempt to put every possible legal issue into a specific law. *Case law* is based upon British common law and allows for the interpretation of statutes to specific situations. Countries that were influenced by Great Britain often have a case law legal system.

These two legal systems operate differently. For example, assume Company A trademarked the name of Business B's established

product in Company A's country. In a statutory law country, Company A may have the right to the name if it trademarked the product first. In a case law country, Business B could take Company A to court to prove that Business B had used the name first and, therefore, that Company A had no right to the name. When a company wants to introduce a new product or new brand name around the globe, it often needs to patent or obtain a trademark in every country where it plans to do business.

Corruption is a problem for international businesses in countries with weak legal systems. *Corruption* is the misuse of an official position for one's own benefit. Countries have been rated on their level of corruption, with a score of 10 being the most corrupt. Sweden, Singapore, and New Zealand are rated as the least corrupt, scoring below 1. Haiti, Bangladesh, and Nigeria are viewed as the most corrupt, scoring above 8.5. The United States scores 2.5. Russia scores 7.3, and China scores 6.6.

Contract Law

A **contract** is any legally enforceable promise or set of promises made by one party to another. Contracts lower the risks of doing business by stating each party's responsibilities. For example, a contract can set the price of products or services. It can help guarantee that payments will be made when products are purchased on credit.

Weak contract enforcement can hinder business operations in a country. Business transactions may need to be paid in cash instead of by credit. Companies may not want to sell products internationally because they fear that copyrights and patents will not be enforced.

The development of free trade areas has helped businesses operate internationally. Trading regions unify their legal systems and set regulations for the enforcement of contracts. For example, a business can patent a product in one European country, and the patent will be enforced throughout the EU.

Sustainability

Sustainability is a worldwide movement to allow for economic development while minimizing negative impacts on the environment. Many countries around the world have enacted "green" laws for business conduct to maintain sustainability. Germany has enacted laws

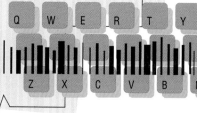

Tech Zone

Technology is increasing the standard of living of poor people in less-developed countries. In India, lower-class citizens used to have to pay corrupt government officials up to $22 for a copy of land deeds. Now these citizens are able to use computer kiosks to access records for as little as 30 cents. This helps farmers obtain loans so that they can plant their crops. This is an example of e-government, which is technology used to meet the needs of a government and its citizens. This technology allows even the poor to have access to information. India also uses e-government to allow people to find farm supplies and obtain health information. The computer kiosks use solar power in towns without electrical power.

THINK CRITICALLY

Describe the impact that e-government has on the lives of poor people in India. Specify how the e-government kiosks can help limit corruption and aid economic development.

requiring manufacturers to take products back for recycling when the product is no longer used. For example, a company that sells computers is responsible for collecting and recycling the computer when it is no longer needed.

There also are a large number of international treaties that are designed to develop sustainable business practices. The Kyoto Protocol is a set of agreements on global air pollution. It is designed to limit global warming. Over 140 countries around the world have signed this U.N.-sponsored treaty. The United States was one of the lone major holdouts on signing the treaty. This lessens the impact on companies doing business in the United States, but any company engaged in business in another country will have to abide by the Kyoto Protocol.

Checkpoint

Describe the two types of legal systems.

World Stars   J.R. O'NEAL

Joseph Reynold (J.R.) O'Neal was born in 1911 in the British Virgin Islands (BVI). The British Virgin Islands are protectorates of Great Britain. At the time, the Virgin Islands were not economically developed. O'Neal became one of the BVI's earliest entrepreneurs and conservationists, helping to move the BVI from a less-developed group of islands to a developed country.

O'Neal received his certification as a pharmacist, but he started in the family business of raising cattle. Eventually, he used his entrepreneurial skills to develop a combined pharmacy, dental service, and photo shop. Other ventures included inter-island shipping and a large-scale general merchandising business. O'Neal also invested in the construction of trading ships. He also developed a hydrofoil ferry service between BVI and the U.S. protectorate islands of St. Thomas and San Juan.

O'Neal was concerned that economic development could endanger the BVI's natural beauty. He became chairman of the BVI's National Parks Trust. He headed the reforestation of two mountain parks. His contributions to conservation work were honored by Queen Elizabeth II of England.

THINK CRITICALLY

Explain the impact that a single individual can have on the economic and environmental development of a country. Determine which skills allowed O'Neal to succeed.

Understand Marketing Concepts

Circle the best answer for each of the following questions.

1. A form of government where citizens elect representatives who, in turn, vote on laws is a
   a. democracy
   b. republic
   c. one-party state
   d. theocracy

2. Which of the following allows for the interpretation of statutes to specific situations?
   a. statutory law
   b. case law
   c. contract law
   d. government law

Think Critically

Answer the following questions as completely as possible. If necessary, use a separate sheet of paper.

3. Briefly describe the concept of contract law and why this is important to international marketers.

_____

_____

_____

_____

_____

4. Write a paragraph explaining why most developed countries are democratic mixed economies. Specify which comes first, the economic development or democracy.

_____

_____

_____

_____

_____

Chapter Assessment

Review Marketing Concepts

Write the letter of the term that matches each definition. Some terms will not be used.

_____ 1. Shows the number of males and females within different age groups in the population

_____ 2. Allows for direct elections by a country's citizens

_____ 3. Looks at the distribution of income in a population by quintiles or fifths

_____ 4. Countries with a high per capita income, a high standard of living, and a strong diversified economy

_____ 5. A system that combines the market economy with varying levels of government control

_____ 6. Countries with low personal incomes, low levels of industrialization, and poor infrastructure

_____ 7. A worldwide movement to allow for economic development while at the same time minimizing negative impacts on the environment

_____ 8. Government controls the production, distribution, and pricing of goods and services

_____ 9. A group that is differentiated from others in a society based on criteria such as income and net worth

_____ 10. A form of government where religion plays a role

a. contract
b. democracy
c. developed countries
d. developing countries
e. economic system
f. free trade area
g. legal system
h. Lorenz curve
i. market economy
j. mixed economy
k. newly industrialized countries
l. one-party state
m. planned economy
n. political risk
o. political system
p. population pyramid
q. republic
r. social class
s. sustainability
t. theocracy
u. traditional economy

Circle the best answer.

11. Most developed countries have what type of economy?
    a. market economy
    b. mixed economy
    c. planned economy
    d. traditional economy

12. Which of the following strategies should a business use to limit political risk?
    a. develop contingency plans
    b. act as good corporate citizens
    c. purchase political risk insurance
    d. all of the above

Think Critically

13. List and explain each of the demographic factors outlined in the text. Explain why these factors are important to international marketers.

_____

_____

_____

_____

_____

14. Identify the differences between a market economy and a mixed economy. Explain why most developed countries operate under a mixed economy instead of a pure free-market economy.

_____

_____

_____

_____

_____

15. List the reasons why a planned economy does not lead to economic development.

_____

_____

_____

_____

_____

16. Russia and China have taken two different paths in reforming their political economies. Explain why one plan is better than the other. Justify your answer.

_____

_____

_____

_____

_____

Make Connections

17. Research Use the Internet to research a U.S. Free Trade Agreement, such as NAFTA or CAFTA. What are the benefits of this agreement? What are the drawbacks?

_____

_____

_____

_____

_____

18. Geography Use a map of the world to identify two countries. Develop a PowerPoint presentation of each country's demographic, political, and legal environments. (*Hint:* The CIA World Fact Book web site is one good source for this data.)

_____

_____

_____

_____

_____

19. History Research the history of China. Identify China's historical political systems. Explain why China's political system may affect its movement toward democracy.

_____

_____

_____

_____

_____

20. Research Create a diagram as shown on p. 91. Choose five countries not already included. Research these countries and indicate where they would be placed.

_____

_____

_____

_____

_____

21. Marketing Math One of the strategies of the Kyoto Protocol is the trading of carbon credits. This strategy allows businesses to own and sell the right to release carbon dioxide, or CO_2, into the atmosphere. Assume your company owns the right to release 10 tons of CO_2. Company X has found that it will cost $1 million to clean up its production in order to reduce CO_2 by 10 tons. It will cost your company only $400,000 to control 10 tons of CO_2. How much will Company X be willing to pay your company for the CO_2 credits? Justify your company's sale of the carbon credits.

_____

_____

_____

_____

_____

_____

_____

_____

PUT MARKETING ON THE MAP

International Marketing Plan Project

Your international marketing plan must be based upon your understanding of your targeted country's demographic and political economy.

Work with a group and complete the following activities.

1. Use the Internet to research the demographics of the country in which you plan to market. Try to identify each of the categories outlined in the chapter. Specify how these will affect the design, price, or sale of your products.

2. Specify the level of development of the country you are targeting. Use the CIA World Fact Book online to develop a political economy analysis of your country. Indicate how this national profile could affect your marketing plan.

3. Develop a list of the political risks your company will face doing business in your targeted country. Develop a plan to lower these risks.

4. Specify the legal system used in the country you are targeting. Indicate how strong contract law is in that country.

5. Determine if your targeted country is a member of any global free trade zones. Indicate if your targeted country has a commitment to sustainability. Specify how these factors will affect your marketing plan.

Case Study

MINUTEMEN—GUARDING THE BORDER

Tightening up the border between the United States and Mexico has become a heated issue. Illegal aliens cross the border each day to work in the United States for higher wages and a better life. The construction, manufacturing, and agricultural industries count heavily on illegal labor from Mexico. Employers pay lower wages to illegal aliens. They also avoid paying Social Security, federal, and state taxes. However, the influx of people from Mexico has put a burden on schools, medical care, and the labor market.

Many citizens in bordering states like Texas, Arizona, and California are becoming increasingly frustrated with the number of illegal aliens entering the United States. Their frustration is not only focused on the number of illegal aliens crossing the border but also on employers taking advantage of the situation and government not responding to the illegal activity.

The increased level of terrorism also raises concerns about illegal aliens crossing the border. Americans are becoming concerned that terrorist cells harbored in Mexico will easily cross the U.S. border.

Concerned citizens in California, Arizona, New Mexico, and Texas have formed a new Minutemen organization to guard the border. Minutemen are volunteers who want to stop illegal aliens from crossing the border. They also want to report businesses that hire illegal aliens.

Patrolling the border is not an easy task. Border patrols cannot stop all of the illegal traffic into the United States. The Minutemen project has attracted hundreds of volunteers from across the country. Many of the volunteers legally carry guns and wave flags while keeping watch on the border. They also use cell phones or radios to alert the Border Patrol when they see people crossing the border. During the second day of operation, the Minutemen project in Arizona helped the Border Patrol apprehend 141 illegal aliens.

The Minutemen project has drawn criticism from the American Civil Liberties Union (ACLU), immigrants' rights groups, and the U.S. Department of Homeland Security. These groups are monitoring Minutemen activities to make sure they are legal—an ironic twist to perhaps protect illegal activity.

THINK CRITICALLY

1. What threats are posed to the United States by illegal aliens from Mexico?
2. Why do some businesses not approve of the activities of the Minutemen?
3. What might be the political backlash for tightening up the border and supporting Minutemen activities?
4. What types of penalties should be given to businesses that hire illegal aliens?

MARKETING MANAGEMENT SERIES EVENT

The Marketing Management Series Event consists of two major parts: a written comprehensive exam and a role-playing event. Participants are given a written scenario to review. Participants have ten minutes to review the situation and to develop a professional approach to solving the problem. This must then be presented to the judge. Participants may use notes made during the preparation time during the presentation, but no note cards may be used.

Ten minutes are allowed for students to present their plan of action to the judge. Five additional minutes are available for judges to ask questions about the proposal.

A major homebuilder is keenly aware of the public's concern over a large number of illegal aliens hired by the U.S. construction industry. Unfortunately, the hiring practices of some builders have led to a stereotype for all builders. The stereotype is of greedy homebuilders that hire cheap, unsupervised, or illegal labor to cut back on wages and taxes paid. Society is also critical of the losses of American jobs to illegal aliens.

You have been asked by the homebuilder to design a rough draft of an advertising portfolio that will be given to potential customers. The portfolio should include facts about the homebuilder's business and pictures of the various models of homes offered by the homebuilder. It also should tastefully assure customers that they are receiving an all-American-made product that involves no illegal activity.

Performance Indicators Evaluated

- Understand the public's perception of mass construction.
- Outline the major information to communicate to potential customers.
- Demonstrate critical thinking and problem-solving skills when creating the portfolio.
- Prioritize information to include in a marketing portfolio.
- Communicate a plan to assure customers of an all-American-made product.

Go to the DECA web site for more detailed information.

THINK CRITICALLY

1. Why is the public so concerned with the construction industry and illegal workers?
2. What might happen to the price of a home if no workers from Mexico are involved with the project?
3. What ethical issues do builders face in this case?
4. Why do you think illegal aliens are willing to work for such low wages?

www.deca.org

International Marketing Opportunities

© DIGITAL VISION

Point Your Browser

▶ ▶ ▶ ▶   intlmarket.swlearning.com

Furniture Opportunities

Most people would say that either Bill Gates with $47 billion or Warren Buffett with $43 billion is the richest person in the world. People don't think about Ingvar Kamprad, the founder of IKEA. His personal fortune is estimated to be $53 billion. IKEA is a global furniture retailer with more than 200 stores in 32 countries and territories.

In 1943, when Ingvar was 17, he received a gift from his father for doing well in school that he used to start a business. He sold pens, wallets, watches, and other items at a reduced price. He called the business IKEA. The name combined his initials (I. K.) and the first letters of the farm (Elmtaryd) and the village (Agunnaryd) where he grew up. Today, IKEA sells through a unique store concept where shoppers enter on the first floor. Then they wander through multiple aisles and floors to reach an exit. IKEA also sells through catalogs and the Internet. It prints 145 million catalogs in 48 editions and 25 languages. In 2004, IKEA had sales of $15.5 billion. Eighty-one percent of sales were from Europe. Sixteen percent of sales were from North America. Three percent of sales were from Asia and Australia.

International expansion has not always been smooth. IKEA tried to sell Scandinavian-designed beds to Americans. The beds were the wrong size for U.S. bed linens. Americans also prefer traditional rather than modern designs. IKEA tried to sell four-legged desks to Germans, who preferred five-legged desks.

IKEA sells inexpensive and stylish furniture designed for small spaces. This appeals to Asia's upwardly mobile professionals in cities such as Beijing and Shanghai. IKEA sees Russia as a strong growth market. It has three stores in Moscow. One is in the second-largest mall in Europe. With 4.5 million visitors annually, the Russian store has more customers than any other IKEA. IKEA's global expansion has helped sales stability.

Think Critically

1. Explain why IKEA would want to sell in more than just its home Scandinavian market.

2. Why would IKEA's furniture appeal to developing markets such as China and Russia?

Lesson 5.1

Identifying Markets

Goals

- Define *market segment*.
- Describe the market segments within consumer markets.
- Describe the market segments within industrial markets.
- Discuss how to meet the needs of domestic intercultural markets.

Terms

- market segment
- profile
- qualified market

- undifferentiated segmentation strategy
- concentrated segmentation strategy

- differentiated segmentation strategy
- demographics

Going Global

The Jeep brand name is one of the most recognized in the world. Jeep started as a military vehicle in World War II. Jeep is now considered to be a lifestyle brand. DaimlerChrysler's Jeep Grand Cherokee was the company's top seller outside of North America. Sales increased particularly in Europe and China. The Jeep Grand Cherokee also is manufactured around the world. There are plants in North America, Europe, and China.

Jeep owners see the brand as fitting the Jeep lifestyle. In Europe, there are Jeep camp events and Jeep clubs. In China, Jeeps often have decals of outdoor lifestyle events such as surfing, camping, or climbing even though these activities are not practiced in China. Jeep reinforces this brand image. It offers outdoor, adventure, and lifestyle products through Jeep-licensed merchandise.

Working with a partner, explain why Jeeps would appeal to customers in North America, Europe, and China. Describe the profile of Jeep's consumers in each of these markets.

MARKET SEGMENTS

MARKETING–INFORMATION MANAGEMENT

The first step in developing a marketing strategy is to determine the market segment you want to target. A **market segment** is a group of individuals or organizations that share similar characteristics. They will respond in the same way to a business's product design, price, distribution system, and promotional campaign. When a product is sold internationally, businesses may find that their current products appeal to a different market segment in foreign markets. For example, the same Jeep model may appeal to different market segments in Europe and Asia. American consumers may buy the Jeep for its off-road ability. Asian and European customers may purchase the Jeep to

---

support a lifestyle. Marketers start the segmentation process by identifying characteristics that create a **profile**, or picture, of the market segment.

Qualifying Markets

Market segments need to be qualified. A **qualified market** will have three characteristics. The first is a *need* or desire for the product. The second is the *ability to pay*. The third is the *authority to purchase*. Qualified markets will differ by product and by culture. For example, soft drinks often are sold to youth markets in the United States. In many other countries, young people may have a need or desire for soft drinks, but they may not have the ability to pay for them. In some cultures, only the head of the household may make major purchases. Others in the family may not have the authority to purchase a product.

Business markets are qualified in the same way. An *industry* includes businesses that produce similar products. Many businesses within the same industry may have the same need for a product. The ability to pay and the authority to purchase can vary greatly across international business markets.

Time Out

Product use can vary widely around the world. U.S. citizens on average drink 216 liters of carbonated soft drinks per year. This amount is more than half a liter per person per day. Britons consume 96.5 liters. Germans consume 72 liters. The Japanese consume only 21.6 liters.

Segmentation Strategies

When companies pursue new opportunities, they must choose a segmentation strategy. International marketers typically follow three strategies. The first is an **undifferentiated segmentation strategy**. Using this strategy, a company looks at all customers as one market. This strategy works when a market is too small to be profitable to target. It also works when a small group uses the majority of the product or when a brand is dominant in the market. Companies such as Coca-Cola and KFC use this strategy in some international markets.

A **concentrated segmentation strategy** is used when a business focuses on one clearly defined market segment. A **differentiated segmentation strategy** is used when a company targets two or more segments with unique strategies.

Businesses look for markets where they can obtain profits with a low risk. This may be achieved using a concentrated segmentation strategy where a business looks for a small market with few potential competitors. On the other hand, it could look for markets that are large or growing. In this case, a business should use a differentiated segmentation strategy to pursue multiple segments or market multiple products. This strategy is part of the reason that many companies are looking at markets such as China. It is a large and rapidly growing market. Of course, not all Chinese customers react to the same marketing strategies in the same way. There are considerable differences among China's 1.4 billion people.

Name three characteristics of a qualified market.

Checkpoint

CONSUMER MARKETS

MARKETING–
INFORMATION
MANAGEMENT

Consumer market profiles are created from a combination of variables. These variables include demographic, cultural, geographic, and product usage characteristics. A single consumer can be in different market segments for different products. Also, a single product can appeal to different market segments, especially across borders.

Demographic Segmentation

Demographics are population characteristics such as age, gender, race, income, and education. Within a culture, individuals who share common demographic characteristics may react to a marketing strategy in the same way. This is not necessarily true worldwide. Globally, there can be considerable differences in consumers' needs and wants even if the same demographic characteristics exist.

Demographic trends are valuable indicators for identifying new markets. These trends include projections for growth in incomes or population. The ability to use demographic data as a planning tool depends upon a business's ability to collect and access it. Most countries do not have the ability to use computer databases to link demographic information to product sales.

Cultural Segmentation

Culture can be defined by *lifestyle* characteristics including values, activities, interests, and opinions. Lifestyles often are a reflection of the larger culture. For example, many Scandinavian cultures have a strong health, family, and work orientation. Southern European countries may have more leisure-oriented cultures and lifestyles. Advertisements for many consumer products are designed to show how a product fits or supports a lifestyle.

The consumer's current lifestyle is not always important. Many products are sold to support a customer's *idealized lifestyle,* or the preferred lifestyle the customer would like to live or project to others. Jeep fits European and Chinese customers' idealized lifestyles. Although these customers may not take their Jeeps on adventures, they want to be seen as adventurous.

Tech Zone

There can be considerable differences in the ability to use technology to target markets across borders. In the United States, consumer information is the property of the business that collects it. U.S. businesses use computer databases to collect, sell, and analyze consumer information. This information includes demographic, lifestyle, and product usage factors. Companies use computer databases to develop consumer lists that are sold to help businesses reach customers.

In Europe, consumer information is the property of the consumer unless the consumer releases the information. Most developing countries do not have the technological ability to collect information to help marketers identify customers.

THINK CRITICALLY

Describe the advantages to marketers of having the ability to capture consumer information. Discuss the advantages and disadvantages to consumers of having personal information collected in databases.

Lifestyle characteristics are good predictors of customer choice. However, it is much harder to get data on lifestyles. This data is collected from surveys and purchases.

Geographic Segmentation

Markets can be segmented based on where consumers are located. This is called *geographic segmentation*. Geographic characteristics can be strong profiling criteria for some products. Individuals who are raised in rural, farm areas may use products in the same way and may share many of the same needs and desires. Some products have heavy geographic concentration usage. Coffee shops in large cities often are clustered together to meet the needs of individuals who work, live, or shop in the area.

Geographic segmentation also looks at the economic development of a country. Within a country there can be varying levels of development. Consumers in large metropolitan areas in developing countries may have more in common with city dwellers in other larger countries than they do with rural customers in their own country.

Product Usage

Product usage characteristics are related to the amount of a product used. Some customers are considered to be *heavy users*. These individuals purchase and use a large amount of a product. Soft drinks have heavy user market segments. These individuals consume a large percentage of total soft drink sales. Youth markets are heavy soft drink users.

Many consumers use products based on the benefits derived from the products. Because of this, *product benefits* also are used as a segmentation variable. Consumers who react to product benefits can vary widely on other segmentation characteristics. For example, consumers in all market segments benefit from low-priced products, such as low-end televisions and appliances.

Fitting Products to Consumer Markets

The knowledge that companies gain while serving markets lowers their risk when introducing new products. Wal-Mart has considerable experience selling to global markets. This experience and the information in Wal-Mart's databases help ensure success when introducing new products to current customers.

When a company sells existing products to new markets around the world, it must first determine if the products will appeal to the same market profiles. Introducing new products to new markets is a risky strategy. Businesses must conduct marketing research to lower risks.

Name four ways that consumer markets can be segmented.

Checkpoint

INDUSTRIAL MARKETS

Industrial markets profile businesses based on the type of organization, the industry served, and the purchasing situation. Additionally, a different marketing strategy may be needed to meet the rules and regulations that apply to sales in each country. For example, it is unlikely that an automotive parts supplier could consider the auto industry around the world as the same market segment. Most countries have rules and regulations pertaining to the production and sale of manufactured auto parts. In addition, the buyers in each region may have different buying motives.

Organization characteristics include business size, ownership, geographic location, and the amount of product used. Large global businesses may have centralized purchasing offices or systems. They may purchase large amounts of products. This situation requires a different marketing strategy than when selling in markets where most manufacturing is controlled by small, independently owned companies.

Factors related to the *industry served* include product categories and product benefits. Another consideration is the end market served, or the business's customers. Often companies around the world that are in the same industry have the same types of customers. They need the same benefits in the products they purchase. For example, a business may sell to high school markets around the world. The types of products needed, the customers served, and the end results desired would be very similar.

The *purchasing situation* variables include the stage of the buying process and other factors that may influence the buying process, such as culture. Business customers that are ordering a new product for the first time must be dealt with differently than businesses that are simply reordering. International salespeople must be able to devise strategies to sell in purchasing situations that are culture-specific. For example, the process of developing business relationships in Asia will differ from developing business relationships in Western Europe. Regional and cultural differences will require different sales strategies.

Trading Bloc Regulations

The development of trading blocs enables international marketers to look at industrial markets by country groups. Given the European Union's common trading rules and regulations, a company may be able to use the same sales strategy across countries. The United States is a member of both NAFTA and CAFTA. This membership makes it easier to plan for business sales in North America and Central America. An international salesperson will still need to take into consideration cultural differences.

Name three ways that industrial markets can be segmented.

_____

_____

DOMESTIC INTERCULTURAL MARKETS

MARKETING-INFORMATION MANAGEMENT

Marketers do not need to cross borders to find international markets. The United States has a culturally diverse population. Large groups of individuals maintain lifestyles closer to their cultural heritage than to mainstream American culture. Two examples of these cultures are Asian-Americans and Hispanic-Americans.

© GETTY IMAGES/PHOTODISC

The U.S. Census Bureau defines Asian-Americans as those having a heritage from the Far East, Southeast Asia, or the Indian subcontinent. These segments share cultural values of strong family ties, a strong work ethic, and an emphasis on education. Asian-Americans are the wealthiest segment tracked by the U.S. Census Bureau. Between 1990 and 2000, the Asian-American population increased nearly four times the rate of the U.S. population as a whole. Asian-American dual-income households have an average income eight percent higher than non-Hispanic white households. Asian-Americans working full time earn more than their non-Hispanic white counterparts.

"Hispanic" refers to the original settlers of the southwestern United States. It also refers to immigrants whose backgrounds are from Spanish-speaking countries in Latin America. Hispanics share values of strong family ties, strong religious affiliations, and a strong work ethic. Hispanics have a median age of 26.7 years compared to white America's median age of 39.6. The Hispanic birth rate is twice the national average. Hispanic household income is growing, with 38 percent earning over $40,000 in 1999. By 2008, Hispanic spending could reach more than $1 trillion.

Geographic Concentration

Domestic intercultural markets often are geographically clustered. For example, Hispanics are heavily represented in the southwest United States. They also have populations of over one million in both Illinois and New York. Smaller domestic intercultural markets often are clustered within the United States and Europe. For example, Chicago has the second-largest ethnically Polish population outside of the Polish capital of Warsaw. France has a large number of people with a Muslim heritage from countries such as Algeria, Morocco, and Tunisia.

Businesses target these markets by changing to meet cultural needs. A fast-food restaurant in Paris called Beurger King Muslim allows devout Muslims to eat burgers in accordance with their religion. All of its meat is prepared in accordance with Islamic dietary laws.

Explain what a domestic intercultural market is.

Checkpoint

Passport

Understand Marketing Concepts

Circle the best answer for each of the following questions.

1. Which of the following is *not* a characteristic of a qualified market?
   a. ability to pay
   b. authority to purchase
   c. need or desire
   d. loyalty

2. Which consumer market segment is characterized by values, activities, interests, and opinions?
   a. cultural
   b. demographic
   c. geographic
   d. product use

Think Critically

Answer the following questions as completely as possible. If necessary, use a separate sheet of paper.

3. Develop a profile of a market segment using demographic factors. Describe a product that would appeal to this market.

   _____

   _____

   _____

   _____

   _____

   _____

   _____

4. Research Use a magazine to find a lifestyle ad. Describe the lifestyle the ad is presenting. Explain if the ad is for people who actually have this lifestyle or if it is showing an idealized lifestyle.

   _____

   _____

   _____

   _____

   _____

   _____

   _____

Market Opportunity Analysis

- Explain why it is important to pursue new market opportunities.
- Describe the screening process used to evaluate market opportunities.

- portfolio of markets
- screening
- buildup method
- market share

Going Global

International express delivery companies are looking at China as a new marketing opportunity. Chinese middle-class consumers are ordering products from overseas markets. Chinese businesses are finding that time is an important consideration when shipping parts, products, and documents. China's membership in the World Trade Organization now allows independently owned international express mail businesses to operate in China. Growth is expected to continue. Within five years, every Chinese person is expected to have a credit card and to be making purchases online.

UPS's business with China doubled in one year, and it plans to have 60 distribution centers in China to meet expected demand. FedEx moved its Asian hub from the Philippines to a new $150 million facility in southern China. DHL has been in China the longest. It developed a partnership with the Chinese company Sinotrans in 1980. DHL-Sinotrans has the largest network in China with 56 branches covering 318 cities.

Working with a partner, discuss why express delivery companies view China as an opportunity.

IDENTIFYING MARKET OPPORTUNITIES

SELLING

Pursuing new market opportunities is important for all businesses. Old markets often disappear over time. New markets and products are needed to help businesses grow.

Pursuing new international opportunities increases uncertainty and risk. A business must operate in different economic, cultural, and political/legal environments. International marketers attempt to lower uncertainty by carefully researching and evaluating global markets. Opportunities exist with new products and new markets. A company can pursue four basic strategies.

- pursue no new products or markets
- introduce new products into existing markets
- introduce existing products into new markets
- introduce new products into new markets

Identifying new market opportunities is the first task for international marketers. Next, they need to determine if they are going to pursue these international opportunities or remain in their domestic market. Then, they will need to identify new or existing products to meet the needs of the new markets. Finally, they will need to devise a strategy to successfully pursue these opportunities.

Market Opportunity Analysis

Businesses find international markets in a number of ways. Often a business will receive an unsolicited request for a product. Businesses that do not have international experience may ignore these requests. Not taking advantage of international orders results in lost opportunities.

A business can lower the cost of finding new markets by enlisting the help of third parties. Third parties can include national or state trade missions. Often these trade missions will show products, distribute promotional material, and help develop contacts. Once the contacts are found, it is up to the business to pursue them further.

Finally, a business can actively attempt to identify new markets. This often requires conducting research. It also may involve participating in international travel. It can be easier to sell to business markets internationally than to consumer markets. The needs of business markets often are more similar across national borders than the needs of consumer markets. Selling to international consumer markets often requires the development of new marketing strategies, such as new distribution channels.

Developing a Portfolio of Markets

A **portfolio of markets** is a collection of different products in different market locations. By having an array of products and markets, businesses lower their risks. A company should have new products to replace old products or markets that dwindle. Not having new products or markets can increase risks. An international portfolio of alternative products lowers the risk of having all sales attached to one product or market. For example, after the September 11, 2001, terrorist attacks, IKEA's U.S. sales decreased but not Russia's sales. In addition, its stores in China will provide future growth opportunities if sales slow in Europe and North America.

Having multiple products in multiple countries creates an international portfolio. If done correctly, it can lower overall risks for a business. Today, international marketers are looking for growth in developing countries. Because increased competition and low growth are common in developed countries, there are often more opportunities in developing countries. Markets in Asia, Central and Eastern Europe, Central and South America, and parts of Africa are seen as large potential growth markets.

Checkpoint List the four strategies a business can use to pursue opportunities.

SCREENING PROCESS

Screening is the process of identifying potential market opportunities to pursue. Often international marketers start by looking at a large number of options. Then they will screen these options to arrive at a smaller number. Screening for new opportunities involves a four-step process.

1. **Identify markets** The first step is to determine the market segments that a business could pursue.

2. **Identify competitive advantages** This step requires identifying competitors and competitive products for each of the potential markets. It often requires marketing research.

3. **Estimate industry sales** Industry sales include all of the sales within a business category. For example, the fast-food industry could include a variety of restaurants, such as hamburger, chicken, and sandwich restaurants. Each of these restaurants also could be viewed as an individual industry.

4. **Estimate share of market** A market share is the percentage of a market that a business could capture.

Identifying Sales Potential

MARKETING-
INFORMATION
MANAGEMENT

Determining sales potential starts with an estimate of total sales within an industry category. This estimate generally is provided by a reliable source. The U.S. government is one of the largest data collectors in the world. Information on industry sales in developed countries is often easier to obtain than information on developing or less-developed countries.

Data Collection The U.S. Census Bureau is a good source for facts and statistics. It collects and provides information on a variety of industry categories. This information often is very broad, such as data on "all restaurant sales."

Trade and professional associations serve businesses with common interests. These organizations often collect and sell information that focuses on more narrowly

Ethics Around the World

Are children an ethical target market? Children around the world share the same needs and desires. However, they cannot be easily targeted as market segments. In the United States, most products children are able to buy can be legally advertised to children. In Sweden and Norway, advertising aimed at children under the age of 12 is forbidden. Direct mail advertising to children under the age of 16 also is illegal in Sweden.

As in the United States, it is lawful in Great Britain to target children with advertising. British children are targeted with more food advertising than children in any other country in Europe. The majority of products advertised in Great Britain are for products that encourage poor eating habits. British citizens have one of the greatest problems with obesity in Europe.

International marketers use advertising as a tool for dispersing information to new markets. Rules and regulations will differ on how these tools can be used to reach selected markets, such as children.

THINK CRITICALLY

1. Why do you think Sweden and Norway would ban advertising to children?
2. Argue for or against a ban on advertising to children. Consider both the pros and cons of this policy.

targeted products or markets. For example, Euromonitor International found that sales of ice cream in Western Europe were $20.3 billion in 2004. It also found that Western Europeans like fruit flavors because they are perceived as healthy and pleasurable. These trade studies are usually for sale.

It is harder to determine industry sales for less-developed markets. International marketers can estimate regional sales by assuming that markets develop in similar ways. For example, express shipping companies would be interested in statistics on credit card use by Chinese shoppers. By estimating total online credit card sales, the shipping companies could then calculate the total amount of express shipping. This is the **buildup method** of estimating sales, which starts with an estimate of individual behavior and then extends it to the entire market. For example, U.S. online customers may average two purchases per month. These online purchases result in twenty-four shipped packages per year per customer. Let's assume that the same holds true for middle-class Chinese shoppers in larger cities. A total estimate of shipments can be made by multiplying the average number of times individuals have packages shipped by the number of expected Internet shoppers.

Market Share To help identify sales potential, a company must estimate its market share. **Market share** is the percentage of industry sales a company is able to capture from competitors. Market share can be estimated by comparing a company's advantages and benefits to its competitors. This process is easier when a company has a history of competition. For example, McDonald's can estimate market share when it enters new markets because of its past experiences. A new company with a new product must be able to make an estimate with less information. This process often will require marketing research.

Checkpoint

List the steps involved in a screening process.

Passport

Understand Marketing Concepts

Circle the best answer for each of the following questions.

1. Which of the following is *not* a step involved in screening for potential opportunities?
   a. identify markets
   b. identify competitive advantages
   c. estimate government purchases
   d. estimate share of market

2. A method of estimating sales that starts with an estimate of individual behavior and then extends to the entire market is called a
   a. market potential method
   b. market segmentation method
   c. sales potential method
   d. buildup method

Think Critically

Answer the following questions as completely as possible. If necessary, use a separate sheet of paper.

3. Explain how the screening process helps businesses select international markets.

   _____

   _____

   _____

   _____

   _____

   _____

4. **Research** Use the Internet to find the total industry sales for automobiles. Try to find information on total market sales for the United States and at least one other country or bloc of countries. Explain how an international marketer could use this data.

   _____

   _____

   _____

   _____

   _____

   _____

International Marketing Research

- Describe the marketing research process.
- Identify international data collection problems.

- marketing research
- environmental scanning
- sample

- survey
- cross-cultural equivalence

Going Global

Want to be a *cool hunter*? This is a real occupation in which people use observational research to spot new trends. Companies want to know what young people between the ages of 14 and 30 are likely to buy in the future. Traditional research will not work because these individuals have not seen the products. Youth Intelligence is a consulting and marketing research company. It uses focus groups, online surveys, and interviews in neighborhoods, schools, and homes to spot new trends.

But marketing research does not need to be conducted only through surveys. New marketing opportunities often are spotted through careful observation. One cool hunter noticed clothing worn by young people in Italy. The clothing was then introduced through fashion stores in the United States. Another entrepreneur found that young Europeans were fond of drinking high-caffeine soft drinks. When he returned to the United States, he brought this idea with him and started a company selling a soft drink with three times the caffeine of colas.

Break into small groups. Discuss why a business would hire cool hunters to identify new products. Consider future trends you have seen. Do you think a business would pay you for these ideas?

THE MARKETING RESEARCH PROCESS

MARKETING-INFORMATION MANAGEMENT

International marketers conduct research to lower the risk involved in developing new products or pursuing new markets. Marketing managers must be able to make informed decisions. When marketing managers are faced with a specific problem, they often will conduct marketing research. **Marketing research** is the systematic process of gathering information to help make marketing decisions. Marketing research follows a scientific process consisting of a number of specific steps.

There are a number of problems that international marketing managers must overcome when collecting international marketing research. In some countries, there is no infrastructure for collecting information. Individuals in some cultures may not want to respond to surveys because they do not trust researchers. Given this, marketers might have to resort to other methods of collecting data. **Environmental scanning** is the process of collecting information from various sources. These sources may include international business journals, news programs, the Internet, and industry trade magazines.

Steps in the Marketing Research Process

The steps in the marketing research process follow a systematic method of collecting and analyzing data. Each of these steps is dependent upon the previous steps.

1. **Define the problem** This first step is the process of identifying the area to be researched. Marketing managers must be able to define the problem. For example, if product A's sales in a country drop, the researcher must find the cause. It could be due to problems with the product. It also could be due to increased competition or some environmental factor. Studying each of these factors may require a different research strategy.

2. **Analyze secondary data** *Secondary data* is data that has been previously collected. It could be a public source such as census data. It could be information held within a company. Developed countries often have secondary data available. It can be more difficult to find reliable secondary data in developing countries. Marketers often find there is a problem in the comparability of secondary data. For example, the employment rate in a population is often calculated differently in different countries.

3. **Collect primary data** Data not previously collected is called *primary data*. Collecting primary data involves two processes—designing a data collection plan and then actually collecting the data. If a company uses surveys, it must be able to develop a plan to send the surveys, have respondents answer, and then collect the data. Researchers usually collect data from a sample of the larger population. A **sample** is a smaller number of people who have the same profile as the larger population. There are a number of considerations related to primary data collection in international markets.

Marketing Myths

Marketing research is designed to provide information to help marketing managers make decisions. No matter how good research is, there are always surprises in decision making. Coca-Cola learned this lesson in the 1980s.

Coke's research showed that it was losing market share to Pepsi. Coke conducted marketing research and found that customers' taste preferences were changing. Coke tried new formulas. It found that a new Coke formula was rated higher than old Coke. This New Coke tasted more like Pepsi. Coca-Cola did not want to split its market share, so when it introduced the New Coke, it pulled the old Coke.

Coca-Cola did not realize that Coke was viewed by customers as part of their idealized American lifestyle. Customers revolted, and the old Coke was reintroduced. Coke's marketing research needed to include more than just taste testing. It needed to include lifestyle analysis.

THINK CRITICALLY

1. Explain why Coke would consider replacing its original cola.
2. Describe the mistakes that Coke made in its research process. Recommend how it could avoid these mistakes in the future.

© GETTY IMAGES/PHOTODISC

4. **Perform data analysis and decision making** The data collected must be analyzed in a systematic manner. Managers then must use the results to make decisions.

Data Collection Methods

There are two methods of data collection—quantitative and qualitative. *Quantitative* data collection obtains data in a way that allows for statistical analysis. *Qualitative* data collection uses techniques such as interviews or focus groups to obtain non-numeric information.

A **survey** is one of the most common quantitative marketing research data collection methods. A survey typically has a number of questions that ask respondents to choose between answers, such as "strongly agree" and "strongly disagree." *Focus groups* and *in-depth interviews* are qualitative data collection methods in which interviewers ask respondents open-ended questions. The responses are then compiled and analyzed.

Companies often will create test markets. *Test markets* are small segments of customers who share the same profile as a larger market. In this way, companies can determine if the product will appeal to the larger market before spending the money for a full introduction.

Checkpoint

List the four steps in the marketing research process.

_____

_____

_____

INTERNATIONAL DATA COLLECTION PROBLEMS

MARKETING–
INFORMATION
MANAGEMENT

The purpose of marketing research is to lower the risk involved in making decisions. The more problems researchers have with data collection, the less likely they are to trust the information they collect. International marketers prefer to enter a market with good information instead of entering a market with high uncertainty.

Equivalence Data Collection Problems

There are a number of factors that international marketers must consider when conducting research. One factor relates to **cross-cultural equivalence**, or how similar research results are across cultures. For example, assume a marketing researcher is trying to determine if a new product would sell better in Europe or Asia. The individuals chosen to participate in the data collection process are called the *subjects*. The subjects are likely to differ across borders. The researcher would need to devise a data collection method that allows for comparison across different countries and cultures.

Cross-cultural equivalence presents itself in many different forms. The researcher's first concern may be *conceptual equivalence*. A question asked in one culture may not have the same meaning in another culture. Even asking if an individual is likely to buy a product could have a conceptual difference. In some high-context cultures, individuals don't like to say "no." They believe that saying "no" could be offensive. These cultural differences could lead to inaccurate data when customers indicate they will buy a product when they actually have no intention of buying it.

Translation equivalence is a problem when using multiple languages. The data should be translated by natives of both countries using a back translation process to ensure the same meaning exists in each language.

Sample equivalence also can occur. The people chosen to answer the surveys may have the same demographic profile. However, they may not share the same needs and desires or have the same authority to purchase. Marketers may also encounter a *measurement equivalence* problem. This occurs when survey results differ because individuals in a culture respond differently to survey questions.

Data collection equivalence exists when researchers are not able to collect data in similar ways across cultures. Even if it is possible to conduct survey research across cultures, there can be a number of problems with data collection.

Other Data Collection Problems

Primary data collection and analysis is dependent upon the researcher's ability to collect and analyze data. International marketers increase their risks of obtaining faulty data when they enter markets where there are data collection problems.

There can be a number of infrastructure problems for researchers attempting to use surveys. Researchers may find that some countries do not have reliable mail delivery or telephone systems. It also can be difficult to identify the segments a researcher wants to sample. For example, there may not be a way to find a list of people who have a specific profile. Even if a researcher has a list, some countries' privacy laws do not allow the researcher to contact subjects without prior approval.

Willingness of subjects to respond to marketing research is another problem. Individuals from countries with a one-party government often fear anyone who asks for their opinions. It can be safer to not have an opinion. If they do respond to questions, they may not answer honestly. Often questions related to income need to be avoided. People may fear that the information will be used for tax purposes.

© GETTY IMAGES/PHOTODISC

Global Research Organizations

International marketing researchers must overcome many obstacles to obtain the data needed by marketing managers for the decision-making process. There are a number of global research companies that specialize in collecting data across many cultures. You probably have heard of the Nielsen television ratings. You may not know that ACNielsen is one of the world's leading marketing information companies. ACNielsen has more than 21,000 employees worldwide serving more than 100 countries. Businesses use companies such as ACNielsen to conduct market research and information analysis. This information helps companies find new opportunities and develop marketing and sales campaigns.

Checkpoint Name four types of cross-cultural equivalence.

_____

_____

World Stars | OSCAR DE LA HOYA

Oscar De La Hoya came from a family of boxers. His first boxing match was at the age of six with his cousin. He lost. Thirteen years later in 1992, De La Hoya won the Olympic gold medal for boxing. He went on to claim world championships at a number of boxing weights. He then won the world welterweight title. But De La Hoya is more than a boxer. He always wanted to be a singer. He produced a CD that topped Billboard's Latin Dance charts. A single recording also was nominated for a Grammy.

De La Hoya's newest venture is in business. He is targeting the fast-growing Hispanic market. De La Hoya and his investors plan to open restaurants, health clubs, storage facilities, and banks in the Hispanic inner-city neighborhoods of Southern California. De La Hoya has noted that there are Asian and Cuban banks but no Mexican banks. Latinos make up one-third of California's population and will be the largest population segment by 2030. They are currently the majority in Los Angeles County.

The Hispanic market is a large and growing segment in the United States. This cultural group has its own unique profile, needs, and desires. Targeting this segment in the United States requires an understanding of its distinct differences. De La Hoya's business ventures serving the Hispanic market in California can act as a springboard to the larger Hispanic market throughout North America.

THINK CRITICALLY

Explain why De La Hoya sees the Hispanic market as a unique market segment to target. Why does De La Hoya understand this market? What skills does he have that would help him achieve success in business?

Understand Marketing Concepts

Circle the best answer for each of the following questions.

1. The process of systematically gathering information to help make market decisions is
   a. marketing research
   b. environmental scanning
   c. surveys
   d. focus groups

2. A research method that typically uses a number of questions for data collection is a(n)
   a. focus group
   b. environmental scan
   c. test market
   d. survey

Think Critically

Answer the following questions as completely as possible. If necessary, use a separate sheet of paper.

3. List and define the two types of data collection methods.

_____

_____

_____

_____

_____

_____

_____

4. **Research** Use the Internet to find web sites for two trade associations. List the types of industry support that these associations provide.

_____

_____

_____

_____

_____

_____

_____

Chapter Assessment

Review Marketing Concepts

Write the letter of the term that matches each definition. Some terms will not be used.

_____ 1. The process of identifying potential market opportunities to pursue

_____ 2. A way to estimate sales based on an estimate of individual behavior which then is extended to the entire market

_____ 3. A collection of different products in different market locations

_____ 4. A smaller number of people who have the same profile as the larger population

_____ 5. The systematic process of gathering information to help in making marketing decisions

_____ 6. A picture of the market segment

_____ 7. The process of collecting information from various sources such as journals, news programs, the Internet, and industry trade magazines

_____ 8. The percentage of industry sales a company is able to capture from competitors

_____ 9. Characteristics of the population including age, gender, race, income, and education

_____ 10. A quantitative research method that asks respondents a number of questions

a. buildup method
b. concentrated segmentation strategy
c. cross-cultural equivalence
d. demographics
e. differentiated segmentation strategy
f. environmental scanning
g. market segment
h. market share
i. marketing research
j. portfolio of markets
k. profile
l. qualified market
m. sample
n. screening
o. survey
p. undifferentiated segmentation strategy

Circle the best answer.

11. A group of individuals or organizations that share characteristics and will respond in the same way to a business's product design, price, distribution system, and promotional campaign is a
   a. demographic
   b. market profile
   c. market segment
   d. market lifestyle

12. A(n) _____ is used when a company targets two or more segments with unique strategies.
   a. undifferentiated segmentation strategy
   b. differentiated segmentation strategy
   c. concentrated segmentation strategy
   d. focused segmentation strategy

Think Critically

13. Explain why a company should consider new international markets.

_____

_____

_____

_____

_____

_____

14. Think of a product or service you recently purchased. Create a profile of the typical consumer who purchases this product or service.

_____

_____

_____

_____

_____

_____

_____

15. Using the same product or service described in Question 14, explain why you were qualified to make this purchase.

_____

_____

_____

_____

_____

_____

16. Why is it important to have a portfolio of markets?

_____

_____

_____

_____

_____

_____

_____

Make Connections

17. **Research** Using the Internet or other sources, find the total population of your city. What is the population breakdown for ethnic or cultural groups in your city? How could this data be helpful to marketers?

_____

_____

_____

_____

18. **Communication** Refer to the matrix shown at the right. Describe the pros and cons of following each of these marketing strategies.

Old Product Old Market	New Product Old Market
Old Product New Market	New Product New Market

_____

_____

_____

_____

_____

_____

_____

_____

_____

19. **Marketing Math** Your research has found that 10 percent of U.S. customers spend an average of $20 per month to purchase your industry's product. You are expanding into Europe. You believe that 5 percent of European customers will spend an average of $5 per month to purchase your industry's product. Assume that the U.S. population is 300 million and the European population is 400 million. Calculate the yearly industry sales for both countries.

_____

_____

_____

_____

20. Research Assume you work for a bicycle manufacturer. Use the environmental scanning process and the Internet to identify sources of information for this product. List a few sources and a trade association for this product or product category.

_____

_____

_____

_____

21. Problem Solving Choose a product that you think could be modified or improved in some way. Describe how you could follow the steps in the research process to devise a plan to improve the product.

_____

_____

_____

_____

_____

PUT MARKETING ON THE MAP

International Marketing Plan Project

Your international marketing plan must identify the market segments you want to target as well as new marketing opportunities. You must also develop a marketing research plan that will help you make decisions.

Work with a group and complete the following activities.

1. Develop a profile of the international market segment(s) you would like to target with your products. Use the Internet to research the population size of the market segments in your targeted country. (_Hint:_ Try the NationMaster.com web site to locate demographic data.)

2. Specify the segmentation strategy your group would like to follow. Justify using an undifferentiated, concentrated, or differentiated segmentation strategy.

3. Use the Internet to identify the competitors you will have in the country you are targeting. Specify your competitive advantage.

4. Use the screening process to determine your product's market share. Use the Internet to find data to help you determine total industry sales for your product category.

5. Use the Internet to identify sources of information for your product. Indicate how these sources will help you understand your market.

6. Recommend a marketing research strategy for your company that will help lower the risk of entering a new market. Specify how your research strategy will ensure cross-cultural equivalence.

Case Study

CHILD LABOR AROUND THE WORLD

The International Labor Organization (ILO) estimates that 250 million children between the ages of 5 and 14 work in developing countries. One hundred twenty million children work full time. Sixty-one percent of the children are from Asia. Thirty-two percent are from Africa, and seven percent are from Latin America. Industries that use child labor include agriculture, domestics, trade, services, manufacturing, and construction.

Some children work long hours. They are exposed to dangerous, unhealthy conditions. Lasting physical and psychological injuries are often the result for children working in unhealthy conditions.

Working at rug looms has left some children with eye damage, lung disease, and stunted growth. They also are susceptible to arthritis. Children making silk thread in India get blisters from dipping their hands in boiling water. They breathe smoke and harmful fumes from machinery. They also handle dead worms that cause infections.

Children harvesting sugar cane in El Salvador use machetes to cut cane in the hot sun for up to nine hours each day. Injuries to hands and legs frequently go untreated.

Child labor abuse occurs when children work for too many hours for too many days and earn too little or no pay. Many of these children are subjected to physical abuse. They are exposed to dangerous pesticides and required to use unsafe tools.

Bonded labor occurs when a family receives an advance payment to hand over a child to an employer. Usually the child cannot work off the debt, and the family cannot raise enough money to buy the child back. Bonded labor is outlawed by the U.N. Abolition of Slavery. However, millions of children still work as bonded child laborers around the world.

Cheaper manufacturing in other countries has raised awareness of child labor abuse. Big brands like Nike and Liz Claiborne have been criticized for manufacturing clothing and shoes in countries that use child labor.

Reports of child labor abuse in the production of popular merchandise frequently result in backlash against the offending company. Sales can decline because of the negative publicity surrounding the company's products.

THINK CRITICALLY

1. Why is child labor abuse prevalent in less-developed countries?

2. List two advantages for children working in a family business.

3. Why do major clothing and textile manufacturers have many of their products manufactured in India and Taiwan?

4. What would be the incentive in a less-developed country to have a large family?

GENERAL MARKETING RESEARCH PROJECT

The General Marketing Research event provides an opportunity for participants to demonstrate skills needed by management personnel. The marketing research event consists of the written document and oral presentation. The written document is worth 70 points. The oral presentation is worth 30 points.

One to three students may work on the Marketing Research Project. The written document is limited to 30 pages, including the appendix. Major sections that must be included in the written document are Executive Summary, Research Methods Used in the Study, Findings and Conclusions of the Study, Proposed Strategic Plan, Bibliography, and Appendix.

Participants will have ten minutes to present their plan to the judge. Five minutes are allotted for the judge to ask additional questions about the project.

You have been hired by a major homebuilder to develop a strategic plan to enhance the current employee training program. You must first review the current training program and research its effectiveness. The program must take into consideration the diverse workforce employed by the construction industry.

Performance Indicators Evaluated

- Clarify the business's current objectives for its employee training program.
- Design marketing research to determine actual results of the current training program.
- Conduct actual market research.
- Prepare a strategic plan based on the market research.
- Present the research findings and proposed strategic plan.
- Demonstrate effective communication skills as a team.

Go to the DECA web site for more detailed information.

THINK CRITICALLY

1. Why is the employee training program important?
2. What special circumstances in the home building industry must be considered when training employees?
3. Why is the employee training plan worthless without a strategy for putting it into action?

www.deca.org

International Marketing Strategies

© GETTY IMAGES/PHOTODISC

Point Your Browser

▶ ▶ ▶ ▶ intlmarket.swlearning.com

Racing to the Lead

In 1937, Toyota Automatic Loom Works started a new division, Toyota Motor Co. Ltd. This company began by manufacturing trucks for the Japanese army. The trucks were direct copies of U.S. Chevy trucks. After World War II, Toyota began producing small cars. In 1959, Toyota started its international expansion with the production of vehicles at a small plant in Brazil. By 2005, Toyota was the second largest manufacturer of automobiles in the world. In less than 50 years, Toyota rose from being a small manufacturer to being a global leader. One of the keys to Toyota's growth has been the production of high-quality cars at a low cost. Under the leadership of Taiichi Ohno, Toyota developed just-in-time manufacturing. This process is designed to minimize inventories and control waste. Toyota also applied a process of continuous improvement called *kaizen*. These manufacturing processes were copied by other Japanese manufacturers and later by American manufacturers. In the 1970s, American auto manufacturers lost market share to Japanese manufacturers because of low-quality products.

Toyota also has succeeded by introducing new products. It was one of the first to introduce a hybrid car, the Prius. Toyota has not been able to keep up with demand for this car. Toyota runs 47 plants in 26 overseas markets. Seventy percent of its profits come from outside of Japan. Toyota has had a tradition of localizing production for local markets. It is now looking at the world as a global marketplace. It is building products and platforms that it can use around the world.

To continue expanding, Toyota will have to push into new markets. One of the new markets that Toyota is considering is China, where it is currently behind Volkswagen, GM, and Honda in sales. Toyota even plans to manufacture Prius hybrids in China. Toyota plans to expand in Japan with its Lexus luxury cars. In the United States, Toyota now is competing against American automobile manufacturers in the truck market.

Think Critically

1. Explain the reasons for Toyota's growth in the international marketplace.

2. Describe the nature of Toyota's competitive advantage.

International Competitive Advantages

- Identify strategies to gain competitive advantages.
- Describe company resources needed to gain competitive advantages.
- Explain ways to contend with international competition.

- competitive advantage
- value relationship
- economies of scale
- productivity
- micro-loans
- research and development
- distribution channel
- direct competition
- indirect competition

Going Global

Volkswagen began in Germany in the 1930s. Volkswagen means "people's car." The original car was designed to carry five people and be very inexpensive. It cruised at 62 miles per hour and got 33 miles per gallon of gasoline. The Volkswagen Beetle entered the United States in the 1960s. This inexpensive car met the needs of young people at that time. Volkswagen's sales in the United States peaked in the 1970s.

Volkswagen's main problem is manufacturing costs. Labor costs in Germany are too high, and productivity is too low. It is difficult for Volkswagen to move manufacturing outside of Germany. German state governments own over 18 percent of its stock. Volkswagen also has problems with quality. It was ranked 33rd out of 37 in customer car complaints.

New management at Volkswagen is looking to the United States for growth. It wants to expand market share in the United States. It is even putting cup holders in U.S. cars. Volkswagen finally understands Americans well enough to realize that they eat in their cars.

Working with a partner, discuss why Volkswagen has had problems competing around the world. Recommend a strategy for Volkswagen to regain U.S. market share.

COMPETITIVE ADVANTAGES

PRODUCT/SERVICE MANAGEMENT

Competition is a major force for change. Businesses are facing a tremendous amount of international competition. Businesses must find a competitive advantage to survive in this environment. A **competitive advantage** exists when a product has greater value in benefits or price than competitive products. A **value relationship** is the amount of benefits received given the price paid for a product.

The United States operates in a much more competitive environment than it has ever before faced. At the end of World War II, the United States was the only country to benefit economically. The U.S. business infrastructure was undamaged. The GI Bill created an educated workforce. The emerging struggle with the Soviet Union locked out Central and Eastern Europe and Central Asia from international competition.

In the 1960s, Europe attempted to create an ideal society through large social spending. Japan was just beginning to recover. In the 1970s, Japan, South Korea, Taiwan, Singapore, and Hong Kong began to rise. Japanese manufacturers focused on total quality management. India was educating its massive population. But the United States was still dominant in technology, capital, and political power.

In the 1980s, China began to open to trade, and Russia reformed. European unity was well underway. Asia began creating a highly educated workforce.

In the 1990s, Europe restructured its educational system. Asia began building new universities. The United States' struggle with the Soviet Union came to an end, but U.S. spending on its military was still more than the rest of the world. Since the year 2000, Asia has been growing. It has an educated workforce and a low-wage pay scale.

Today, more countries are able to produce high-quality products with a high-quality workforce. Global competition is increasing. Companies are increasingly using production and management resources around the world. The advantages that the United States had 50 years ago are now disappearing. U.S. companies must now devise strategies to gain competitive advantages to compete in a global marketplace. There are three generic competitive advantage strategies: differentiation, low costs, and focused. Companies often follow a combination of differentiation and low-cost strategies.

Tech Zone

Enterprise resource planning (ERP) systems are computer systems that integrate workflows throughout a business. For example, an ERP system tracks inventory, sales orders, manufacturing, shipping, payment flows, and service. ERP systems are designed to create efficiency and lower costs. Most ERP systems use Internet-based interfaces.

It does not matter to ERP systems if data flows within a six-mile radius or 6,000 miles away. ERP systems can link suppliers around the world. They can track sales worldwide. They can link service centers to customers anywhere. For example, if a customer orders a custom-made laptop, inventory parts can be ordered from China and Taiwan. Once the customer has the laptop, if there is a problem, the customer can use a call center and talk to someone in India. That person can look up parts and schedule maintenance in the United States. ERP systems facilitate globalization.

THINK CRITICALLY

Describe the advantages an ERP system can bring to a business. Describe how ERP systems accommodate global business processes.

Differentiation

PRODUCT/SERVICE MANAGEMENT

To create value and competitive advantage, businesses try to differentiate as much as possible from competitors. With a differentiation strategy, a business tries to find an area where it can be unique in comparison to competitors. It could produce a higher-quality product. It could have a strong brand image. It could offer greater service or meet needs faster. It could perform additional aspects related to product design and delivery.

The international automotive industry provides a good example of a differentiation strategy. High levels of competition have forced auto manufacturers to produce high-quality products. These companies have produced new models. They have increased services and warranties. When customers view products as having equal benefits and quality, they then look for the lowest-priced product.

Low Costs

If products cannot be differentiated, companies must be able to lower costs. One strategy to lower costs is to obtain economies of scale. **Economies of scale** exist when a large amount of product is produced, which in turn lowers the cost of each individual product. Increasing productivity is another strategy used to keep costs down. **Productivity** is the amount of a product that can be produced with a given set of resources. One of the keys to U.S. competitiveness has always been its high productivity. Research and development and technology are used to increase productivity. Another strategy is maintaining strict control over costs. This strategy often requires the lowest-cost resources available to produce a product. Low-cost resources can be in various forms, such as materials and labor.

China has been viewed as a low-cost producer. Its competitive advantage comes from economies of scale, the use of manufacturing technology, and low-cost labor. As China and other developing countries move into the future, they plan to differentiate themselves with new products or processes. They also plan to produce their own high-quality products.

Focused

A third generic strategy for a company is to focus on a single market within a single country. This method is a focused strategy. If it is done successfully, a business can avoid competitors.

Average hourly wages in the manufacturing industry differ among countries as shown below. (Values are in U.S. dollars.)

United States—$13.92
Mexico—$1.33
Japan—$18.01
Taiwan—$5.42
Germany—$24.30
Spain—$9.97
United Kingdom—$12.31

Checkpoint

Name three competitive advantage strategies.

_____

_____

COMPANY RESOURCES

Global competition can be a challenge for companies. International managers must find the resources and create a capability to compete. International companies find resources in a number of different areas. These resources include human, financial, manufacturing, and marketing resources. Some of these resources are used to create higher levels of product benefits. Others allow for low costs.

Human Resources

Human resources include both management and labor. Many global corporations hire top managers with considerable international experience. The CEO of Toyota, Fujio Cho, supervised the first U.S. Toyota factory. To be successful, he needed to learn how to manage U.S. employees. U.S. employees ask questions. They want to understand why they should work a certain way. This experience was new to Fujio Cho. Japanese employees don't ask questions. He also learned about U.S. culture and customers while living in the United States.

Toyota has had problems taking its manufacturing processes around the world. It took time for the U.S. labor force to follow *kaizen*, or continuous improvement strategies. Once a labor force is trained in a manufacturing process, it typically can operate at high productivity rates.

Much in the same way that companies can have competitive advantages, countries can too. A country's human resources can be a big part of its competitive advantage. The United States has had a competitive advantage with a high-quality management and labor workforce. Developing countries, such as China, have been viewed as having advantages in low-labor costs. Past government control in China had kept a generation of managers from developing. Today, most Chinese managers are younger than 40 years of age. India and Southeast Asia have both improved their educational systems. They now are producing a new generation of global managers. More than ever before, it is important for U.S. managers to understand the global marketplace to stay competitive.

Financial Resources

Business operations require financial resources to obtain other needed resources. Businesses in some countries have access to large amounts of financial capital. These countries have active stock markets or banks that lend money. One of the problems in developing countries is the lack of capital sources to provide financing.

One way for countries to make capital more accessible to businesses is to charge low interest rates. Bank loans in Japan can have very low interest rates. They sometimes are as low as one or two percent. This type of government policy toward lending encourages business development. However, it also presents some problems. The banking industries in Japan and China both have large amounts of bad debt because of easy lending practices.

Small businesses, especially in developing countries, can have problems obtaining financial resources. One strategy that has proved successful is the development of micro-loans. **Micro-loans** are very small loans, typically around $100. They allow entrepreneurs to start businesses and make money. Micro-loans have a high repayment rate. They have allowed many low-income people, especially women, in developing countries to make money for their families.

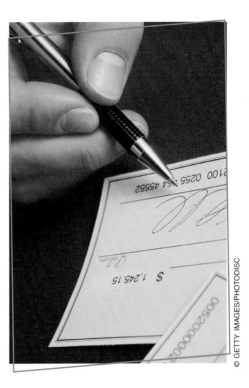

© GETTY IMAGES/PHOTODISC

Manufacturing Resources

Manufacturing consists of a set of processes that use raw materials to produce final goods. Some countries have gained advantages in producing specific types of products. For example, Japan is the world's leading auto manufacturer. It produces over eight million cars per year. Germany is in second place. The United States is third. Japan's advantages do not come from just one manufacturer. The Japanese auto industry has developed a set of suppliers that produce high-quality products. They use a just-in-time inventory system and kaizen improvement processes.

China's rise as a global manufacturing power is the result of a planned government policy. In the 1980s, China developed "shell" plants in workers' towns. Large empty factory shells were built. They were surrounded by large apartment complexes. International manufacturers brought equipment and raw materials into the factories. Chinese workers lived in the apartments and walked the short distance to work.

Research and development (R&D) is the process of using funds to create new products and processes. Companies engage in R&D to produce new products and lower costs. Countries in Asia are starting to compete through increased R&D spending. Japan and South Korea spend about 3 percent of their gross domestic production on R&D. The United States spends about 2.7 percent. China has set an R&D spending target of 1.5 percent. Asian countries are directing their spending toward the next wave of innovation: biotechnology, nanotechnology, and information technology. R&D helps companies use their manufacturing resources more efficiently, giving them a competitive advantage.

Marketing Resources

MARKETING–
INFORMATION
MANAGEMENT

To be successful in the international marketplace, a business must understand the marketing environment. It must understand customers, supply and distribution networks, and competitive products. The more experience an international firm has in a market, the better it will understand customers in that market. Marketers always have an advantage when they are selling within their own culture because they share a cultural heritage with their customers.

Distribution channel relationships also develop over time. A **distribution channel** consists of the companies and individuals who participate in the exchange of goods and services. Some international firms find it difficult to enter new markets. They often cannot find ways to distribute their products and have difficulty finding sources of supply. Japan has a tradition of having a large number of small distributors. U.S. firms have found it difficult to enter the tight social networks of the Japanese distribution system.

A strong global brand image can give a business an advantage. International firms use resources to create brand names such as McDonald's, Coca-Cola, and Nike. The strength of these brand names creates consumer demand. This demand allows these firms to enter distribution networks and capture additional market share.

Checkpoint   Name the four resources companies use to gain competitive advantages.

_____

_____

ANALYSIS OF INTERNATIONAL COMPETITORS

MARKETING-INFORMATION MANAGEMENT

In a global marketplace, it is difficult to predict where the next competitor will come from. Competition can be direct. **Direct competition** refers to competitors working within the same industry. Competition also can be indirect. **Indirect competition** comes from the sale of products that provide similar benefits. Honda manufactured motorcycles before it entered into the automotive market. It is an example of a business moving from indirect competition (motorcycles) to direct competition (automobiles) against U.S. auto manufacturers.

International competitors are evaluated on their ability to apply resources and capabilities within an industry. For example, it is no secret that Wal-Mart has global expansion plans. Wal-Mart is known for having competitive advantages in management talent. It also is known for using technology to understand the marketplace and for having economies of scale. When Wal-Mart entered the British grocery marketplace, the stock price of British grocery companies dropped before Wal-Mart sold its first product. It was evident that the direct competition from Wal-Mart would affect the business of other British grocery companies.

Building Barriers

Businesses do not just seek competitive advantages. They also attempt to build barriers to competitive firms. Most of these barriers take advantage of the political and legal environment in which the business operates. Regulations within a country can hold off some competitors. One type of barrier is the use of intellectual property laws. Patents, trademarks, and copyrights build barriers for other firms trying to enter the marketplace. Weak intellectual property laws, such as those in China, allow businesses to work around these barriers.

Trade policies also can act as barriers. Quotas, tarriffs, and license requirements act as barriers to competition. Typically these barriers benefit a business. But they do not necessarily benefit customers. The complicated Japanese distribution system has kept out international firms. This barrier raises costs to Japanese customers.

Some businesses use market power as a barrier. *Market power* exists when a firm can control pricing in an industry. Monopolies and firms with large market share often have market power. This market power allows these firms to lower prices, which drives out new businesses in the marketplace that cannot compete with the lower prices.

Name three types of barriers used to keep out competition.

Checkpoint

Passport

Understand Marketing Concepts

Circle the best answer for each of the following questions.

1. A _____ exists when a product has greater value in benefits or price over competitive products.
   a. value relationship
   b. value position
   c. competitive difference
   d. competitive advantage

2. Competitors working within the same industry are
   a. indirect competition
   b. direct competition
   c. competitive partners
   d. trade associates

Think Critically

Answer the following questions as completely as possible. If necessary, use a separate sheet of paper.

3. Communication Create a matrix like the one shown below. In each box, list businesses and products with which you are familiar. Identify strategies that the businesses in each box use to compete.

High Differentiation Low Cost	High Differentiation High Cost
Low Differentiation Low Cost	Low Differentiation High Cost

_____

_____

_____

_____

4. Research Select an industry other than the automotive industry. Use the Internet to develop a list of international competitors. Determine how each of these businesses attempts to gain competitive advantages against the others.

_____

_____

_____

_____

International Product-Markets

Terms / Goals

- Explain how companies expand product-markets.
- Describe the screening process used for product-markets.

- product-market
- lead time
- brand recognition

Going Global

In 1937, Soichiro Honda began manufacturing piston rings and other auto parts for Toyota. After World War II, Honda attached engines to bicycles to create cheap, efficient transportation for the Japanese. By the 1970s, Honda was the largest producer of motorcycles in the world.

In the early 1960s, Honda produced cars mostly for the Japanese market. These cars were too small for the United States. In 1972, Honda introduced the Civic to the United States. The Civic was larger than Japanese models. Its high gas mileage fit U.S. customers' needs. The Accord, introduced in 1976, was a big hit. By 1982, Honda began manufacturing cars in the United States.

Honda determined that there was an opportunity for a separate luxury line of vehicles in the United States. In 1986, a new brand, Acura, was introduced. It included modified versions of Hondas. These cars were sold in separate dealerships. These same models were sold in Japan under the Honda brand.

Working with a partner, list the product expansion that Honda went through over the years. Explain why Honda has been successful following this strategy.

PRODUCT-MARKETS

PRODUCT/SERVICE MANAGEMENT

The smallest unit for which businesses develop strategies is called a product-market. A **product-market** is the name given to a single product in a single market. For example, product A in market A is a different product-market than product A in market B. Product B in market A is a different product-market than product B in market B.

An example in the automobile industry can be found with the Honda corporation. Japan tried to enter into a new market, the United States, with the same product it had been producing for its Japanese market. This strategy did not work. Honda later decided to try to sell to a new, more upscale automobile market. But Honda needed a new product. Honda also decided that it needed a new brand name for the U.S. market that would identify the new luxury design. It introduced the Acura product line in the United

States. One of the products in this line was the Acura Legend. The Acura Legend and a luxury-oriented customer segment is one product-market.

Honda has expanded into new product-markets throughout its history. International marketers look to expand into new product-markets in three different directions. The first is in new markets. The second is through product expansion. The third is with new technology.

New Markets

When international marketers are making decisions about new markets, they must determine whether they will pursue new markets in their own country or expand into new international markets. Honda made a decision to expand into new markets outside of Japan. These new markets included the United States as well as other countries. Within Japan, Honda also expanded into the luxury market with models like the Legend.

Product Expansion

Honda expanded its products in a number of different ways. It started by building auto parts for Toyota. It then expanded its products into a related area by putting motors on bicycles. This move led directly to the manufacturing of motorcycles. Honda built upon this expertise to produce cars. Honda has stayed in the motor industry. It has expanded production into motorized products that have new forms and functions.

International businesses make decisions about product design when they enter new markets. Businesses must determine if they will sell the same product or change a product for new markets. The basic design of

© WALLY MCNAMEE/CORBIS

McDonald's restaurants is the same throughout the world. The process of preparing and selling the menu items in McDonald's restaurants also is basically the same. McDonald's does change menus to meet local market needs. The amount of change a product requires depends upon the differences in cultural needs.

Honda must make at least one major change when it manufactures cars for international markets. In Japan, cars drive on the left side of the road. The more changes that a business must make for local markets, the higher the costs will be because companies lose the advantage of economies of scale.

New Technology

Most companies expand product lines into areas where they have expertise. Companies look at their own skill base before they consider producing new products. For example, Honda has used its technology expertise in manufacturing and engineering to produce new products. Honda manufactures power equipment such as lawnmowers, marine engines, and other small-engine machines. As an extension of its technology expertise, Honda has created a new product—a humanoid robot called ASIMO. ASIMO was designed to walk and perform tasks to assist humans.

New technology is important. New processes that result from technology can lower costs. In addition, new intellectual property can be a barrier that provides protection from competition. By being innovative, a company can set itself apart from competitors. An *innovation* is a new product or process. Eventually old products will be replaced by new products. If a company does not have the skill base to develop new products, it is likely to disappear in the long run.

List three ways product-markets can expand.

THE PRODUCT-MARKET CHOICE

MARKETING – INFORMATION MANAGEMENT

In pursuing opportunities, businesses start with a large number of product-market choices. Then a screening process is used to determine the best product-markets based on market factors, competitive advantages, and strategic considerations.

- **Market factors** An attractive market will be large and have a high growth rate. Markets also are appealing if the company already has some experience with a market. Experience can reduce the risks and expense of entering the market. A market must be qualified based on its need for the product, its ability to pay for the product, and its authority to purchase the product.

- **Competitive advantages** When a product has a greater perceived value than competitive products, competitive advantages exist. This perceived value extends to products that are directly competitive as well as products that are indirectly competitive. McDonald's cannot enter a market and charge more than other similar restaurants. One of its competitive advantages is quality food at low prices.

- **Strategic considerations** Factors such as lead time and brand recognition must be considered. **Lead time** is the amount of time a company is ahead of its competition in pursuing a strategy. If a company is able to enter a new market with a long lead time, it has time to create brand recognition, customer loyalty, or distribution systems before its competitors. How well a product's name is recognized in a market is known as **brand recognition**. Competitors that have to catch up face increased costs.

   The possibility of economies of scale in production or distribution gives a business a cost advantage. Wal-Mart must have a minimum number of outlets to be successful. The distribution systems Wal-Mart uses to gain an advantage are very expensive. These costs need to be spread over a large number of stores.

Marketing Myths

Free movement of resources is one of the most important factors involved in creating efficient global companies. This free movement applies to capital, materials, and labor. But labor movement can be a problem.

U.S. labor is very fluid. Workers are willing to move across the country to find jobs that take advantage of their skills. When labor is in high demand in certain parts of the country, U.S. workers will move to that market. In some countries, individuals are not willing to move to new locations to pursue new jobs. Europeans do not often cross country borders to find new employment. Often this reluctance is due to language differences. Even within the borders of a country, European labor may not want to move.

In the Czech Republic, Skoda, a Czech car manufacturer, wanted to start a new production line. But the Czech labor force would not relocate to a different area due to slight cultural differences. Therefore, Skoda was forced to locate the new factory in a more expensive area. This location increased the costs of manufacturing the cars.

THINK CRITICALLY

1. Explain why the free movement of labor would be good for a society.
2. Speculate on the reasons that workers in the Czech Republic would not want to change locations.

The ability to overcome or build barriers also is a strong strategic consideration. Lack of intellectual property protection will keep companies out of markets. Many companies are reluctant to send product samples to countries like China. They are afraid that the products will be copied by a Chinese company that will then compete against them. Countries that have stronger intellectual property laws are more attractive to marketers.

Attractive Countries

Expanding product-markets into new countries also requires an evaluation of how attractive the country is for new opportunities. Part of this evaluation is a review of the risks involved in doing business in the country. Businesses must determine the types of barriers they will face. They need to find resources that are available to help sell the product or reach markets within the country. They must find out how large the market is and its potential for growth. The more positive these factors are, the more attractive the country will be for expansion.

Many industries are being drawn to China because it has strong markets for products. For example, in the 1990s, the United States was the world's leader in chemical production. U.S. manufacturers also were the world's leaders in chemical use. Today, manufacturing is moving to China. Companies that supply products to manufacturers must be located close to them. Fifty new chemical plants costing over $1 billion are being built in China. By comparison, only one plant is being built in the United States. Many of these chemicals are the same, but shipping costs are lower when manufacturers and suppliers are located nearby. There also is a strong incentive to be first in these markets to take advantage of new business relationships. These chemical plants will draw engineer and management talent. China could become the next center for chemical innovation.

Checkpoint

List three factors involved in product-market choice.

Passport

Understand Marketing Concepts

Circle the best answer for each of the following questions.

1. A name given to a single product in a single market is a
   a. product-market
   b. competitive advantage
   c. country market
   d. share of market

2. The amount of time a company is ahead of its competition in pursuing a strategy is
   a. competitive advantage
   b. advantage time
   c. differential time
   d. lead time

Think Critically

Answer the following questions as completely as possible. If necessary, use a separate sheet of paper.

3. Choose a company that you know well. Identify the product-markets it serves. Determine how closely these product-markets are related.

_____

_____

_____

_____

_____

_____

_____

_____

4. Use the company you identified in Question 3 above. Explain the strategy this company could use to expand into foreign markets.

_____

_____

_____

_____

_____

_____

_____

International Labor Markets

Goals

- Explain why there is a global war for talent.
- Discuss why companies outsource parts of their value chain.

Terms

- immigrant
- expatriate
- glass ceiling
- value chain
- outsourcing
- offshoring

Going Global

Where do video games come from? *Myst, Prince of Persia,* and Tom Clancy's *Splinter Cell* come from a company called Ubisoft. Ubisoft is based in Paris, but it uses programmers in Canada, China, Morocco, and Romania. Creating a video game is not cheap. Development for PlayStation 3 games can cost $20 million. By using programming and design resources in other countries, Ubisoft has a per-employee cost that is one-third of the industry average. This gives Ubisoft a competitive advantage.

Ubisoft uses teams to develop games. These teams can be located in one country or across borders. A development team in Shanghai, China, was assigned to develop a racing game. They needed help from other team members because none of them knew how to drive. Ubisoft's competitors are now planning to use programmers in these same locations. This increase in the demand for labor will cause salaries to increase.

Working with a partner, discuss why Ubisoft would want to use programmers in four different countries. Identify the skills these game programmers need to work for a company like Ubisoft.

THE GLOBAL TALENT WAR

MARKETING-INFORMATION MANAGEMENT

There is a global recruiting war for talent. Businesses must find employees who understand international marketing for three reasons. First, business operations are now global. For example, a manufacturer is likely to obtain supplies and sell products around the world. Even service firms, like hotels, convenience stores, and food franchises, are global businesses. To work in these companies, managers must be able to manage locally but develop strategies globally.

Second, growth opportunities are in new markets such as China, India, and Central and South America. Businesses must be able to enter these markets and compete against other global businesses. A third issue facing developing countries is that the birthrate is falling below the population replacement rate. Just to maintain current employment rates into the future, businesses must be able to find new employees. These factors are leading international corporations to search the world to find people who have a global perspective.

Businesses in a country can benefit by drawing talent from around the world. Before the terrorist attacks on September 11, 2001, the United States allowed for immigration in fields such as information technology, engineering, and medicine. An **immigrant** is someone who leaves his or her home country and goes to another country to live. Leaving one's home country is called *emigration*. After September 11, 2001, companies found it harder to bring expatriates into the United States. An **expatriate** is someone from one country who works in another country. Canada allows for immigration at three times the level of the United States.

The global war for talent is not just for managers. Other jobs moving to other countries include manufacturing and service jobs and high-skill jobs such as programming, medicine, accounting, and education. Job shifts are easier because of changes in transportation and technology.

Gender Discrimination

In the race for global competitiveness, a culture cannot afford to leave half of its talent base behind. Gender discrimination has been an issue in most countries. It is still a major issue in many countries today.

The United Nations measures *gender empowerment*. This is the measure of the participation of women in legislatures, in higher positions in public and private employment, and in academic and technical work. It also measures estimated income. Women in Scandinavian countries are the most empowered. They are followed by Europe and the United States. Women are the least empowered in some Middle-Eastern countries. Lack of empowerment can directly affect the types of jobs that women pursue.

Women around the world have bumped into a glass ceiling. A **glass ceiling** describes a barrier that prevents individuals from moving into top management positions. In the United States, less than one percent of the CEOs in the top 500 corporations are women. In continental Europe, there have been no women CEOs in the largest companies. Twenty years ago in Japan, women were not supposed to work past 5 p.m. Today, a few women have made it into top management.

Part of the reason women don't move to the top of global corporations is due to lifestyle choices. But there are other major reasons. Women are excluded from informal men's networks. Women are stereotyped in many cultures. Also, there are too few women who are CEO role models of major global corporations. Women will benefit as the search for global talent intensifies.

Time Out

According to a report by the United Nations Development Fund for Women, the number of women employed around the world increased by 200 million between 1993 and 2003. Latin America showed the largest increase from 25 percent in 1980 to 33 percent in 1997.

List three reasons there is a global talent war.

Checkpoint

VALUE CHAIN OUTSOURCING

PRODUCT/SERVICE MANAGEMENT

A business consists of a number of unique functions that work together to create value. A **value chain** breaks a business into functional areas. It shows how the business obtains materials, produces and distributes products, markets products, and provides customer support. In order for a business to gain an advantage, it must be able to perform some function in its value chain better than its competitors. At the same time, it also must effectively perform all other functions to maintain its competitive advantage. Businesses often find that they can be more efficient by having another provider perform part of a value-chain function.

Outsourcing involves finding an outside source to perform a job function. For example, advertising has traditionally been outsourced from businesses to advertising agencies. Shipping has traditionally been outsourced to trucking companies or shipping lines. Companies outsource part of their value chain when someone else can do the job more efficiently.

The major reason that global companies outsource is to reduce costs. Outsourcing also allows a company to concentrate on what it does best. In situations where it is important to have low-cost manufacturing, companies have outsourced to low-wage countries.

Offshoring Pros and Cons

Offshoring is the outsourcing of jobs to other countries. One of the top offshoring countries is India. India has a highly educated workforce that speaks English. Low-cost communication has allowed India to focus on service for English-speaking countries. One Indian service center hires young Europeans to work in its call centers. These young people earn only $5,000 to $8,000 a year, but they have free housing and vacation time.

There is much debate about whether offshoring is good or bad for a country's economy. Some economists say that for every dollar of jobs off-

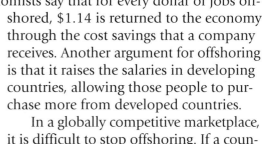

shored, $1.14 is returned to the economy through the cost savings that a company receives. Another argument for offshoring is that it raises the salaries in developing countries, allowing those people to purchase more from developed countries.

In a globally competitive marketplace, it is difficult to stop offshoring. If a country or company develops rules against offshoring jobs to lower-wage countries, it could find itself noncompetitive in the world marketplace. Volkswagen is an example. German state ownership has limited Volkswagen's ability to outsource and cut costs. It has made Volkswagen less competitive.

© DIGITAL VISION

Understand Marketing Concepts

Circle the best answer for each of the following questions.

1. Someone who leaves his or her home country and goes to another country to live is a(n)
    a. immigrant
    b. emigrant
    c. expatriate
    d. foreigner

2. Finding an outside source to perform a job function is called
    a. offshoring
    b. value chaining
    c. expatriating
    d. outsourcing

Think Critically

Answer the following questions as completely as possible. If necessary, use a separate sheet of paper.

3. Explain the meaning of "glass ceiling." List reasons why more women do not move to the top of global corporations.

_____

_____

_____

_____

_____

_____

_____

4. Research Use the Internet to identify how two countries compare to the United States in areas such as educational level, productivity level, and gender equity. Indicate which country has a competitive advantage in human resources.

_____

_____

_____

_____

_____

_____

_____

Chapter 6 Assessment

Review Marketing Concepts

Write the letter of the term that matches each definition. Some terms will not be used.

_____ 1. Amount of a product that can be produced with a given set of resources

_____ 2. How well a product's name is recognized in a market

_____ 3. The amount of benefits received given the price paid for a product

_____ 4. The sale of products that provide similar benefits

_____ 5. The companies and individuals who participate in the exchange of goods and services

_____ 6. A name given to a single product in a single market

_____ 7. Exists when a very large amount of product is produced, which in turn lowers the cost of each individual product

_____ 8. Outsourcing of jobs to other countries

_____ 9. A barrier that prevents individuals from moving into top management positions

_____ 10. The process of using funds to create new products and processes

a. brand recognition
b. competitive advantage
c. direct competition
d. distribution channel
e. economies of scale
f. expatriate
g. glass ceiling
h. immigrant
i. indirect competition
j. lead time
k. micro-loans
l. offshoring
m. outsourcing
n. productivity
o. product-market
p. research and development
q. value chain
r. value relationship

Circle the best answer.

11. A(n) _____ breaks a business into functional areas showing how it obtains materials, produces and distributes products, markets products, and provides customer support.
    a. outsourcing process
    b. value chain
    c. competitive chain
    d. market analysis

12. Which of the following is *not* a reason women hit a glass ceiling?
    a. women can't break into male networks
    b. lack of CEO role models
    c. women don't do as well as men in school
    d. stereotyping

Think Critically

13. Choose two competing products. Make a list of the benefits that each product offers. Compare the products' prices. Which product would be considered to have a greater value relationship?

_____

_____

_____

_____

_____

14. Make a list of products that compete by differentiation. Make another list of products that compete based on price. Indicate what the products within each list have in common.

_____

_____

_____

_____

_____

_____

15. Choose an industry. Specify if that industry needs to concentrate on human resources, financial resources, manufacturing resources, or marketing resources to gain competitive advantages in international markets.

_____

_____

_____

_____

_____

_____

16. Choose a product category that is sold internationally. Develop a list of products that are indirectly competitive. Indicate if any of these products could become directly competitive.

_____

_____

_____

_____

_____

Make Connections

17. **Communication** Develop a PowerPoint presentation indicating how other countries have gained competitiveness against the United States. What policies should the United States have adopted over time to maintain competitiveness?

_____

_____

_____

_____

_____

18. **Research** Use the Internet to research micro-loans. Identify countries that are using micro-loans. Indicate why these loans can help economic development in these countries.

_____

_____

_____

_____

_____

19. **Marketing** Develop a presentation to management indicating how a company can gain marketing advantages in international marketplaces.

_____

_____

_____

_____

_____

_____

20. **Technology** Use the Internet to learn more about the new Honda ASIMO robot. Explain how this kind of new technology could help a company compete globally.

_____

_____

_____

_____

_____

RETAIL MARKETING RESEARCH PROJECT

The Retail Marketing Research Project provides an opportunity for participants to demonstrate skills needed by management personnel to increase sales of goods in a retail environment product line.

The marketing research event consists of the written document and oral presentation. The written document is worth 70 points, and the oral presentation is worth 30 points.

One to three students may work on the marketing research project. The written document is limited to 30 pages, including the appendix. Major sections that must be included in the written document are Executive Summary, Research Methods Used in the Study, Findings and Conclusions of the Study, Proposed Strategic Plan, Bibliography, and Appendix.

Participants will have ten minutes to present their plan to the judge. Five minutes are allotted for the judge to ask additional questions about the project.

You have been hired by a local furniture store to research current sales trends and promotions. You must propose new strategies to assure success in the furniture industry. The furniture store sells high-ticket domestic and imported products. Its competition includes high-volume furniture companies that are enticing customers with special credit promotions.

Performance Indicators Evaluated

- Define the purpose of the marketing strategy.
- Explain effective strategies that should be retained.
- Describe new marketing strategies to increase the market share in the furniture industry.
- Design marketing research to determine actual results of the current sales promotions.
- Conduct actual market research.
- Prepare a strategic plan based on the market research.
- Present the research findings and proposed strategic plan.
- Demonstrate effective communication skills as a team.

Go to the DECA web site for more detailed information.

THINK CRITICALLY

1. What are the store's competitive disadvantages?
2. Why is it important to determine current successful strategies used by the store?
3. How can imported furniture be used as part of the marketing strategy?
4. Why would it be helpful for the store to identify a product-market that it can serve?

www.deca.org

International Product and Brand Management

7

© DIGITAL VISION

Point Your Browser

▶ ▶ ▶ ▶ intlmarket.swlearning.com

Diamonds Are Forever

Diamonds are made from carbon, which is one of the most common materials on earth. Diamonds are at least one billion years old and are found in just a few places on earth. Until the end of the 1800s, only India and Brazil produced diamonds. In the late 1800s, diamonds were discovered in South Africa. Ownership of the South African mines was joined under a company called De Beers. The company was named after the farm where the diamonds were found. New diamond mines were later established in Australia, Siberia, and Western Africa. This increased supply threatened to drive down the price of diamonds. De Beers organized the Central Selling Organization to control the sale of diamonds around the world. De Beers limits the supply of jewelry-quality diamonds. Limiting the supply keeps prices high.

In 1947, De Beers began creating a brand image for diamonds. The slogan "Diamonds are Forever" was designed to promote diamonds as the ideal jewel for engagement or wedding rings. It positioned diamonds as a symbol of eternity and love. De Beers promoted diamonds by showing them as wedding gifts in popular romantic movies. De Beers published stories in magazines and newspapers linking diamonds to romance. Diamonds were associated with celebrities, fashion designers, trendsetters, and the British royal family. Jewelers were taught by De Beers to persuade men to spend two or three months' wages on a diamond engagement ring. After World War II, De Beers ran a campaign in Japan that successfully promoted diamond rings as a Western status symbol. Japan now has gone from having no diamond tradition to being the second largest retail market for diamonds. De Beers has opened stores in London, Tokyo, and New York. De Beers still controls over 65 percent of global diamond distribution.

Think Critically

1. Explain why diamonds can be sold at a high price.

2. Describe how De Beers was able to create a global brand image for diamonds.

International Product Strategies

- Discuss the factors that influence standardization-versus-adaptation decisions.
- Describe how companies create global brand positions and equity.

- product
- brand
- product positioning

- brand equity
- grey market
- family brand

Going Global

Samsung was founded in 1938. The name means "three stars" in Korean. The company originally sold dried Korean fish, vegetables, and fruit to Manchuria and Beijing. It expanded into several other markets over the years, but it wasn't until the 1980s that Samsung started focusing its efforts on the electronics market. In the 1990s, Samsung decided to create a global brand name for its products. It increased the quality of its products through design and innovation. By 2005, Samsung was rated as the twentieth top brand in the world, ahead of Sony. Samsung has set a goal of being the world's best. It has the largest global market share for thirteen of its products.

Samsung has used a variety of strategies to create its global brand image. It used product placement in the movie *The Fantastic Four*. It also tripled the size of its global design staff to meet the design needs for a global marketplace. Samsung's efforts have paid off. From 2001 to 2002, Samsung's brand value increased by almost $2 billion. Its global brand ranking increased almost 20 percent from 2004 to 2005.

Working with a partner, describe the strategy that Samsung is using to create a global brand image. Describe how this strategy is helping Samsung.

INTERNATIONAL PRODUCTS

International marketers face a number of decisions when they take products around the world. A **product** is something offered to a market that satisfies a want or a need. Products contain both tangible and intangible parts. The *tangible* parts of a product include those things that can be seen and felt. They include packaging, brand name, quality, and design. *Intangible* parts of a product include the warranty, after-sale service, delivery, credit, and installation. Services are mostly intangible products.

Products are designed to meet a market's wants or needs. These wants or needs can vary greatly across cultures. International marketers must design their products to gain competitive advantages. They must decide if they can standardize products for all markets or if they need to make adaptations to meet special market needs. They also must design strategies to create brand images that set their products apart from competitors'.

Standardization Versus Adaptation

International marketers have four choices when they move products into new markets.

- keep their home country of products the same

- adapt an existing product for new markets

- design new products for new markets

- design one product for a global marketplace

Businesses may want to design a standardized global product for several reasons. A global product can create economies of scale in R&D, production, and marketing. A global product with a global brand image allows a company to compete against other global marketers.

Developing a global product is not always possible. Products may be used in different environments. They may have to operate in different political and legal environments. Consumers may have different cultural needs and norms. Local competition in foreign markets may be different than in domestic markets. Product customization may be necessary.

When making decisions between production standardization and adaptation, marketers need to evaluate market characteristics, product characteristics, and company characteristics. The more similar each of these factors is between markets, the less adaptation is needed.

Market characteristics include political and legal regulations, customer characteristics and preferences, purchasing patterns, and distribution systems. They also include the country's stage of economic development, the climate and geography, and the nature of competition.

Product characteristics include the nature of the product, the ability to create a global brand, and the purpose for which the product is used. They also include the perception of product quality, the perception of the product's country of origin, and the required after-sale service.

Company characteristics include the financial resources the company has to create a global brand. The international orientation of management and the ability of the company to find and take advantage of international opportunities are other company characteristics.

Global Brands

A **brand** is a name, word, or design that identifies a product, service, or company. Brands create a certain expectation in the minds of customers. Ideally, these global brands will not require much design change as they move around the world. In order to compete with local brands in local markets, global brands need a competitive advantage.

Global brands can be subject to a *country-of-origin effect* when people see a country as a brand. For example, in the 1950s, the phrase "Made in Japan" meant low quality to consumers. But by the 1990s, Japan's brand image had changed. Now "Made in Japan" signals high quality. Today, "Made in China" can mean low quality.

Time Out

According to Interbrand Corporation, the top ten world brands in 2005 were Coca-Cola, Microsoft, IBM, GE, Intel, Nokia, Disney, McDonald's, Toyota, and Marlboro.

Checkpoint Name three factors that influence adaptation-versus-standardization decisions.

PRODUCT POSITIONING

PRODUCT/SERVICE MANAGEMENT

Product positioning refers to using a brand to create an image. When you think of a BMW car, you may think of quality German engineering and a fast, sporty automobile. Disney may bring to mind wholesome family entertainment. Global brands face the challenge of obtaining a consistent global position in consumers' minds across cultures.

Traditionally, companies have relied heavily on advertising to create brand image. Today, companies are shifting promotions from traditional advertising and media, such as television, to new means, such as the Internet, live events, cell phones, and movies.

Global Brand Equity

Brand equity is the additional value that a brand name brings to a product or company. Interbrand Corporation tracks world brands. It estimates Coca-Cola's global brand equity at over $67 billion. This figure is based on a projection of what the brand can deliver in future sales. If a brand image slips, brand equity can drop. Sony outspends Samsung in advertising, but Sony lost $2 billion in brand equity from 2004 to 2005. Competitive products, such as Apple's iPod, have threatened Sony's brand dominance.

Counterfeits, forgeries, and grey markets can diminish brand equity. A **grey market** exists when products are sold outside of an established authorized distribution system. Grey markets can have a negative effect on the brand image and equity because the product

Tech Zone

BMW was an innovator in using the Internet to deliver streaming movies featuring BMW automobiles. BMW hired top Hollywood movie directors to create short films. BMW produced these movies in 2001 before broadband was widely used in customers' homes.

The market that BMW was targeting included high-income individuals who likely had high-bandwidth Internet access at work. The short films would attract people to BMW's web site. Once there, they could then use the web site to design their dream cars. They could choose colors, components, and interiors. BMW's brand image has gone up while Mercedes' and Volkswagen's brand images have gone down.

To create a brand image with the youth, BMW also has created comic books for teenagers based on the films. This approach does not seem like advertising.

THINK CRITICALLY

Describe the advantages of using streaming video to promote BMW automobiles. Describe how BMW creates its brand image using technology.

may be perceived as cheap if not sold by an authorized dealer. Some companies have had difficulty gaining brand equity in China. Counterfeits of designer Gucci bags that say "Made in Italy" can sell in China for $15.

Packaging and Design

Product packaging and design can have a strong impact on product image and sales. Samsung has used product design to gain competitive advantages. In 2004, Samsung won five Industrial Design Excellence Awards (IDEAs). Research is conducted in many countries around the world to help designers study how consumers use products.

The Japanese beverage company Suntory used research and product design to reposition an ice tea beverage. Suntory's first attempt was a product made from an aged Chinese tea, but Japanese consumers did not like the product. Research showed that Suntory's target consumers wanted green tea, so Suntory redesigned the product, switching to green tea. The bottle was redesigned to look like a traditional Japanese bamboo flask colored green. The product was renamed *Iemon* after the founder of a tea house. The name created the image of calmness and reassurance. Sales of this new product reached close to one billion dollars in 2005.

Global Brand Names

Finding a global brand name is not easy. A brand name must be unique to the product and its market. It must not be a name used by any other product or company. The name Exxon was chosen because almost no language around the world uses two x's together. The brand name should not have any undesirable meaning across languages.

To avoid these problems, companies hire naming firms. These firms evaluate names and products that will fit into a global market. Accenture was originally Arthur Andersen Consulting. When it became a separate company, it needed a new name. It used a number of consulting firms to come up with a list of 5,500 potential names. Once the company reduced the list to the top ten names, it chose Accenture because the *Ac* linked back to the old company. The name also implies an accent on the future.

Some family brands are well recognized around the world. A **family brand** is typically the brand name of a company. For example Ford Motor Company and Kellogg's are family brands with individual product brand names. Samsung moved from having individual product names to creating a family brand. This move allowed Samsung to create greater brand equity.

Companies also need to have pictorial images, such as *logos* and *trademarks*, that translate well across cultures.

Describe a strategy that can be used to position a product globally.

Understand Marketing Concepts

Circle the best answer for each of the following questions.

1. Something offered to a market that satisfies a want or a need is a
   a. brand
   b. brand equity
   c. product
   d. tangible part of a product

2. When a brand is used to create an image, this is known as
   a. family branding
   b. country-of-origin effect
   c. brand equity
   d. product positioning

Think Critically

Answer the following questions as completely as possible. If necessary, use a separate sheet of paper.

3. Research Find a product that is sold around the world. Describe the tangible and intangible parts of that product.

   _____

   _____

   _____

   _____

   _____

   _____

   _____

   _____

   _____

4. Communication Assume you work for a company that wants to create a global brand. Develop a PowerPoint presentation outlining how your company can do this.

   _____

   _____

   _____

   _____

   _____

   _____

Consumer and Business Markets

Goals

- Explain how companies develop brand images for consumer markets.
- Describe the characteristics of international business markets.

Terms

- price
- purchasing power parity
- raw materials
- component parts
- derived demand
- commodity products
- cost-plus method
- marginal-cost method

Going Global

Which plug do I use in this country? When travelers cross the world they often need to take a variety of electrical plug adapters. Different countries use different electrical currents, and they also use different types of plugs. The United States uses either two flat blades or a three-blade, grounded plug for 110 volts. Continental Europe uses two round prongs while Great Britain uses a rectangular-blade plug with 220 volts. Japan uses the same plug and current as the United States while China uses an oblique, flat blade with ground.

What is the reason for all of the differences? Harvey Hubbell II created the first U.S. electrical plug in 1904. As different countries developed their own electrical grids, they patented different styles of plugs. In addition, these unique plugs acted as a barrier to companies wishing to sell into new markets. Each market needed to have a different plug design. This requirement increased costs for exporting companies.

Working with a partner, describe why countries have different plug designs. Explain how an exporting company can overcome this type of barrier.

CONSUMER MARKETS

PRODUCT/SERVICE MANAGEMENT

Consumer products are targeted toward end users. Consumers' needs and wants vary greatly across cultures. Consumer product companies are more likely to use adaptation strategies for local markets. Targeting diverse consumers requires a strong understanding of local markets.

A local company's understanding of local markets often can give it an advantage over global marketers. A number of companies in China are developing local Chinese brands. Names like Gome Electronics, Lenovo computers, BIRD mobile phones, and Geely cars are not well known in Western countries. Neither were WiseVIEW, Tantus, and Yepp. These were Samsung's product brand names before they went under the Samsung family brand. Chinese companies can use their brand development in China to develop a base to move across Asia and other global markets.

Consumer market promotion is moving heavily to the Internet and other alternative brand-building venues. Web sites for global companies often have the same design even when languages change between countries. Yao Ming, the Houston Rockets NBA player, has been used by a number of global marketers trying to build a brand presence in China. In 2004, more than 200 million Chinese were estimated to have watched Yao Ming play exhibition games with the Houston Rockets in China. Yao has helped promote products for McDonald's, Pepsi, Disney, and Reebok.

Pricing

A **price** represents what a customer forfeits in exchange for receiving a product or service. Typically this is a payment of money. In some cases, barter is used instead of money. *Barter* involves the exchange of one product or service for another product or service.

Individual incomes vary widely around the world. Consumers in China earn less than consumers in the United States or many European countries. In turn, many products sold in China are priced lower than in other foreign markets. Likewise, individuals in Switzerland have higher incomes, so everything costs more. Even though Chinese consumers have lower incomes, they still have money to purchase products. Often an international marketer will look at **purchasing power parity (PPP)** when determining the price of a product. The PPP measures how much of a product a currency can buy in a country. It takes into account the average price of identical products in different countries. The non-PPP-adjusted GDP per capita (person), or nominal GDP, for individuals in China is $1,269 while the GDP for the United States is $39,900. When GDP is adjusted for PPP, China's adjusted PPP per capita is $5,642.

Global companies must make a decision about how to price their products around the world. Companies can adopt a standard global price or a price for local markets. It often is more difficult to have a global world price for consumer products. Distribution costs, taxes, and other expenses can differ in each market where the product is sold. For consumer products, companies are likely to adopt more than one pricing strategy.

Luxury Markets

Targeting luxury markets often allows international marketers to use a global standardization strategy. Luxury products typically target individuals with high incomes. These individuals are likely to have similar needs and wants and an equal ability to pay. Given this, luxury products are much more likely to have a global price. Otherwise, products could be purchased in cheaper markets and returned to local markets possibly to enter into a grey market.

Time Out

In 2004, the price for McDonald's Big Mac around the world in dollars was:
- U.S., $2.90
- Switzerland, $4.90
- Sweden, $3.94
- Egypt, $1.62
- China, $1.26
- Saudia Arabia, $0.64

Louis Vuitton competes against global luxury fashion brands such as Prada, Gucci, Hermes, and Coach. Vuitton has sales of over $3.8 billion a year. Fifty-five percent of its income comes from Japan. Vuitton is looking for growth in the United States, China, and India. Vuitton's image as a luxury designer allows it to sell handbags for prices from $600 to over $2,000 each. It is no wonder that Vuitton products are heavily counterfeited in countries such as China. But high-end Chinese customers do not buy counterfeited handbags. Counterfeits are shipped primarily to the United States and Europe.

When might global consumer product companies use a standardization strategy?

BUSINESS MARKETS

Business markets include companies or organizations that purchase products for the operation of a business or the completion of a business activity. Business markets purchase products that are used to produce other goods and services. Products purchased can include raw materials, equipment, supplies, or services. The final products then enter other business markets, including wholesalers, distributors, and retailers.

- **Raw materials** Unprocessed products that are used to produce other products are called **raw materials**. Raw materials can include chemicals, minerals, and agricultural products. Many countries specialize in the production of raw materials that are exported around the world.

- **Equipment** Business markets use two types of equipment. *Capital equipment* includes land, buildings, and expensive pieces of equipment. Tool-and-die equipment used to make industrial parts is an example of capital equipment. Germany and Sweden specialize in making tool-and-die equipment. *Operating equipment* includes smaller, less expensive equipment, such as personal computers.

- **Supplies** Products and materials that are consumed in the operation of the business are *supplies*.

- **Component parts** Parts that are partially completed by one manufacturer to be used by another manufacturer are called **component parts**. At one time, manufacturers of component parts were located close to the final assembly plant. Today, improved global distribution systems allow manufacturers of component parts to ship products around the world.

- **Services** Business markets use a large number of different services. They can include transportation, banking, promotional, accounting, and many others.

Business markets differ from consumer markets in a number of ways. Total sales in business markets are larger than in consumer markets. Business markets operate based on **derived demand**, which is the demand that comes from the end purchaser. Raw materials are sold to manufacturers that create component parts. The component parts are sold to assembly plants. Their final products are sold to distributors and finally to retailers.

Businesses that sell industry products often compete on price. They also attempt to gain economies of scale. Exporting is also more common in businesses that sell to business markets.

Industrial Markets

MARKETING–
INFORMATION
MANAGEMENT

An industrial market is a type of business market. Industrial markets have distinct characteristics that impact international marketing strategies.

- **Classification** Industrial markets are often segmented by the types of products they produce or by how products are used in a business. The products and processes are less likely to vary across industrial markets. For example, automobile manufacturers use the same types of supplies and the same types of production processes.

- **Industrial Buyers** The motives, authority, and negotiating style of industrial buyers can differ across cultures. Industrial buyers make complex decisions and often have service needs. They also are very value oriented.

- **Relationship Development** Industrial markets work within a network of relationships. Sellers and buyers become dependent upon each other. If a supplier is unable to send materials to a manufacturer, employees are laid off and revenue stops. In many Asian countries, strong personal relationships develop between individuals in businesses. These personal relationships help build strong links between businesses.

- **International Orientation** Today most industrial relationships are global. Raw materials and component parts are shipped across borders to assembly plants with low labor costs. Final products are shipped to individual markets worldwide.

- **Uniformity** Industrial products have much less variation than consumer products. Industrial salespeople with an expertise on products can apply that expertise in any market because of the product's uniformity. However, salespeople will have to understand the cultural differences of the people with whom they work.

Commodity Products

Commodity products include goods that cannot be easily differentiated. Commodity products include grains, minerals, and petroleum. These products typically are pooled together by the producers. For example, farmers in the United States pool their grains in storage areas. The grains are then sold in bulk through commodity markets. Commodities often are traded in global commodity markets. In these markets, a global price is set based on the supply of the commodity and the worldwide demand. All sellers in the global market accept the global price.

Perhaps the best-known commodity market is for oil. Producers around the world sell oil in a global market. Increased demand and limited supply can drive prices higher. Developing economies in China, India, and other countries are increasing the demand for oil needed for energy production and transportation. This increase in derived demand has been pushing up prices worldwide.

© GETTY IMAGES/PHOTODISC

Business Pricing

PRICING

Businesses that sell to business markets are more likely to export and ship products around the world. When exporting products, companies can incur costs of modifying the products for foreign markets. They also can incur operational costs involved in exporting the products. Finally, they can encounter tariffs, taxes, and other costs involved in entering a market.

All of these factors can lead to differences in costs for products in different markets. If the company wants to maintain a standard worldwide price, profits in foreign markets may be lower due to shipping, distribution, and other costs. Companies often develop a *dual-pricing* system for domestic and export markets. They may adopt a **cost-plus method** where all export costs are included in the price of the product. This method can result in very high costs in export markets. To maintain competitiveness, some firms may use a **marginal-cost method**. Using this method, firms will look at the price they need to set to be competitive in foreign markets. Then, they must look at their costs to be sure that they are meeting a minimum profit.

List two ways a business market differs from a consumer market.

Checkpoint

Understand Marketing Concepts

Circle the best answer for each of the following questions.

1. Which of the following would *not* be true of a consumer market?
   a. branding is important
   b. adaptation is more likely
   c. commodity products are a common purchase
   d. all of the above are true for consumer markets

2. Unprocessed products that are used to produce other products are called
   a. raw materials
   b. equipment
   c. supplies
   d. component parts

Think Critically

Answer the following questions as completely as possible. If necessary, use a separate sheet of paper.

3. Identify a luxury brand that is sold globally. Use magazine ads to describe how this product is positioned. Develop a profile of a global consumer for this product.

_____

_____

_____

_____

_____

_____

4. Identify an industrial product. Determine how this product impacts consumer usage. Generate a list of global factors that could create derived demand for this industrial product.

_____

_____

_____

_____

_____

_____

_____

International Service Marketing

Goals

- Explain the nature of international services.
- Describe international service growth areas.

Terms

- intangibility
- inseparability
- heterogeneity
- perishability
- ISO standards

Going Global

Is Yum! Brands yummy? Yum! Brands is expanding rapidly in international markets. It is opening one new restaurant in China every single day. Yum! Brands is not a Chinese company. It is the parent company of Kentucky Fried Chicken, Taco Bell, and Pizza Hut. Yum! Brands has 34,000 restaurants around the world.

Seventy-five percent of Yum! Brands restaurants are locally owned and managed by franchisees. Yum! Brands has used its size to gain economies of scale when working with global service providers, such as advertising agencies and suppliers. However, this cost savings may not counteract the potential decline in Yum! Brands' sales. Fast-food companies could face a decline in customer demand in developed countries because of concerns about obesity.

The U.S. market may well be over-saturated. China may be the answer. China is seen as a growth market, with five hundred million urban Chinese that can afford to eat at a Yum! Brands restaurant. This number doesn't include an additional 800 million Chinese that could still enter the market.

Working with a partner, discuss why Yum! Brands would want to expand globally. Explain why Yum! Brands would not use its corporate brand name for its individual restaurants around the world.

INTERNATIONAL SERVICES

PRODUCT/SERVICE MANAGEMENT

Most products have a combination of tangible and intangible parts. The after-sale service components of products are becoming an important part of gaining competitive advantages. Service businesses provide mostly intangible benefits. Banks, for example, hold funds, provide investment advice, make loans, and offer a variety of other services to customers.

As individuals across the world become more affluent, services become more important. These services include not only banking but also educational, medical, travel and tourism, and others. Services are a major part of the world's economy. Services account for a large percentage of the GDP in developed countries. In 2004, services in the United States accounted for 80 percent of its GDP. Services were 33.3 percent of China's GDP, 71 percent of Japan's GDP, and at least 70 percent of many E.U. countries' GDPs.

Services are crossing borders. Technology is aiding the movement of information worldwide. Service businesses are looking for global expansion to gain economies of scale in their areas of competitive advantage. For example, investment banks have advantages in corporate financing. This expertise can be offered to a larger set of international customers.

Nature of International Services

Services have four characteristics, each with unique international aspects.

In many countries, a large number of employees work in service businesses.
- U.S., 80 percent
- E.U., 70 percent
- Japan, 65 percent
- China, 29 percent

- **Intangibility** implies that a service cannot be physically possessed. Service businesses offer mostly intangible benefits. These benefits typically are consumed immediately, even though benefits can remain long after. For example, education is an intangible service, but the benefits remain throughout your lifetime. Many services are based on information that can flow easily across borders. Many after-sale services are outsourced. These service centers are linked electronically to customers around the world.

- **Inseparability** suggests that service businesses cannot be separated from their providers. International communication networks are bringing service workers directly to customers. These service workers can be in almost any country in the world.

- **Heterogeneity** indicates that services can vary from provider to provider. Companies need to ensure that the same level of service is provided in each global location. There has been a country-of-origin effect perception in some service industries. Faced with international competition, global corporations have developed global standards of quality for products and services around the world.

- **Perishability** means that services cannot be stored. They can be very time-dependent, which works in favor of local businesses. For example, it may be cheaper to hire a plumber from India to work in the United States, but the time it would take for the plumber to arrive limits this option.

ISO Standards

ISO standards are a set of global quality standards. The International Organization for Standardization (ISO) sets global standards for quality. The ISO network includes national standards institutes from 156 countries. They agree on quality standards for the manufacturing of tangible products and the delivery of services. There currently are two widely used ISO families of standards. ISO 9000 standards refer to quality management requirements in business-to-business markets. ISO 14000 standards relate to environmental standards. Companies that meet these global standards have demonstrated that they provide top quality products and services.

Checkpoint

List the four characteristics of services.

_____

_____

_____

INTERNATIONAL SERVICE GROWTH

The global service industry offers extensive international marketing opportunities. Because a service cannot be manufactured and exported, global expansion will require businesses to work with service providers in foreign markets. Consumers are also aiding the growth of international services by traveling to other countries to take advantage of cheaper services.

Banking and Financial Services

Banks act as a depository for savings. They also are a source for lending to both businesses and consumers. Banks help ensure that funds flow smoothly throughout the economy. For this reason, banks typically are heavily regulated.

Banks look to foreign markets for growth. The Royal Bank of Scotland has purchased close to 30 U.S. bank groups to increase its presence in the United States. Global banks also have tremendous opportunity for growth in developing countries. As India and China develop economically, millions of new customers will be looking for banking services.

Medical Services

India is becoming a center for medical tourism. In 2003, nearly 150,000 people traveled to India for surgeries. They came from countries with state-controlled medical systems because they did not want to wait for surgery. They also came from countries with private medical systems because medical procedures in India can be one-third the cost of those in developed countries. It is estimated that by 2012 India could have a medical tourism service industry worth $2 billion. Other areas for medical tourism include Southeast Asia, South Africa, and South America.

Restaurants

People in developed countries spend up to 50 percent of their food dollars in restaurants. Companies like McDonald's have huge global opportunities. In the United States, there are over 43 McDonald's restaurants for every million people. In China, there is only one McDonald's restaurant for every four million people.

Ethics Around the World

Is a diamond worth a single life? Conflict diamonds, or blood diamonds, are names given to diamonds from West African countries in conflict, such as Angola, Liberia, Sierra Leone, and Guinea. These diamonds do not flow through De Beers. They most often enter into a *black market* where products are bought and sold illegally. Funds from conflict diamonds often are used to support terrorism and military action against governments.

It is very difficult to distinguish conflict diamonds from legally mined diamonds. The U.N. has proposed a "Certificate of Origin" for each diamond to show that it is mined from a legitimate government-controlled area. This proposal will require a standardized certificate for all diamond-exporting countries. For this system to work, diamond trade will need to be structured. Sales also will need to be audited and monitored.

In 2000, between $350 and $420 million of Angolan diamonds were smuggled into neighboring countries. These countries were required to seize all Angolan diamonds without a government certificate of origin. But not a single illicit Angolan diamond was intercepted. It was as if the diamonds vanished into thin air.

THINK CRITICALLY

1. Do you think the diamond trade supports conflicts in these areas, or does the conflict support the trading of diamonds?
2. Describe the difficulty in developing a system to stop the trading of conflict diamonds.

Tourism

In 2003, international tourism revenue was over $474 billion, with the United States receiving nearly $65 billion. France is the number one tourist arrival destination, receiving over 67 million tourists per year and close to $37 billion in foreign tourist revenue. By 2020, global tourism is expected to increase from about 700 million travelers to 1.6 billion travelers.

Checkpoint

Name at least three areas of international service industry growth.

World Stars | STAN SHIH

Most people in the United States have never heard of Stan Shih or Acer Inc., but he is well known in Asia and Europe. Acer is the fifth largest seller of PCs, and it is the fastest growing. Acer laptops are top sellers in Italy, Germany, and the Netherlands. In the 1990s, Stan Shih transformed Acer from a contract component manufacturer into a global brand company. Shih graduated from the National Chiao Tung University in Taiwan with degrees in electrical engineering. In 1971, he began working for Unitron Industrial Corp. where he designed Taiwan's first desktop calculator. In 1976, he co-founded the company that was the forerunner of Acer.

Shih was a management pioneer in Asia. Many of his management principles went against Chinese tradition. He minimized Acer's management structure and moved voting control to a large number of shareholders. He used outside directors and paid managers in stock. He expected his employees to openly express their opinions. He assumed that people were naturally good, not self-serving. He banned his children from working for Acer. He thought the pressure would be unfair to his children and his work associates. It also could block qualified managers from top positions.

Fortune magazine chose Shih as "One of 25 People You Ought to Know for Doing Business in Asia." Shih has received numerous awards. In 1976, he was one of the "Ten Most Outstanding Young Persons" in Taiwan. In 1999, he was awarded the International Business Executive of the Year award from the Academy of International Business. In 2003, he received an award from the Taiwan Ministry of Economic Affairs for "Outstanding Contribution to Brand Building in Taiwan." He became the first Asian CEO to receive an honorary degree of Doctor of International Law.

THINK CRITICALLY

Describe how Stan Shih ran his company differently from traditional Chinese companies. Speculate on how this could have helped his company grow. Explain how this could have led to the international recognition Shih has received.

Understand Marketing Concepts

Circle the best answer for each of the following questions.

1. _____ suggests that service businesses cannot be separated from their providers.
   a. intangibility
   b. inseparability
   c. heterogeneity
   d. perishability

2. _____ indicates that services can vary from provider to provider.
   a. intangibility
   b. inseparability
   c. heterogeneity
   d. perishability

Think Critically

Answer the following questions as completely as possible. If necessary, use a separate sheet of paper.

3. Choose a service business. Describe the business using the four characteristics of a service. Indicate how these four factors would differ if this was an international service.

_____

_____

_____

_____

_____

_____

4. Research Use the Internet to learn more about ISO standards. Describe the types of ISO standards that service businesses would strive to meet. (*Hint:* Visit the ISO web site.)

_____

_____

_____

_____

_____

_____

_____

_____

Chapter Assessment

Review Marketing Concepts

Write the letter of the term that matches each definition. Some terms will not be used.

_____ 1. Something offered to a market that satisfies a want or a need

_____ 2. Exists when products are sold outside of an established authorized distribution system

_____ 3. Typically the brand name of a company

_____ 4. Represents what a customer forfeits in exchange for receiving a product or service

_____ 5. Additional value that a brand name brings to a product or company

_____ 6. Pricing method that includes all export costs

_____ 7. Demand that comes from the end purchaser

_____ 8. Goods that cannot be easily differentiated

_____ 9. Using a brand to create an image

_____ 10. Implies that a service cannot be physically possessed

a. brand
b. brand equity
c. commodity products
d. component parts
e. cost-plus method
f. derived demand
g. family brand
h. grey market
i. heterogeneity
j. inseparability
k. intangibility
l. ISO standards
m. marginal-cost method
n. perishability
o. price
p. product
q. product positioning
r. purchasing power parity
s. raw materials

Circle the best answer.

11. Partially completed parts from another manufacturer are called
    a. outsourced parts
    b. component parts
    c. equipment parts
    d. raw material parts

12. When people see a country as a brand, a _____ occurs.
    a. national brand
    b. global brand
    c. country effect
    d. country-of-origin effect

13. _____ measure(s) how much of a product a currency can buy.
    a. ISO standards
    b. GDP
    c. purchasing power parity
    d. derived demand

Think Critically

14. Identify a product that you have recently purchased. If this product were to be sold globally, determine if it would follow a standardization or adaptation strategy based on the market, product, and company characteristics. Explain why.

_____

_____

_____

_____

_____

15. Make a list of five countries. Specify the country-of-origin effect for products exported from these countries. Determine if these countries specialize in the manufacture of any products.

_____

_____

_____

_____

_____

_____

16. Find a product with an appealing design. Specify how the design characteristics enhance the product's brand equity.

_____

_____

_____

_____

_____

17. Make a recommendation to a business on how it can use technology and other non-traditional promotions to create an international brand image.

_____

_____

_____

_____

_____

_____

_____

Make Connections

18. Marketing Identify a raw material that is often supplied to the United States by a foreign country. Identify which business markets would have a high derived demand for this raw material. Explain why.

_____

_____

_____

_____

_____

_____

_____

19. Research Watch a movie. Make a list of the products that you view throughout the movie. Specify how the use of the products in the movie helps create a brand image.

_____

_____

_____

_____

_____

_____

_____

_____

20. Communication Develop a PowerPoint presentation to persuade the management of an organization to adopt ISO standards. Consider both the ISO 9000 and ISO 14000 standards.

_____

_____

_____

_____

_____

_____

_____

_____

21. **Marketing Math** Assume your company has a product that sells for $100 in the United States. It costs $75 to manufacture the product. The average price this product sells for in foreign markets is $110. Per unit shipping costs are $5. Taxes and tariffs are $12 per unit. All other expenses are $8 per unit. Your company requires a 10 percent return on manufacturing costs. Can this product be profitable in foreign markets?

_____

_____

_____

_____

_____

PUT MARKETING ON THE MAP

International Marketing Plan Project

Your international marketing plan must recommend a branding strategy for your business. You also must identify the tangible and intangible components of your product or service. Finally, you must determine how you will provide services to support your business.

Work with a group and complete the following activities.

1. Make a list of the tangible and intangible components of your products. Specify how these may need to be adapted for the different markets you want to target.

2. Identify market, product, and company characteristics to help you decide whether to pursue a standardization strategy or an adaptation strategy. Justify a recommendation for the strategy you select.

3. Identify the brand name you will use for your products. Use the Internet to conduct a brand name search to be sure the name is not already being used. Check the translation in at least three languages to be sure you know the meaning.

4. Create a positioning statement for your brand to describe the image you want to project. Make a recommendation for how your company will create this brand image in customers' minds. Indicate if you believe there would be a country-of-origin effect in the countries in which you want to sell.

5. Research the purchasing power parity (PPP) in the countries in which you want to sell. Specify how you plan to price your product in the foreign markets.

Case Study

PRODUCT BRAND STRATEGIES

The war of the colas continues with strategies ranging from new products to sponsorship of events that attract large target markets.

During the 1970s, Pepsi conducted taste tests to show that cola drinkers preferred Pepsi to Coca-Cola. Coca-Cola realized that some consumers preferred the flavor of Pepsi. So, it created a sweeter-tasting New Coke in 1985, but the new product fizzled.

New products come and go, reflecting changing cultural trends. Pepsi developed a clear Pepsi One, but many people did not buy into the idea of a clear cola. Both Pepsi and Coca-Cola also have tried a series of flavors, including cherry, lemon, lime, and vanilla.

Diet Coke and Diet Pepsi were produced for a health-conscious society. The diet formulas have been changed to accommodate the latest diet trends. Coca-Cola Zero was created to give consumers a diet product with zero carbohydrates and full cola flavor.

Coca-Cola has become a part of the culture in other countries. Sudan is the largest country in Africa, and Coca-Cola plays a big role in its economy. Coca-Cola generates a multiplier-effect in Sudan's employment. Every job created by Coca-Cola in Sudan results in the creation of ten additional jobs in related industries.

Coca-Cola is also a part of India's culture. Coca-Cola has made significant investments in India including new production facilities, waste water treatment plants,

distribution systems, and marketing equipment. Coca-Cola indirectly employs 125,000 people in India, and almost all goods and services required to produce and market Coca-Cola are made in India.

Coca-Cola and Pepsi continue to intensify their marketing plans in the United States. Major college and professional sports arenas pledge allegiance to whichever cola sponsors their team or league. Coca-Cola has captured the loyalty of much of the Baby Boomer generation. Pepsi has made inroads with the younger generation through music and commercials.

Now the cola industry must develop international marketing strategies to earn the loyalty of customers throughout the world.

THINK CRITICALLY

1. Why do Coca-Cola and Pepsi spend large sums of money on marketing when their products already are well known?

2. What are some marketing adjustments that colas must make to sell in other countries?

3. Why does Coca-Cola have a web site that shows how its presence has benefited other countries?

4. A popular commercial for Coca-Cola in the 1970s included the song *I'd Like to Teach the World to Sing in Perfect Harmony*. This song was recently brought back for Coke advertisements? Why did Coca-Cola do this?

FOOD MARKETING SERIES EVENT

The Food Marketing Series Event consists of two major parts: a written comprehensive exam and a role-playing event. Participants are given a written scenario to review and present to the judge. Participants have ten minutes to review the situation and develop a professional approach to solving the problem. During the presentation, participants may refer to notes made during the preparation time, but no note cards may be used.

Ten minutes are allowed for students to present their plan of action to the judge. Five additional minutes are available for judges to ask questions about the proposal.

Coca-Cola has developed a new product that has no calories, no carbohydrates, and full Coca-Cola flavor. Coca-Cola Zero has been on the market for several months with disappointing sales results. Most consumers have formed a loyalty to Diet Coke, Diet Pepsi, Coca-Cola, Pepsi, and other established flavors of cola.

Coca-Cola has hired you to design an effective strategy for increasing sales of Coca-Cola Zero. Coca-Cola believes that consumers will become fans of the product once they taste it.

You must develop a strategy to acquaint large numbers of consumers with the Coca-Cola Zero product. Six-ounce plastic bottles are available to use for this special promotion.

You must explain a strategy to use in major shopping malls and supermarkets to build a customer base for Coca-Cola Zero.

Performance Indicators Evaluated

- Understand product loyalty.
- Explain creative strategies to introduce consumers to Coca-Cola Zero.
- Demonstrate critical-thinking and problem-solving skills.
- Provide incentives for consumers to purchase a new product.
- Describe the best locations to introduce a product to large numbers of people.

Go to the DECA web site for more detailed information.

THINK CRITICALLY

1. Why is it difficult for a new cola to successfully enter the market?
2. Give two examples of effective promotion strategies to generate consumer interest in a new product.
3. List two product features or benefits of Coca-Cola Zero that should be used to market the new product.
4. How can Coca-Cola use brand equity to its advantage?

www.deca.org

International Marketing Channels

CHAPTER 8 · CHAPTER 8 · CHAPTER 8 · CHAPTER 8 · CHAPTER 8

8

© DIGITAL VISION

Point Your Browser

intlmarket.swlearning.com

Open All Night Everywhere

Where do people go when they need something in the middle of the night? For many people around the world the answer is 7-Eleven. Founded in Dallas, Texas, in 1927, 7-Eleven started as an ice company. It sold milk and eggs as a convenience to customers. The president of 7-Eleven realized that electric refrigerators were going to put an end to the ice business, so he pioneered the idea of convenience stores. Originally these convenience stores were open only from 7:00 A.M. to 11:00 P.M. Today they are open 24 hours a day.

In the 1980s, 7-Eleven was not an efficient company. Stores would receive as many as 80 deliveries a week. The situation was different in Japan. Japan's second largest retailer, Ito-Yokado, licensed the 7-Eleven brand. It centralized distribution and brought fresh food into stores. It developed an information network that allowed managers to tailor inventories to customer needs. The 7-Eleven stores became a cool hangout where customers would stop up to five times a day.

Today's 7-Eleven stores control inventories through technology. Store managers can find out which products are selling best at their store and throughout the country. Slow-moving items can be discounted to clear inventory. Bakeries and kitchens surround 7-Eleven distribution centers to deliver fresh food to stores by 5:00 A.M.

There are almost 28,000 7-Elevens around the world. The convenience stores are both franchise- and corporate-owned. Surprisingly, there are fewer than 6,000 in the United States and Canada. The remainder can be found in countries as diverse as Japan, Australia, Mexico, Taiwan, Singapore, the Philippines, the United Kingdom, Sweden, Denmark, South Korea, Thailand, Norway, Turkey, Malaysia, China, Singapore, and Guam. Although 7-Eleven started in the United States, today majority ownership is held by 7-Eleven Japan. It operates almost 11,000 7-Eleven stores in Japan.

Think Critically

1. Explain what contributed to the trouble 7-Eleven faced in the 1980s. Describe what changed to improve profits.

2. Why does 7-Eleven have more convenience stores in Japan than in the United States?

International Channel Design

Goals

- Describe the role of marketing intermediaries.
- Discuss how businesses develop channel relationships.

Terms

- channel of distribution
- logistics
- marketing intermediary
- total cost concept
- channel captain

Going Global

Coca-Cola is the world's number one brand. But being number one does not guarantee worldwide success. No matter how well recognized a brand is, it will not sell unless it is on a store shelf. Coke's channel of distribution has traditionally followed three routes. Coke provides syrup to bottlers. The bottlers receive bottles and cans from manufacturers. The bottlers then distribute the final product to retailers and vending machines.

Most of Coke's distributors around the world are independent businesses.

Coca-Cola is the dominant cola drink in Germany, but it has been facing some problems. Its share of the total market dropped from 62 percent to 55 percent. One of the reasons for this decline is a reverse channel recycling law. Retail stores did not want to bother with the collection of used cans and bottles, so they pulled Coke and other soft drinks from their shelves. Retail stores demanded a new container that did not require recycling. In addition, new retail discounters began to pressure Coke to lower prices. To meet these demands, Coca-Cola has decided not to renew distribution contracts with many bottlers. Coke believes this decision will allow it to introduce new products faster and control the distribution channel. Some business people in Germany think that relationships developed by bottlers may disappear.

Working with a partner, describe Coke's distribution model. Explain why Coke would not renew the German bottlers' contracts. Describe the risk that Coke takes by not using the German bottlers.

MARKETING CHANNELS

DISTRIBUTION

Efficient distribution systems are important to global competitiveness. Brand recognition and product quality will not matter if a product is not available where customers shop. International marketers must establish a **channel of distribution**, which is the path used to move products from their source to the customer. Channels of distribution work hand-in-hand with logistical systems. **Logistics** includes activities that create an orderly and timely acquisition and transportation of products through the channel of distribution.

Coca-Cola has established a distribution system. Coca-Cola receives raw materials from around the world to produce its syrup. It then must ship its syrup to bottlers. Container manufacturers must produce and store cans and bottles for bottlers. Bottlers must establish relationships with retailers and find ways to get inventories to store shelves while minimizing costs. This distribution system must operate efficiently at low costs. The soft drink industry is extremely price competitive, so the total cost of distribution must be kept down.

Channel Length

Products don't usually move directly from a manufacturer to a customer. They typically move through a number of intermediaries. A **marketing intermediary** is an independent business that assists the flow of goods and services from producers to customers. Intermediaries include agents and brokers, wholesalers, and others. The intermediaries take possession of products and then sell to other channel members.

There is a general movement in all markets to shorten channels of distribution. A *short channel of distribution* means that there are a few intermediaries. The shortest channel is a *direct channel* from producer directly to the customer. A *long channel of distribution* implies that there are many intermediaries. Consumer goods typically have a longer or *indirect channel of distribution*. At a minimum, these channels include manufacturers, wholesalers, and retailers. Industrial markets can have shorter channels of distribution. If an order is large enough, Manufacturer A could sell directly to Customer B without an intermediary.

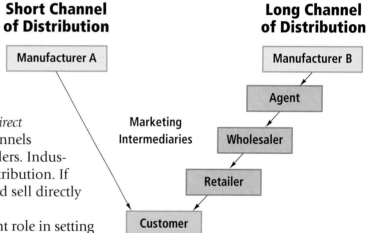

Marketing intermediaries have an important role in setting up distribution channels. Wholesalers and retailers provide a series of services to their customers by breaking the large bulk created by other channel members into an assortment of products for others to buy. They also provide information to others in the channel. They store products until others need them. They may transport products, provide financing, and help promote products. For example, a retailer may buy from a wholesaler that has a large assortment of products from different manufacturers. Retailers break the bulk that wholesalers have purchased and offer an assortment of products to consumers. When international marketers enter new locations, they also must break the bulk of their inventory in order to have the right assortment of products for customers.

Channels of distribution have become a key to international competitiveness because they can:

- **Facilitate just-in-time (JIT) inventory** With *JIT inventory* systems, products arrive just as they are needed. This process works for both manufacturers and retailers. Computerized inventory and point-of-sale systems provide constant inventory feedback to warehouses and suppliers. These systems limit the amount of inventory a business needs to carry. JIT is becoming a standard for manufacturers and retailers around the world. Producers and shippers must deliver the right product to the right location at the right time.

Tech Zone

Universal Product Codes (UPCs) are on nearly every retail product sold. UPCs allow checkout scanners to identify products, assign prices, and keep track of inventory. Each UPC must be passed in front of a laser scanner for checkout.

Radio frequency identification (RFID) tags can identify products without a laser scanner. RFID tags are silicon chips with a built-in antenna that can transmit data to a wireless receiver.

The smallest RFID tags are used to identify products and require no batteries. At this time, they are considerably more expensive than printing a UPC code on a package. Larger battery-operated RFID tags are used in a number of transportation areas. They allow drivers to automatically pay tolls without stopping, eliminating delays. Shippers use RFID tags to track products and shipping containers on container ships and trains. Trucking companies use them to track trucks and trailers in shipping yards. Since January 2005, Wal-Mart has required its top 100 suppliers to apply RFID tags to all shipments. This technology has increased shipping efficiency. It also improves production and distribution planning.

THINK CRITICALLY

Describe the advantages that RFID tags offer for international logistics. Explain why RFID tags would be better than UPC codes.

- **Lower costs** There is a worldwide drive to lower the costs of moving products from manufacturing through channels of distribution to the customer. This requires designing the most efficient system for delivering products. Considerable saving can be found through efficient channel design.

- **Speed up distribution** Intense international competition requires that companies find a way to get products to customers faster than competitors can. In addition to speed, the reliability of distribution systems also is important.

- **Support expansion into new markets** New international market opportunities require that companies either establish a new distribution channel to reach customers or work with an existing network. In either case, companies must be competitive in these markets and at the same time provide the lowest-cost system possible.

Large international firms are gaining cost savings and efficiencies by gaining control both forward and backward in the channel. For example, as a manufacturer, Coke is near the beginning of the distribution channel. It has moved its channel ownership forward by gaining control of its bottling operations in Germany. Wal-Mart, which is near the end of the channel, has moved channel ownership backward to gain control of its warehousing and distribution systems.

International Channel Design

International marketers have two choices when they enter new markets. They will either establish a new channel of distribution or work within an existing channel. When international businesses use existing channels, they often redesign the distribution channel to increase efficiency. To gain greater efficiencies in Japan, 7-Eleven Japan redesigned its distribution channel.

A number of factors must be taken into consideration when designing a channel of distribution. These factors include the nature of the product, customer needs, competition, costs, communication systems, control issues, company goals, and available resources. For example, Coca-Cola may spend up to $2 billion to gain control of its German distribution system. The main reason Coca-Cola is spending this money is to gain the ability to react more quickly to changes in the marketplace.

Developing a completely new channel of distribution in a foreign market is a high-risk strategy. The business would need to develop relationships with suppliers, arrange for the importing of inventory, develop warehouses, develop delivery systems, choose retail locations, and hire and train all employees to work within the distribution system. Wal-Mart is a company with international expansion plans and the resources to carry them out. As Wal-Mart expands into China, it has to train 500 new employees for each supercenter it opens. Wal-Mart works with local partners to find prime locations to distribute its products in major Chinese cities.

Total Cost Concept

Channel designers develop distribution systems that minimize total cost. A **total cost concept** is the idea that all costs must be taken into consideration when designing a channel of distribution. For example, Coca-Cola could produce its entire bottled product in the United States and then ship it around the world. This design could result in a costly distribution system, considering most of what is shipped is water. Rather than ship bottled products, it is more cost-efficient to produce the product in the country in which it will be marketed. In addition to shipping, costs such as insurance, storage, and inventory losses would result in a very expensive product. Coca-Cola must evaluate alternatives and look for the lowest cost for delivering products to customers.

An international study shows that when customers are faced with out-of-stock products, 21 to 43 percent of them will make that purchase at another store. Retailers lose approximately 4 percent of their sales due to out-of-stock products. This can partially be attributed to distribution problems.

Name four ways distribution channels aid in developing competitive advantages.

Checkpoint

CHANNEL RELATIONSHIPS

Distribution channels consist of a number of different members, each with its own goals. Channel members develop relationships the same way that people develop relationships. When goals and behaviors are compatible, they are likely to work in cooperation. However, it also is possible that conflicts can arise within a distribution channel.

There are a number of reasons why conflicts can form. All distribution systems attempt to achieve the lowest cost possible. This could result in *disintermediation*, or the removal of channel members. For example, Coca-Cola is attempting to disintermediate bottlers in Germany to gain greater control over the distribution channel, including packaging its product in a way that meets the needs of German retailers.

© DIGITAL VISION

Channel Power

Some members of distribution channels have greater power than others. Wal-Mart is the channel captain in its distribution system. A **channel captain** takes the leadership role in organizing a distribution system, which lessens the chances for conflict. Channel captains gain power through their ability to reward or punish channel members and through their knowledge of their product-market.

Coca-Cola is also the channel captain in its distribution system. In Germany, Coke is not taking over all of the bottlers. Seven bottlers will maintain their independence while the rest will not have their contracts renewed by Coke. As the channel captain, Coca-Cola is rewarding some intermediaries while removing contracts from others.

Finding International Partners

International marketers often will look for partners when they enter new markets. There are a number of ways to find partners. They may be located through government sources from both state and federal commerce departments. Contacts also may be found at trade shows. Information often is collected from outside sources such as the Internet. To help identify potential partners, businesses also will use members of the current distribution channel, such as distributors, a sales force, and customers.

Export management companies (EMCs) specialize in helping businesses distribute products. EMCs typically specialize in specific products and markets. An EMC can act as an agent, or broker, for a company. An *agent* brings together buyers and sellers but typically does not take title, or ownership, of the product. Agents usually take a percentage of sales. EMCs also could take ownership of the product, but then they incur the risk of selling the product. By using this strategy, however, EMCs could earn higher profits.

Potential international partners need to be screened. Because potential partners can handle many different products and businesses, each partner needs to be evaluated to be sure there are no conflicts. Potential partners need to have a strong knowledge of the product and the market. They need to be able to provide after-sales service. Finally, they need to be willing to perform these services at a reasonable price.

Checkpoint

Name four ways that businesses can find international partners.

Understand Marketing Concepts

Circle the best answer for each of the following questions.

1. A distribution system with few intermediaries is a(n) _____ channel.
   a. long
   b. short
   c. intermediary
   d. retail

2. Businesses that take leadership roles in distribution systems are called channel _____.
   a. intermediaries
   b. leaders
   c. captains
   d. distributors

Think Critically

Answer the following questions as completely as possible. If necessary, use a separate sheet of paper.

3. Choose an international business. Draw a diagram illustrating the industry distribution channels. Include normal transportation modes and intermediaries.

_____

_____

_____

_____

_____

_____

_____

4. Using the distribution channel illustrated in Question 3, indicate how this distribution channel can help create competitive advantages for the international business.

_____

_____

_____

_____

_____

_____

_____

_____

Exporting and Logistics

- Explain what is involved in the exporting process.
- Discuss the importance of having an efficient logistical system.

- exporting
- importing
- indirect exporting
- direct exporting
- customs
- customs broker
- intermodal transport

Going Global

Containerized shipping has revolutionized the transport of international cargo. Malcolm McLean is credited with inventing the shipping container. He knew that at foreign ports products were transferred from a truck to a ship to be sent overseas. Once the cargo arrived at the destination port, it was removed from the ship and placed back into a truck. McLean thought that a modified truck trailer could act as a cargo container. These containers could go directly onto a ship, and goods could be moved in and out much faster. Today about 90 percent of all cargo is containerized for shipping. Large container ships can cross the oceans safely because international weather systems can reroute travel around storms.

The world's largest container shipping company is A.P. Moller-Maersk. Moller-Maersk has more than 380 ships and moves over one million containers each year. Each container meets ISO standards. Sending cargo by shipping containers also has many other advantages. Containers aid in clearing customs. Damage and theft also are reduced, which can lower insurance costs.

Working with a partner, describe how cargo systems would help make distribution systems more efficient.

EXPORTING

DISTRIBUTION

When international marketers have foreign customers, they must export their products to those markets. **Exporting** is the process of shipping a product to another part of the world for trade or sale. **Importing** is receiving exported products. Once sales are made to foreign customers, products need to be exported. Exporting includes preparing products for shipment, arranging all documentation, and planning the shipping and delivery of products. Businesses can engage in direct or indirect exporting. When a company is not fully committed to international marketing, it may engage in indirect exporting. In **indirect exporting**, a business uses brokers or agents to help find customers and export products. Indirect exporting can increase the total cost of the sale. When a company is more fully committed to foreign markets, it may engage in direct exporting.

With **direct exporting**, a company actively controls finding markets and exporting products.

Exporting requires that a company identify customers and then find a way to move products from a domestic location to a foreign customer. This method requires arranging for shipping, documentation, clearing customs, and delivery in the foreign market. Companies can use an *export trading company* as a global distribution intermediary. Export trading companies provide services such as buying and selling products, conducting market research, and distributing products abroad.

Mitsubishi is one of Japan's largest export trading companies. Japan's trading companies, known as *sogo (general) shoshas (trading company)*, do more than just export. They have banks for funding, shipping companies, suppliers, and manufacturers that work together. The sogo shoshas control more than half of Japanese imports and exports.

Even when a company engages in direct exporting it often will use intermediaries to help in the exporting process. An *international freight forwarder* acts like a travel agent for cargo. It ships products to customers in foreign countries.

Documentation

When products enter into foreign markets they must "clear" customs. A country's **customs** acts as immigration control for products entering the country. Customs agents inspect shipments to ensure that the imported products are properly documented. They also collect customs fees, and they ensure that restricted products do not enter the country. Restricted products could include dangerous products, embargoed products, fake products, or products made from endangered species.

There are companies that specialize in helping products clear customs. A **customs broker** is an intermediary that helps products move through customs. In the United States, customs brokers are licensed by the U.S. Department of the Treasury. They must understand the tariff schedules and customs regulations enforced by the United States. They must be familiar with the 500 pages of customs regulations and thousands of tariff items. Depending upon the item, a customs broker also may work with the Department of Agriculture, the Environmental Protection Agency, the Food and Drug Administration, or any other regulatory agency. They also work with transportation logistics to ensure that products reach their final destination.

There are a number of important documents that must accompany exported/imported products. A *bill of lading* is a document issued by a carrier (transporter) to a shipper (exporter) acknowledging that the carrier has received the goods. It describes the kind and quantity of goods the carrier receives from the shipper. It also indicates how the goods will be shipped and specifies the destination. A *certificate of origin* is a document that indicates the country in which goods being exported are obtained, produced, manufactured, or processed. To determine import duties, countries consider the country of origin of imported goods. They also consider the country of origin when deciding whether the products can be legally imported.

Foreign Trade Zones

A *foreign trade zone* (FTZ) is an area designated by a country as a specialized zone where products may be exempt from duties. Products in these zones can be stored, modified, displayed, or otherwise used for business without paying duties. If a company assembles a product in an FTZ for sale in that country, it can pay a duty at a lower finished-product tariff rate instead of a higher component-part rate. If the products are exported out of an FTZ, no import duties are paid to the country where the FTZ is located. Foreign trade zones are not just on ports. The largest U.S. foreign trade zone is in Kansas City, Missouri. This zone is more than 16 million square feet in size.

Checkpoint

List the two levels of commitment to exporting.

_____

_____

INTERNATIONAL LOGISTICS

DISTRIBUTION

Logistics has become an important part of international business strategy. At one time, it was difficult to predict how long it would take for products to move around the world. Today, weather satellites and global positioning systems (GPS) allow ships to avoid bad weather and limit risks. Container ships can be loaded in one country and can cross the Pacific Ocean to another country in ten days. Individual shipments can be tracked to ensure that inventory arrives JIT (just-in-time).

Logistics and the Total Cost Concept

Transportation costs are a large portion of the total cost involved in exporting a product. When companies use a total cost concept, they must take into consideration all the costs involved in delivering a product to a customer. For example, it may seem logical that the transportation costs of shipping products by water or land would be much cheaper than the costs of shipping products by air. But there are considerations other than the shipping costs. Products shipped by water or land arrive with less certainty than products shipped by air. These products may need to be warehoused and insured for longer periods of time. There also are greater chances for loss, spoilage, and obsolescence. If the total cost of shipping by air is lower than these costs, then shipping by air should be the preferred shipping method.

A computer manufacturer obtains component parts from around the world. One very expensive component is computer chips. These chips are typically small and light. The price on chips can fluctuate rapidly, but most often the price goes down. These products are subject to theft because they can be used in most computers around the world. Given these considerations, airfreight is a good choice for shipping. It limits the shipping time, enhances security and control of the products, and helps ensure that they will arrive when needed by manufacturers.

Power supplies are one of the heaviest parts of a computer. Technology on these components does not change rapidly. If shipped overseas, ocean freight is likely to be used to transport these products. Since this method is less reliable, a larger supply needs to be maintained in inventory to ensure that components are ready for assembly. Maintaining a larger inventory increases the total cost of this component.

Often shipping costs are negotiated. The term *free on board (FOB)* is used to indicate where the shipper pays for the cost of loading and transporting products. For example, if a business in New York sends products *FOB New York*, it means that the buyer pays for shipping from the New York dockside. *FOB destination* means that the seller pays shipping to the receiving point of the buyer. Sellers also can agree to cover *cost, insurance, and freight (CIF)*. A computer manufacturer may want to negotiate with its suppliers an FOB destination contract covering CIF. In this way, it may be able to lower its cost of purchasing products. This type of contract may work for a large buyer of computer products like Dell, but it may not work for a smaller buyer with less negotiating power.

Ethics Around the World

Reverse logistics includes all operations related to the reuse of products and materials. According to the international working group on reverse logistics, RevLog, reverse logistics includes all logistic activities related to collecting, disassembling, and processing used products, product parts, and/or materials in order to ensure a sustainable, or environmentally friendly, recovery.

New laws in Europe, especially Germany, are forcing manufacturers to recover waste products. There are a number of economic benefits in re-entering products into the production process instead of paying for disposal. There also is a growing environmental consciousness by consumers.

At one time, Estèe Lauder destroyed more than a third of its cosmetics returned by retailers. It sent about $60 million of returned products to landfills each year. The company developed a reverse logistics system using scanning technology. This system looked at the expiration dates for products and determined if products could be sold in other markets, employee stores, or given away to charities. The first year this system was used Estèe Lauder saved $475,000 in labor costs alone.

THINK CRITICALLY

1. Why do you think countries have implemented reverse logistics laws?
2. Describe the advantages and disadvantages for companies using reverse logistics.

Transportation Modes

There are a number of different transportation modes that exporters use when they ship products. Each of these alternatives has advantages and disadvantages.

Water Transportation Water transportation may be used for transport either within a continent or across oceans. Barges often are used to transport products within a continent on rivers and lakes. Barges most often carry large bulk items and commodities such as grain or minerals. Ocean-going water transportation has changed considerably with containerized shipments. About 90 percent of the world's trade is transported in cargo containers. Almost half of the value of U.S. imports arrives by container ships. This amounts to nearly nine million cargo containers offloaded at U.S. seaports each year.

Air Cargo Also called airfreight, *air cargo* is a growing part of international shipping. Just as containerized oceangoing ships have revolutionized ocean shipping, containerized jumbo jets are able to carry over 90 tons of products. The largest air cargo shipper in the world is FedEx. Air cargo allows for direct shipping of products from airport to airport just about anywhere in the world. While shipping costs with air cargo can be high, this method cuts down on the need for warehousing. It also limits the possibility of theft.

Land Transportation There are two major types of land transportation—rail and truck. Rail transport is typically used for bulk products. These modes of transportation require land connections. Products can move by land across Europe and Asia and by ferry into Africa. Products also can move between North and South America. Moving products over large distances increases the chances of loss, damage, and uncertainty of delivery.

Pipelines Pipelines typically are used for energy-related products such as oil and natural gas. Other products, such as coal, can be put into a slurry (a liquid mixture) and shipped through pipelines.

Intermodal Transport

Often products move by a combination of transportation modes, or through **intermodal transport**. Most often, intermodal transport includes using containerized shipping linked to truck transport.

- *Fishyback* is a term used for the containerized shipping of goods between trucks and ships.

- A *piggyback* system of transportation requires the transfer of containers between truck and rail.

- A *birdyback* system of transportation requires the transfer of containers between truck and air cargo.

Checkpoint

List four types of transportation modes.

_____

_____

Understand Marketing Concepts

Circle the best answer for each of the following questions.

1. When a company is not fully committed to international marketing, it may engage in
   a. direct exporting
   b. indirect exporting
   c. undirected exporting
   d. global exporting

2. Which mode of transportation offers the greatest certainty of international delivery?
   a. piggyback
   b. ocean freight
   c. air cargo
   d. truck

Think Critically

Answer the following questions as completely as possible. If necessary, use a separate sheet of paper.

3. Explain the difference between direct and indirect exporting. What factors would lead a company to choose one form of exporting over the other?

_____

_____

_____

_____

_____

_____

_____

_____

4. List the advantages and disadvantages of each transportation mode.

_____

_____

_____

_____

_____

_____

_____

_____

Lesson 8.3

International Retailing

Goals

- Identify the various types of international retailers.
- Describe the factors international retailers need to consider when developing a global strategy.

Terms

- consumers
- retailer
- specialty store
- convenience stores
- e-commerce
- malls
- franchise

Going Global

Wal-Mart is not the only retailer with global ambitions. Tesco is Britain's largest grocery store. It sells one-third of all British groceries. Tesco was founded by Jack Cohen in 1924. Tesco pioneered a number of concepts that Wal-Mart uses today. It opened its first superstore in 1968. It began selling gasoline in 1974. It started using Internet shopping services in 1995. Tesco has expanded internationally by opening stores in Central Europe, Ireland, and East Asia.

A Tesco Extra hypermarket is about half the size of a Wal-Mart Supercenter. There are Tesco supermarkets, Tesco Metros (small grocery stores), Tesco Express convenience stores, and One Stops (very small stores). Tesco's international expansion has relied upon using partners who understand local needs. Tesco bought 50 percent ownership of 25 hypermarkets in China by partnering with Tsing Hsin International.

Considerable controversy surrounds global grocery businesses entering into developing markets. Some critics say that the large grocers destroy smaller businesses. In fact, 20 percent of competitors are likely to go out of business when large chains enter a market. On the other hand, efficiencies that these large retailers create reduce prices for consumers. They also produce opportunities for new suppliers. The distribution systems these large retailers use require that suppliers operate in modern, efficient logistical systems.

Working in small groups, discuss why Tesco has a number of different types of retail stores. List the advantages and disadvantages of large retailers moving into developing markets.

FROM MARKETS TO MALLS

SELLING

Individual buyers are often the **consumers**, or end users, for products. A **retailer** is a member of a channel of distribution that sells to the end user. Retailing can include consumer product and food vendors. Most often, retailers offer convenience by providing an assortment of products for consumers. Retail businesses have moved from being small businesses serving local market needs to being giant global businesses serving worldwide markets.

The earliest type of retailing was most likely conducted between individuals who produced a surplus to sell to or trade with individual buyers. These early retailers often gathered in market places to sell their wares. Markets have existed for at least 5,000 years. One of the oldest excavated cities in the world is called Uruk. This ancient city was a market and trading center in Asia Minor prior to 3,000 B.C.

Around the world, many markets have remained unchanged. Products still are brought in from producers and are offered for sale under temporary shelters. Prices are negotiated at the point of sale. In some cultures, price negotiation is a standard buying method. Food markets have been a tradition in many countries. In developing economies where refrigeration has not been widely available, consumers have a tradition of purchasing fresh food almost daily.

Traditional and local retailers are under pressure today from new retail stores and international retail giants. Many retailers are developing a global perspective and are entering new markets. They are changing local retail market conditions.

Types of International Retailers

In addition to local markets, there are a number of different types of retailers. Retailers are typically categorized by function, size, and product depth and width. Stores are considered to have wide product *width* when there are a variety of product categories. Product categories have *depth* when there are many variations within a category.

Specialty Stores Specialty stores are a natural evolution from a market-based retailer. A **specialty store** is typically a smaller store that specializes in a product category, such as a jewelry store. It has narrow width but product depth. These stores often have higher levels of service and product expertise. Specialty stores were at one time the dominant store type. Cities and towns were designed with centralized shopping and stores that specialized in baked goods, knives, boots, and other types of products. In the United States, these smaller specialty stores often were located in central business districts. Over the last 30 years, many of these stores in the United States closed as discount stores and malls grew in dominance. Discount stores and malls have grown in Europe over the last 20 years and are now growing throughout Asia.

Specialty stores have not disappeared. They often can be found in the modern equivalent of the ancient market—the shopping mall. Most of these specialty stores sell higher-end designer products to differentiate themselves from discount chains.

General Merchandise There are a number of different types of general merchandise stores. These stores have both product width and depth. *Department stores* consist of a number of individual departments that

China wants to promote the development of its retail sector. In 2003, retail sales in China were 5.2 trillion yuan ($628 billion U.S.). In 2004, retail sales in the United States were more than $4 trillion.

Time Out

Marketing Myths

A kiwi is both the name of a small flightless bird from New Zealand and a small fuzzy fruit with a green center. The kiwifruit also is called a Chinese gooseberry. This fruit was an export crop for New Zealand. The kiwifruit became known as a kiwi in the United States and Europe. This name was not trademarked, so regardless of where the fruit is grown, it is called a kiwi.

A new version of the kiwifruit has been developed in New Zealand. This new kiwifruit is marketed under the brand name *Zespri*. This name is trademarked by a New Zealand marketing company called ZESPRI. The new kiwifruit has a golden flesh and a tropical taste. New Zealand does not want to lose this trademarked product.

THINK CRITICALLY

1. How did a lack of a trademark on the kiwifruit affect New Zealand?
2. Explain why trademarking the Zespri is important for New Zealand.

specialize in specific products. The first modern department store was Bon Marche started in Paris in 1838. Discount department stores such as Wal-Mart have captured large market shares around the world. Wal-Mart has competition not only from Britain's Tesco but also from France's Carrefour and Auchan Group. These discount retailers operate *superstores* and *hypermarkets* that combine groceries and other discount department store products. Most often these stores are located outside of cities.

Convenience Stores Located around the world, **convenience stores** have a limited inventory offering width but little depth. Taiwan has the world's highest concentration of convenience stores per person and the largest number of 7-Eleven stores per person in the world.

Vending Consumers can purchase products from a vending machine. In the United States, vending machines sell mostly soda and snacks. In many countries around the world, vending machines sell meals, sodas, adult beverages, and other convenience items. With sales of just over $22 billion, vending is a small part of U.S. sales. Japan has over 4.5 million vending machines, which is the highest number of vending machines per person in the world. Vending machine shops carry over 200 product lines. Total vending sales in Japan in 2002 were over $48 billion.

E-Commerce

E-commerce involves using the Internet to aid in the sales process. This sales system has grown in popularity in the United States and other developed countries. E-commerce is less sucessful in developing countries. On-line sales require that a customer have access to the Internet. Individuals also must have a credit card. Additionally, there must be an efficient delivery system to get products to customers.

The Malling of the World

Trajan's Mall, also called Trajan's Forum, is likely to have been the world's first mall. It was established in Rome in 112 A.D. Trajan's Mall was multi-level with 150 shops and offices. Customers could shop for clothing, flowers, silk, and food from all over the world. Other ancient malls could have been found in tenth-century Iran and eighteenth-century London.

Malls, or *shopping centers*, are buildings that host a variety of stores. Shopping centers can be totally enclosed or open air. The shopping center leases space to individual stores. Today, malls are established around the world. The trade organization for shopping centers, the International Council of Shopping Centers, has members from 80 countries.

Taipei 101, in Taipei, Taiwan, is currently the world's tallest building. This skyscraper is built in conjunction with a modern mall. The mall has fashion and other high-end global specialty stores. Currently, the largest shopping center in the world is West Edmonton Mall in Edmonton, Alberta, Canada. This shopping center has 5.3 million square feet, over 800 stores, 25 restaurants, a casino, an amusement park, an indoor wave pool, a dolphin lagoon, and 26 movie screens in two theater complexes.

© GETTY IMAGES/PHOTODISC

Checkpoint

List five types of retailers.

_____

_____

_____

INTERNATIONAL RETAILING STRATEGY

SELLING

International retailers have the same concerns as every international marketer. They must understand the needs of the local market, ensure that they have a product that meets those needs, and ensure that they are able to create a brand image that will appeal to customers.

International retailers cannot expand beyond their distribution system's ability to support them. For example, in order for Wal-Mart to expand into China, it must not only open stores but also develop purchasing, warehousing, inventory, and shipping. Retailers also need to train workers for their stores. If Wal-Mart opens 2,000 stores in China, it will need at least one million workers. These are some of the major reasons that international retailers form local partnerships.

Localized Versus Global

International retailers must decide between a localized and a global strategy. The strategy chosen will depend upon the products and the markets served. Land's End clothing retailer used e-commerce to sell products in Germany. It found that it was not able to use discount pricing because it is prohibited by German laws. Land's End not only had to adopt the language but also had to localize its selling strategies.

Many high-end fashion specialty stores have adopted a global strategy. This strategy allows them to develop a single brand image for shoppers around the world. These specialty stores sell to higher-income individuals who share common characteristics. Consumers often can find the same stores in shopping centers around the world.

International retailers often will act as a *franchisor*, franchising their stores to *franchisees*. A **franchise** is a contractual right to licenses, trademarks, and methods of doing business in exchange for royalties and fees. Franchising allows an international retailer to move quickly into new markets. The franchisee provides funding to develop the franchise. The franchisee's knowledge of local market needs can help ensure that local market conditions are met. Franchises also provide a standardized process to help ensure quality product delivery at all of its locations worldwide.

Coca-Cola franchised its distribution systems to local owners. When Coke decided not to renew its German franchises, it took on the responsibility of meeting local market requirements itself. International retailers must control their global brand image when they franchise their stores. If local franchisees do not maintain store and product quality, it can hurt the image of the larger store franchise.

Checkpoint

Name three factors to consider when developing an international retail strategy.

_____

_____

World Stars   H. LEE SCOTT, JR.

H. Lee Scott, Jr. is the president and CEO of the world's largest retailer, Wal-Mart Stores, Inc. Scott was born in Joplin, Missouri. He received his bachelor degree in business from Pittsburg State University in Pittsburg, Kansas. While Scott was in college, he lived in a trailer and had to work full time to support his wife and child.

In 1979, Scott joined Wal-Mart in the logistics and transportation department. He moved up through the ranks, becoming the Director of Transportation, Vice President of Distribution, Senior Vice President of Logistics, and Executive Vice President of Logistics. His background in logistics placed Scott in a strategic position to take Wal-Mart into the future and the international marketplace.

In 1995, Scott was made Executive Vice President of Merchandise. Scott used Wal-Mart's world leadership in efficient logistics systems to eliminate excess inventory and increase sales. Wal-Mart has been able to roll back prices in large part due to efficiencies gained in distribution and purchasing. By 1998, Scott was president and CEO of Wal-Mart Stores. His promotion reflects both H. Lee Scott's skills and the importance of distribution and logistics to Wal-Mart.

THINK CRITICALLY

Explain why Wal-Mart would consider knowledge of transportation and logistics to be important for a CEO. Describe why H. Lee Scott's background made him a good choice to lead Wal-Mart?

Understand Marketing Concepts

Circle the best answer for each of the following questions.

1. What type of retail store has narrow width but product depth?
   a. convenience store
   b. department store
   c. specialty store
   d. mall

2. Which of the following is *not* true of malls?
   a. They can be enclosed or open.
   b. They lease space to retailers.
   c. They are located around the world.
   d. They came into existence in the nineteenth century.

Think Critically

Answer the following questions as completely as possible. If necessary, use a separate sheet of paper.

3. Describe the differences among the different types of retailers.

   _____

   _____

   _____

   _____

   _____

   _____

   _____

4. Communication Write a memo to a retail CEO listing the strategic factors the CEO needs to consider when moving into the international marketplace.

   _____

   _____

   _____

   _____

   _____

   _____

   _____

   _____

Chapter 8 Assessment

Review Marketing Concepts

Write the letter of the term that matches each definition. Some terms will not be used.

_____ 1. Activities that create an orderly and timely acquisition and transportation of products through the channel of distribution

_____ 2. Independent business that assists the flow of goods and services from producers to customers

_____ 3. A company that takes the leadership role in organizing a distribution system, which lessens the chances for conflict

_____ 4. The process of shipping a product to another part of the world for trade or sale

_____ 5. A combination of transportation modes

_____ 6. Occurs when a business uses brokers or agents to help find customers and export products

_____ 7. Contractual right to licenses, trademarks, and methods of doing business in exchange for royalties and fees

_____ 8. Acts as immigration control for products entering a country

_____ 9. A store that offers product width but little product depth

_____ 10. Occurs when a company actively controls finding markets and exporting products

a. channel captain
b. channel of distribution
c. consumers
d. convenience stores
e. customs
f. customs broker
g. direct exporting
h. e-commerce
i. exporting
j. franchise
k. importing
l. indirect exporting
m. intermodal transport
n. logistics
o. malls
p. marketing intermediary
q. retailer
r. specialty store
s. total cost concept

Circle the best answer.

11. The idea that all costs must be taken into consideration when designing a channel of distribution is ___.
    a. concept costing
    b. total cost concept
    c. accounting
    d. major project funding

12. A(n) ____ is an intermediary that helps products move through customs.
    a. export management company
    b. customs broker
    c. customs agent
    d. export manager

Think Critically

13. Select three industries. Specify how distribution and logistics would play a role in providing competitive advantages in each industry.

_____

_____

_____

_____

_____

14. Today, fresh fruits and vegetables can be found in grocery stores year round. This was not the case 20 years ago. List at least four reasons for this change.

_____

_____

_____

_____

_____

15. Visit a local specialty store. Make a list of the changes that would need to be made to use the same store concept in another country. Specify the reasons for those changes.

_____

_____

_____

_____

_____

16. Make a list of products that would be appropriate for specific types of intermodal transportation. Explain your choices.

_____

_____

_____

_____

_____

_____

Make Connections

17. Research Using the Internet, research how technology is being used in distribution systems. Provide examples of the effect of technology on distribution costs, shipping speed, and just-in-time inventory.

_____

_____

_____

_____

_____

_____

18. Problem Solving Create a matrix as shown below. Choose a product and a set of criteria that would be important to an exporter of that product. Based on the criteria you have chosen, describe the pros and cons of using each of the distribution modes. Present your findings to the class.

Mode / Criteria	Air Cargo	Water	Train	Truck	Intermodal
Transit time					
Predictability					
Cost					
Other					

_____

_____

_____

19. Marketing Math You are considering two alternative transportation modes. Using the total cost concept, determine the alternative that will cost the least amount of money.

Air cargo shipping takes two days. Insurance per day: $0.10. Air freight cost: $4.00. Ground transport: $0.60.

Ocean freight shipping takes 15 days. Insurance per day: $0.20. Ocean freight cost: $1.00. Ground transport: $0.60. Warehousing costs: $0.50. Average inventory loss: $0.20.

_____

_____

_____

_____

_____

20. Research Use the Internet to identify an e-commerce retailer that sells in different countries. Look at the company's web sites for at least two countries. Attempt to identify any design or product differences. Discuss why those differences do or do not exist.

_____

_____

_____

_____

_____

_____

_____

_____

PUT MARKETING ON THE MAP

International Marketing Plan Project

Your international marketing plan must identify a distribution and retail strategy for your products. You must take into consideration not only the physical connections but also the strategic concerns.

Work with a group and complete the following activities.

1. Develop an illustration of the distribution channel you plan to use for your product. Indicate which businesses will play what role in the channel. List the pros and cons of your distribution channel design.

2. Indicate who will play the role of channel captain in your distribution channel. Discuss the use of agents or brokers. Specify who has power in the channel. Explain the importance of trust between channel members.

3. Recommend an exporting strategy. Determine if you will use direct or indirect exporting. Specify any export intermediaries that you plan to use.

4. Develop a matrix as shown in Question 18. List the criteria you would use for evaluating transportation modes for your products. Rate the advantages and disadvantages of each mode using these criteria. Recommend a transportation strategy that you believe will result in the lowest costs.

5. Assume that your product will need a retail sales outlet. Recommend a retail sales strategy for your business. Indicate what type of store would work best, whether you plan to use partners, and whether you will use a localized adaptation strategy or a global strategy.

RIPE FOR EXPORTING

Successful businesses are constantly searching for ways to increase sales. Many companies selling popular, high-demand products are encouraged to export products for increased sales.

American farmers have perfected the production of food sources. Record crop production has increased the desire to export grains. Although many countries throughout the world are in need of food, they may not have the money to purchase the grain. Additionally, government relationships with other countries affect whether the trade will take place.

Americans can purchase fresh flowers year-round for reasonable prices. Many of these flowers come from Colombia and other parts of Latin America. Flower growers who export their highly perishable merchandise count on quick, dependable transportation to get the product to its final destination in good condition. Due to the high level of drug traffic in Central and South America, flower shipments are tightly scrutinized for shipment of illegal drugs. A shipment of fresh flowers may not get out of customs if there is any suspicion of enclosed drugs. And the danger of damage or loss of product during shipment is great, making it essential for flower growers to purchase insurance.

The fashion industry constantly showcases new styles and brands. Designer brands that appear to be all American frequently are produced in Mexico, India, Pakistan, Israel, and many less-developed countries to take advantage of lower production costs. These countries depend on exports to the United States for their livelihood.

Automobile manufacturers in the United States are concerned about lagging car sales. The American automobile industry must compete against successful brands like Honda, Toyota, Hyundai, and Kia. The number of imported cars on American roadways has increased due to lower prices, better fuel efficiency, and perceived better quality. Many of the lower-priced import cars have the advantage of lower production costs in the countries where they are made.

Exporting is definitely a viable strategy to increase market share and sales volume. Careful attention must be given to demand from international customers, their purchasing power, political environment, and a fair trade environment.

THINK CRITICALLY

1. Why is it difficult for a company to enter into a new international market?

2. What must American automobile makers do to gain a bigger share of total automobile sales in the United States?

3. What advantages should American automobile manufacturers emphasize to gain the attention of consumers?

4. Give one example of an American automobile manufacturer that has purchased a foreign competitor.

E-COMMERCE MARKETING MANAGEMENT TEAM DECISION-MAKING EVENT

The E-Commerce Marketing Management Team Decision-Making Event provides an opportunity for participants to analyze elements essential to the effective operation of an e-commerce business.

Each management team must be composed of two members. Each team member will be given a 100-question, multiple-choice, comprehensive exam testing knowledge of e-commerce. Team members also will be given a decision-making case study involving a management problem in a business. Performance indicators that must be addressed by teams include economics, communication, professional development, entrepreneurship, distribution, financing, marketing-information management, pricing, product/service management, promotion, and selling.

Teams will have 30 minutes to study the situation and organize their analysis using a management decision-making format. During the preparation period, teams may consult only with one another. Participants may use notes taken during the preparation time for the presentation.

Participants will have ten minutes to present their strategy to the judge. An additional five minutes will be allowed for judges to ask questions about the plan of action.

Harry and David is a high-end specialty retailer that sells snack foods, jams, salsas, fruits, coffees, and other products. The management at Harry and David is considering using e-commerce to sell merchandise online. You have been asked to explain the advantages of e-commerce. You must present your e-commerce plan of action to the management at Harry and David.

Performance Indicators Evaluated

- Explain the advantages of e-commerce.
- Describe the challenges involved with e-commerce.
- Explain the need to expand sales through e-commerce.
- Communicate a plan to implement e-commerce.
- Demonstrate critical thinking/problem-solving skills.
- Display strong listening skills and effective team management.

Go to the DECA web site for more detailed information.

THINK CRITICALLY

1. Why is it smart for a business to consider e-commerce?
2. What challenges will Harry and David have to overcome when using e-commerce?
3. What unique characteristics about Harry and David should be emphasized on the Web?

www.deca.org

International Marketing Communication

CHAPTER 9 · CHAPTER 9 · CHAPTER 9 · CHAPTER 9 · CHAPTER 9

9

© DIGITAL VISION

Point Your Browser

▶ ▶ ▶ ▶ ▶ intlmarket.swlearning.com

Video Launched the MTV Star

Music Television (MTV) started on August 1, 1981, with these words, "Ladies and gentlemen, rock and roll." MTV took advantage of two emerging trends—cable television and music videos. When MTV started, many of the videos were provided by record companies at no cost.

MTV grew with the expanding cable industry. In 1985, MTV was purchased by Viacom and became part of a media giant. MTV has expanded by producing a number of different shows and alternative channels. In addition to the United States, MTV has launched unique networks for Africa, nine Asian countries, Australia, fourteen European countries, and three Central and South American countries.

MTV has expanded its presence to include more than just cable video. MTV.com is the entrance point to a web site. MTV has designed different web sites for more than 22 countries. MTV also has worked with Virgin Mobile, a British cellular phone company, to place MTV content in people's pockets. It also has a station on XM Satellite Radio and is looking to expand into video games. Each of these media provides an opportunity for advertising.

In keeping with its strategy of multiple media platforms, MTV targets music fans in their teens and twenties. According to Media Metrix, an online media research company, MTV.com is ranked as the number one music content web site for teens. MTV allows advertisers to target teens and twenty-year-olds in multiple countries with a variety of media platforms.

MTV faces a global challenger in Rupert Murdoch's News Corporation's Channel V. Channel V's strategy is to create different channels for each major market. By focusing on local music and presenters, Channel V was able to capture audiences from MTV. This competition forced MTV to redesign its offerings to meet local needs. For example, for Muslims in Indonesia, MTV broadcasts a "funky but respectful" call to prayer five times a day.

Think Critically

1. Explain why MTV was able to grow. Describe the alternative ways that MTV can reach its audience.

2. Explain why MTV would need to develop localized content. Describe the advantages and disadvantages of this strategy.

International Promotional Strategies

Goals

- Explain the communication model.
- Identify the steps used in a promotional campaign.

Terms

- promotion
- AIDA process
- encoding
- decoding
- feedback
- noise
- media

Going Global

Juan Valdez has been working for the National Federation of Coffee Growers of Colombia since 1959. Juan has one of the most recognized faces in the world. He is now the face of a new advertising campaign for the Federation's plans for competing against Starbucks. Juan Valdez and his faithful mule, Lana, are fictitious characters. They represent Colombia's coffee growers. In 2005, Juan Valdez was recognized as one of America's favorite advertising icons.

Decreases in world coffee prices have forced the growers to move toward ownership of retail outlets. The Federation started with eleven Juan Valdez coffee shops in Colombia. International expansion has started with shops in Washington, D.C. and New York. The Federation's plan is to open 300 coffee shops around the world.

The Federation is owned and controlled by a half-million farmers who grow coffee on small farms. The Federation needs to communicate the message that these farmers pick only the best beans when they are ripe, producing a higher-quality coffee. The Federation also supports fair trade coffee because profits go back to the farmers.

Working with a partner, explain why Juan Valdez is one of the most recognized faces in the world. Describe why Juan Valdez is a good symbol for the National Federation of Coffee Growers of Colombia.

MARKETING PROMOTION

International communication requires designing a promotional strategy that is appropriate for each international market given its unique culture, communication infrastructure, and market needs. **Promotion** is any form of communication that is designed to inform, remind, or persuade customers about a company, its goods, or services.

A marketing communication strategy typically will follow an **AIDA process.** This process starts by making an audience *aware* of a company's advantages and product benefits. It then moves to create *interest* and then *desire.* Finally, it calls for *action.* Often, customers need to be reminded so that they will remember what was communicated. Ultimately, companies want customers to engage in some behavior, such as purchasing products or services. So, companies use promotions to persuade customers to act.

The National Federation of Coffee Growers of Colombia has used the Juan Valdez campaign since the 1950s. Its promotional campaign is still designed to inform, remind, and persuade customers. New customers are made aware, and those customers who are familiar with Juan Valdez are reminded of Colombian coffee's benefits. With the current promotional strategy, all customers will be made aware of the new retail outlets, informed of benefits to create desire, and then persuaded to take the action of visiting a retail outlet.

The International Communication Process

Promotional campaigns are designed based on the communication model. The communication model starts with a sender who encodes, or designs, a message. **Encoding** is the process of using language and symbols to design a message. The message design can include cultural context information and non-verbal communication. The message is then delivered through a communication channel where it is decoded by the receiver. **Decoding** is the process of interpreting the message. **Feedback,** which is the receiver's reaction to the message, should be collected by the sender. The sender must then determine if the message has been decoded correctly. All communication is subject to noise. **Noise** is anything that interferes with communication. Ideally, the communication process should first be tested through marketing research before the message is sent to the target audience. It should then be evaluated after the campaign is underway.

The Communication Model

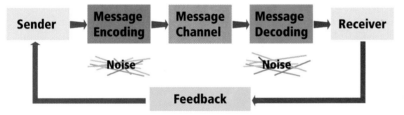

International marketers must be sure that they encode a message in a way that will be properly decoded by the receiver. Individual receivers interpret messages based on cultural understanding. Promotional messages should not just be translated into the target audience's language. For proper decoding, cultural factors also must be taken into consideration. High-context cultures may be especially oriented to background information in an ad, such as the use of symbols or body language. It is often advisable to have messages designed by people who are members of the target culture. Local agencies within the target country can help select the best channel for delivering the message.

Name each of the seven components of the communication model.

Checkpoint

DEVELOPING A PROMOTIONAL STRATEGY

The traditional promotional tools that marketers use to communicate with audiences include advertising, public relations, sales, and sales promotion. Each of these methods is used to develop international promotional campaigns. A communication strategy must take an audience through the AIDA process. Advertising typically plays a major role in making an audience aware of and then creating interest in a company's advantages and product benefits. Desire and action often are achieved through sales promotion and sales techniques. To reach marketing goals, promotional campaigns use the following steps:

1. Identify target audiences
2. Set communication goals
3. Develop a promotion budget
4. Develop a media strategy
5. Select a promotional mix
6. Implement the plan
7. Evaluate campaign effectiveness

Identify Audiences

International marketers are likely to have multiple audiences and goals. If the company is taking an existing product from the home market and moving the product into a new market, it will first need to identify the different markets. The company will have to examine the needs of each market to determine the best promotional campaign to use to inform this new audience about the product's benefits.

Set Goals

One of the Colombian Coffee Federation's long-term goals has been to create a positive country-of-origin effect for Colombian coffee. This positive effect has helped turn a commodity product into a specialty product. As the Coffee Federation's campaign progressed, the goal was to have customers

Ethics Around the World

Promotion is typically used as a tool to communicate with audiences. The role that promotion plays in international marketing strategy differs across national borders. This difference in roles is not just due to legal restrictions on advertising. Some cultures view advertising as rude. Telling customers what they should have may be seen as arrogant.

Marketers often act as a change agent in a culture. They provide new products, ideas, and lifestyle alternatives. But in some cultures, marketing activities represent a threat to established order. Communist economies did not allow for the marketing process to work. Manufacturers were given specific requirements for products. For example, a scientific analysis was undertaken to determine the ideal number of shoes needed for each foot size.

Lack of access to promotional techniques can prevent companies from developing products to meet customers' needs. Rules and regulations that limit promotion can give advantages to existing businesses and can limit competition from entrepreneurs. At the same time, advertising bans can protect customers. China has banned the advertising of medicines because a large number of fake products were being sold.

THINK CRITICALLY

1. Explain the role that marketing communication plays in social change.
2. Describe the advantages and disadvantages of allowing companies to freely engage in advertising without regulation.

look for the Federation's logo. The Federation's logo shows the country of origin and is present on several brands of coffee.

It is possible for a company to have the same communication goals for multiple international markets. When Colombia's Coffee Federation expands its retail outlets into new countries, it will have the same goal of making audiences aware of the benefits and creating interest in these new coffee shops. But given the unique differences in each country and culture, the message design and media strategy used will most likely need to vary.

Develop Budgets

There are a number of methods used to set promotional budgets. These methods include matching the competition, basing promotional budgets on a percentage of sales, spending all the company can afford, and basing budgets on objectives and tasks. The ideal method is *objective-and-task-based budgeting*. This method requires that advertisers predict the amount of promotion needed to reach goals. When entering new markets, it can be very difficult to make this prediction. Without a history, it is difficult to gauge how an audience will react to a new product or service.

Develop Media Strategies

Once international marketers identify target audiences, set promotional goals, and specify a budget, they must design a media strategy and choose a mix of promotional outlets to reach their goals. Promotional **media** are the vehicles used to carry a message to an audience. Media are categorized as broadcast (television and radio), print (newspapers and magazines), outdoor (billboards, posters, and signs), and the newly emerging electronic media (Internet and cellular).

One of the Colombian Coffee Federation's original goals was to show the care that was used in picking coffee beans in Colombia. To reach this goal in the United States, television commercials showed Juan Valdez hand-picking beans in coffee fields at the moment of prime ripeness. This strategy worked well because television advertising can be an efficient mass media tool in the United States.

Select Promotional Mixes

International marketers must design a strategy that will creatively use a mix of media to move an audience toward desired goals. The Columbian Coffee Federation uses a combination of media to reach its

goals. The main role of television is to inform audiences of the benefits of Colombian coffee. Print advertising is used in magazines to remind audiences about the quality of Colombian coffee. Coffee distributors also are targeted through print ads reinforcing the advantages of handpicked Colombian coffee. The Federation also supports a juanvaldez.com web site.

International marketers understand that in order to reach their marketing goals they must develop complex communication strategies that use the entire promotional mix. They must match this promotional mix to the market conditions they are targeting.

Implement the Plan

International promotional campaigns can be very complex. For its new coffee shops, the Colombian Coffee Federation will need to devise a campaign that will work in a number of different countries around the world. Because of these complexities, even large global marketing companies are likely to use local promotional agencies to help develop strategies and implement the marketing plan.

Global marketers are likely to identify target audiences, set communication objectives, and develop promotion budgets. Local marketing companies that understand local market conditions are likely to develop media strategies, select the promotional mixes, and implement the plans. Services provided by international advertising agencies include marketing research, strategic planning, strategic marketing communications, media buying, global branding, creative design, and developing e-business systems.

Evaluate Effectiveness

Evaluating campaign effectiveness requires researching a campaign's impact on the intended audience. This process may work well in markets where there is a marketing research infrastructure. The effectiveness of promotional efforts in many countries is difficult to determine because of limitations on data collection.

Checkpoint

List the steps used in a promotional campaign.

_____

_____

_____

Understand Marketing Concepts

Circle the best answer for each of the following questions.

1. The AIDA process involves creating all of the following except
   a. awareness
   b. interest
   c. desire
   d. activity

2. A web site is an example of what type of media?
   a. electronic
   b. broadcast
   c. print
   d. outdoor

Think Critically

Answer the following questions as completely as possible. If necessary, use a separate sheet of paper.

3. Describe a television commercial you have recently seen. Identify the goals of the commercial in terms of informing, reminding, or persuading. Explain your analysis.

   _____

   _____

   _____

   _____

   _____

   _____

   _____

4. Choose a product that uses a marketing communication strategy (AIDA). Describe the promotional mix that is used to communicate with the target audiences.

   _____

   _____

   _____

   _____

   _____

   _____

   _____

International Advertising

Goals

- Identify the steps involved in developing an advertising campaign.
- Describe the advertising themes.

Terms

- advertising
- product placement
- publicity
- media schedule
- organizational ads
- product ads
- advertising theme

Going Global

When BMW looked for a new international advertising agency, it didn't want to change its slogan, "the ultimate driving machine." BMW has a clear idea of the brand values it wants to communicate to its target audience. Those brand values are technology, quality, performance, and exclusivity. BMW uses these four brand values consistently across its advertising campaigns. These brand values are expressed differently based on the economic, environmental, and competitive changes in each market.

BMW's advertising focuses entirely on the cars. It uses a wide media mix to reach audiences. The advertising agencies that BMW uses must be able to develop campaigns that will be effective in multiple markets. In the United Kingdom, BMW uses television to help brand new car launches. Radio is used for regional markets. Print advertising appears in lifestyle magazines to enhance brand image. Outdoor campaigns are used for high-impact, high-awareness branding for new car launches.

BMW launched a very creative set of short films. These films originally were designed for the Internet. They also have been used in movie theaters and on television. The online BMW short films have been viewed more than ten million times since they were first launched in April 2001.

Working with a partner, describe BMW's advertising strategy. Explain why this advertising strategy may be an effective approach.

ADVERTISING

AdWeek magazine recognized a BMW television advertisement as one of the best ads in 2002. In this ad, four white-collar workers marveled at a BMW car engine's technology and ingenuity. When their boss tells them to return to work, they walk past the space shuttle, under repair in its hangar. The announcer's voice says, "More powerful, more responsive, more efficient. The BMW 4.4-liter, 325-horsepower V8. Perhaps the most advanced engine on Earth."

This ad is designed to reach a set of specific communication goals. BMW wants to remind the public that its cars are "the ultimate driving machine." By using individuals who appear to be NASA engineers marveling at the BMW engine, BMW reminds the target audience about the technology and quality of just one component, the engine. This ad does not try to convey performance and exclusivity factors. Too much information in an advertisement can make the message confusing.

Advertising is any form of paid, non-personal communication. Advertising is one part of the promotional mix. It must be used in combination with other mix components. Advertising is good at creating awareness and interest. It can help create desire, but it is less effective in obtaining action. Action is often the role of sales promotion or person-to-person sales. About two-thirds of worldwide spending on advertising is for business-to-consumer advertising. This ratio changes in many developing cultures where up to 50 percent of advertising can be business-to-business.

Advertising campaigns should parallel and support larger promotional campaigns. The steps involved in developing an advertising campaign include:

1. Identify target audiences

2. Set communication goals

3. Develop an advertising budget

4. Develop a media strategy

5. Create the advertisements

6. Develop a media schedule

7. Implement the plan

8. Evaluate campaign effectiveness

Identify Audiences

Advertising is an effective tool for communicating with audiences around the world. It accounts for about two-thirds of global media spending. An international advertising campaign starts by identifying audiences. A company like BMW may be able to identify a standardized profile of global customers. These customers are likely to be individuals with higher income, social status, and a desire for high-performance cars.

MTV and the Colombian Coffee Federation have audiences that differ across cultures. Even though MTV targeted a global teen demographic, it found that it needed to localize content to meet cultural needs. Coffee drinking also differs around the world. Most countries prefer a stronger coffee than is served in the United States. In addition, coffee shops play a different role. U.S. coffee drinkers often are on the move from one activity to another. For many European countries, a coffee café is for socializing. The shop may not have coffee to go. Many European cars do not have drink holders built in. This difference in audience needs, habits, and social norms will require advertisements to be customized.

Set Goals

Individual advertisements are designed to support the goals of the larger promotional campaign. A new product in a new market will require advertising to create awareness. For existing products in existing markets, the goal may be to remind customers of the factors that create interest and desire.

Develop a Budget

Advertising budgeting is part of the promotional budgeting process. The ideal method to use is the objective-and-task-based budgeting system. Using this method requires that international markets have a good information base to help marketers determine the amount of advertising needed to be effective.

Develop a Media Strategy

Media strategies are based on promotional goals, available media, media characteristics, a culture's media habits, and any regulatory restrictions. In developed countries, international marketers have a wide variety of media choices. They can use broadcast, print, outdoor, or electronic media. Media choices are limited in developing countries.

It is important to understand the preferred media usage for every target audience. With 43 percent of advertising revenue, television is the dominant media in Japan. Japan is followed by Belgium (40 percent) and the United States (37 percent). Radio advertising is dependent upon the number of stations and the number of radios. The United States leads the world with 14,000 radio stations and almost two radios per person. China has only 650 radio stations and averages one radio for every three people. Newspapers may be the preferred advertising outlets in developing countries. India has more than 5,000 daily newspapers.

Media characteristics are another important factor to consider. Advertisements in traditional media, such as broadcast and print ads, can carry only a very short message. Outdoor media, which may have only a few seconds of exposure, are typically designed to remind.

There is a shift in audience media habits worldwide. New technologies, including the Internet and digital television recorders, such as TiVo, are changing viewing patterns. Consumers can bypass advertisements. MTV has devised a strategy to allow companies to advertise across multiple media outlets, including cable, web sites, cellular telephones, and video games.

Many companies often engage in **product placement** where they pay to have their products placed into some other media outlet. BMW cars are often placed into movies and television shows. For reaching younger markets, product placement is used in video games.

Companies often will attempt to obtain **publicity,** which is free communication through the media. Public relations specialists will try to get publicity by sending news releases to different media outlets.

Develop a Media Schedule

A **media schedule** is a calendar that lays out when ads will play and in which media. This tool helps marketers track media exposure. For example, when BMW introduces a new model into a market, it may first use television ads to make the target audience aware of the new model. One ad on one program may not meet communication goals, so multiple shows and times are scheduled. After awareness is created, interest may be generated with a different set of print ads scheduled to come out after the television advertising campaign.

Implement and Evaluate the Plan

After the media strategy has been planned, it must be carried out and evaluated. Advertising campaign effectiveness is difficult to measure. Traditional media measures may be an efficient method of evaluation in developed countries but not in developing countries. Electronic media offer an alternative because they can track individual behavior in databases.

Checkpoint

List the steps involved in an advertising campaign.

CREATE ADVERTISEMENTS

PROMOTION

There are two main types of advertisements. **Organizational ads** promote a company or an entity and its brand image. **Product ads** promote a single product. Taiwan has placed organizational ads in business journals to promote its image as a high-technology manufacturer.

Advertisements often are built around a theme. An **advertising theme** organizes the design of an advertisement and helps to focus communication efforts. BMW has clearly defined its communication goals of showing technology, quality, performance, and exclusivity. These goals limit the types of themes BMW is likely to use. Some of these themes include:

- **Directness vs. indirectness** Many U.S. companies design ads that directly emphasize why someone should buy a product. By focusing on the quality and performance of its car, BMW's ads are more indirect. Many cultures feel that directly telling people they should buy a product is arrogant.

- **Comparative advertising** Directly comparing one product to another is *comparative advertising*. The use of comparative advertising is illegal in many countries. It also can be seen as bragging. BMW is not likely to use comparative advertising in the United States even though it is legal. Comparative advertising could diminish BMW's image by taking away from the perceived uniqueness of the brand.

- **Emotional appeals vs. sophistication** Many companies advertising in the United States use appeals based on emotion. Europeans often expect more sophistication in their products. This attitude matches BMW's communication goals.

- **Humor** International marketers must be careful when using humor. What one culture finds humorous other cultures may not. Humor also should fit the product's image. The use of humor does not match BMW's communication goals.

Time Out

International marketers can use demographics to help create advertising themes. Certain product characteristics appeal to different age groups.
- 20s – novelty, uniqueness
- 30s – stability, family-oriented
- 40s – self-indulgence
- 50s – recognition, power
- 60s – practicality, reliability, bargains

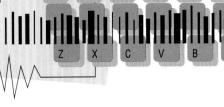

- **Gender roles** Gender roles can vary considerably across cultures. Some cultures have very strict cultural norms for male and female roles. For example, advertising female drivers of BMWs in some Middle Eastern countries would violate cultural norms because women are not allowed to drive alone. BMW's focus on the car allows it to avoid linking its advertisements to specific gender roles.

- **Popular vs. traditional culture** MTV is a very good media outlet for businesses that want to be linked with popular culture. In general, U.S. consumers view popular culture favorably, but consumers in some other cultures do not. Popular culture does not always fit a product. BMW sees its cars as modern classics. Therefore, it is likely to avoid popular culture themes.

International marketers are faced with the challenge of encoding an advertising message in a way that the target audience will properly decode it. They must select a theme that matches the culture and the message being communicated. Advertisements can communicate both verbally and non-verbally. Advertisers must be aware of how social status is conveyed. They also must be aware of how colors and other contextual elements are used.

The BMW NASA ad works well because an audience can form a link between the BMW car and the technological sophistication of NASA. Consumers in countries where there is no prior concept of NASA as a technology leader may not be able to form this link.

Checkpoint List the six types of advertising themes.

Understand Marketing Concepts

Circle the best answer for each of the following questions.

1. Paid, non-personal communication is called
   a. promotion
   b. sales promotion
   c. advertising
   d. publicity

2. Advertisements designed to promote a company or an entity and its brand image are called
   a. company ads
   b. organizational ads
   c. product ads
   d. media ads

Think Critically

Answer the following questions as completely as possible. If necessary, use a separate sheet of paper.

3. View a series of television programs, movies, or video games. Identify products that are placed in the television program, movie, or game. Explain how this product placement enhances the product's image.

_____

_____

_____

_____

_____

_____

4. Choose an ad. Explain the theme used in the ad. Describe how this theme is related to the product, culture, and target market.

_____

_____

_____

_____

_____

_____

International Selling Strategies

Goals
- Describe the selling process.
- Explain the importance of integrated marketing communication.

Terms
- personal selling
- sales commission
- sales promotion
- integrated marketing communication

Going Global

Avon Calling! This is the phrase that millions of "Avon Ladies" use when making sales calls to homes around the world. In 1886, Avon was started by David McConnell as the California Perfume Company. McConnell eventually renamed the company Avon, after William Shakespeare's birthplace.

Avon used a direct-sales approach to bring cosmetics and personal-care products into customers' homes. By 1928, Avon had more than 25,000 U.S. sales representatives. In the United States, women's roles started changing in the 1970s. More women entered the workforce. These women were less likely to be at home and more likely to purchase higher-priced cosmetic products. Many Avon representatives left the company and put their sales skills to work for more prestigious employers. To meet these challenges, Avon trained its sales force to present its products in the workplace.

Avon started selling internationally in the 1950s. In the 1990s, Avon expanded international sales to China and Eastern Europe. By 2001, Avon grew to become the world's largest direct-sales company and the sixth largest global beauty company. In 2005, it had sales of over $7.7 billion and more than 4.9 million sales representatives around the world.

Working in small groups, discuss why Avon's sales model is effective for its target market. Explain why much of Avon's growth is from markets outside of the United States.

CUSTOMER ACTION

SELLING

Marketers ultimately look for some type of action on the part of the customer. In most cases, the action they desire is the purchase of a product. But product purchase is not the only action that marketers desire. Many countries are looking for behavioral change. In the United States and other countries, promotional campaigns have been designed to get people to reduce litter, quit smoking, and wear seatbelts.

Companies use many methods to get customers to take action. Personal selling, sales promotions, electronic media, and sales management all play a role in getting the desired result.

Personal Selling

SELLING

For many products, customer action is obtained through personal sales. **Personal selling** involves face-to-face interaction between a seller and a buyer. Personal selling allows for immediate two-way communication. It allows for instant feedback and the chance to see if the buyer decodes information in the intended way.

The consumer market direct-selling method used by Avon was a common promotional strategy in the United States prior to the 1970s. Door-to-door selling was effective because the salesperson could demonstrate products in a person's home. Most department stores also had professional salespeople on the floor to help sell products to customers. Women leaving the home and joining the workforce is not the only reason for the decline of door-to-door sales. Door-to-door sales is a very expensive method of moving an individual through the AIDA process to obtain action. Today in the consumer market, personal selling is used for products, such as cars, jewelry, homes, and electronics, that involve complex decisions. Also, personal selling should be used only if the product category has a profit margin large enough to pay for the personal attention.

Personal selling is common in industrial sales. Industrial purchase decisions are typically complex and require multiple visits to develop a relationship between the seller and the buyer. The ideal professional salesperson acts as an interface between the selling company and the buyer, ensuring that both parties benefit.

International Sales Process

Personal selling typically follows a multi-step process that includes:

1. approach
2. sales presentation
3. answering objections
4. closing the sale
5. follow-up

The *approach* is the method that the salesperson uses to start the sales process. The approach includes a *pre-approach* process where the salesperson conducts background research to understand the customer's needs. This research helps in crafting the sales presentation. The *sales presentation* is the major communication component in the sales process. If advertising has done its job of increasing awareness and interest, the salesperson can move to creating desire. Buyers often will raise objections that need to be addressed. Objections can arise because the buyer does not understand the presentation. They also may be part of the negotiation process.

In order to close the sale, salespeople need to ask buyers to make the purchase. Once the sale is made, the salesperson should follow up with buyers to be sure they are satisfied. This follow-up can help create goodwill.

The sales process will be successful only if the salesperson has a knowledge of the product being sold and a strong understanding of the customer and local culture. Professional salespeople working for Avon around the world sell the same products. Each of these salespeople must understand the products and product benefits. They also must understand the needs of the local market.

Time Out

Avon considers China its largest long-term growth opportunity. Door-to-door selling was banned in China in 1998. This ban was lifted in December 2004 as required by the World Trade Organization. Avon now expects sales in China to reach $400 million by 2007.

In business-to-business sales, the sales approach may be more standardized. But to succeed, salespeople must be aware of factors that could influence the sales process. Sellers need to understand power relationships inside an organization. They need to understand local negotiation techniques and how to close sales without offending buyers. In many parts of the world, relationship development is the first part of the sales process. Asking for the sale too soon can actually hurt the sales process.

International Sales Management Managing international sales requires that companies carefully hire and train their sales force. Businesses in developing countries can employ a much less expensive sales force because of the low cost of labor. However, the lack of advertising media outlets in developing countries can place a greater burden on the salesperson to create awareness, interest, desire, and action. If salespeople are to succeed, they must receive proper training on the sales process and the company's products.

Avon hires sales representatives around the world. It provides those representatives with training and promotional support to aid their sales process. Area sales managers hold regular sales meetings, training sessions, and support sessions to aid the sales force.

International sales management also requires setting a compensation system. Avon representatives earn a sales commission. A **sales commission** compensates the salesperson based on a percentage of sales. This compensation system is a common practice for many products. Salespeople also can work for a straight salary. A salary provides an incentive for the salesperson to stay with a company. Many industrial sales positions combine a base salary with sales commissions.

Sales Promotion

Companies that sell consumer products will often attempt to obtain consumer action by using sales promotions. A **sales promotion** is an incentive, such as a coupon, rebate, or premium (an addition to the product sold). *Trade promotions* are sales promotions that can be directed to members of the trade or industry as well as to final customers.

Consumer products companies often use coupons to create an incentive to buy. This strategy may work in some international markets, but it may not work in others. Many countries place restrictions on the use of sales promotions. Countries also may not have the infrastructure to support the promotional effort. For coupons and rebates to work, intermediaries must handle the payment process to retailers or end customers. Mailing rebate checks may work in developed countries but not in developing countries.

Marketing Myths

Technology can be a blessing and a curse. Computer manufacturer Dell Inc. learned the hard way that Internet-based blogs can point out problems to the entire world. A *blog* is a web log, or a series of posts on the Internet.

A Dell customer ran into problems with his Dell laptop. He called the technology support center and was routed to India. After a series of frustrating calls, he vented his anger in an online blog. This post led to a number of other Dell buyers adding to the blog and angrily commenting on their experiences with Dell's service.

Dell responded by promising to improve its service center support system. Dell learned that the Internet is a powerful communication system, not just for selling products but also for lodging complaints.

THINK CRITICALLY

1. Describe how customers use blogs.
2. Explain why Dell had to react to a relatively small number of customer complaints in online blogs.

Some countries consider sales promotions to be a form of price competition. Sales promotions can give larger companies an advantage over smaller companies. Premiums, such as a gift or giveaway, can be totally restricted, or they may require special government approval before they can be used. Because of various market conditions, sales promotions often need to be planned locally.

Electronic Media

Electronic media are used to support sales efforts and to host company and product web sites. Electronic media are good at creating interest and desire. The web site can persuade customers to contact a sales representative. Most companies use traditional media to advertise their web address and to create awareness of their web site.

BMW has shifted promotional dollars to the Internet from traditional media. BMW has an extensive web site. It has designed web sites for 90 different countries. Once in the site, visitors can explore cars and technologies, link to car service, set up a customized personal web page, or design a car. Electronic media allow BMW to offer more information at a price lower than traditional media.

© GETTY IMAGES/PHOTODISC

List the steps used in the sales process.

Checkpoint

MARKETING COMMUNICATION

PROMOTION

Developing promotional strategies requires that all elements of the promotional mix are integrated to reach communication goals. **Integrated marketing communication** is a planning process that attempts to ensure that all marketing communication efforts send a consistent message to customers.

To maintain a consistent message, international marketers frequently will set the communication goals and budgets. Then, message design will be outsourced to companies in the local market to ensure that communication is encoded in a way that the local audience will understand the message.

Promotional efforts must be coordinated with sales promotion and personal selling efforts. Avon provides an example of this strategy. Its promotional efforts meet the needs of both its sales force and target markets. It advertises globally so customers are aware of and interested in the products. The sales force is trained to sell the products and maintain goodwill with customers.

Standardization versus Customization

When developing marketing communications for business and consumer markets, international marketers must consider standardization versus customization. In general, business markets need less customization. Business buyers around the world often have the same information needs, just as they have the same product needs. Obviously, proper language translations need to be undertaken. Consumer markets may require a higher level of customization. BMW may target a similar market segment around the world. The need for information may be the same, but the message will need to be encoded in a way that fits with cultural norms.

Checkpoint

Explain what is meant by standardization and customization of marketing communications.

_____

_____

World Stars | ANDREA JUNG

Andrea Jung was raised with multiple cultural experiences. She was born in Toronto, the daughter of immigrants from Hong Kong and China. Her relationship with Avon started as a consultant. She brought her experience as an executive vice president at Neiman Marcus for accessories, cosmetics, and women's intimate apparel. At Avon, she noticed two things. First, Avon was run by "men in suits," who didn't understand the female customers' needs. She also saw that Avon's colors needed freshening, the packaging looked cheap, and products needed improvement.

Jung joined Avon in 1994 as President of the Product Marketing Group and advanced rapidly. By 1996, she was promoted to President of Global Marketing. By 1999, she became Avon's first female Chief Executive Officer. In 2001, she was named Chairman of the Board. Jung is credited with turning Avon around and making it a global powerhouse. She poured millions into research and development. She was also responsible for new ads that used popular celebrities. Jung has given Avon a younger look. Under her leadership, sales have increased 45 percent, and the stock price has increased 165 percent. Jung has received considerable recognition by the business community. In 1998, the American Advertising Federation inducted her into the Advertising Hall of Fame. In 2001, *Time Magazine/CNN* recognized her as one of the 25 Most Influential Global Executives. *Fortune* magazine has ranked her as one of the 50 most powerful women in business.

THINK CRITICALLY

Discuss how Andrea Jung's background has helped her be an effective manager at Avon. What message about Avon do you think Jung is trying to communicate to consumers?

Understand Marketing Concepts

Circle the best answer for each of the following questions.

1. Face-to-face interaction between a seller and a buyer is called
   a. personal selling
   b. sales promotion
   c. promotion
   d. advertising

2. A planning process that attempts to ensure that all marketing communication efforts send a consistent message to customers is called
   a. integrated marketing communication
   b. international marketing communication
   c. advertising
   d. promotion

Think Critically

Answer the following questions as completely as possible. If necessary, use a separate sheet of paper.

3. Explain the differences between personal selling and sales promotion. Describe how a marketer could use both.

_____

_____

_____

_____

_____

_____

_____

_____

4. Explain why companies would use an integrated marketing communication approach with their promotional strategy.

_____

_____

_____

_____

_____

_____

_____

Review Marketing Concepts

Write the letter of the term that matches each definition. Some terms will not be used.

_____ 1. When companies pay to have their products placed into some other media outlet

_____ 2. Any form of paid, non-personal communication

_____ 3. The process of using language and symbols to design a message

_____ 4. A calendar that lays out when ads will play and in which media

_____ 5. Any form of communication that is designed to inform, remind, or persuade customers about a company, its goods, or services

_____ 6. Free communication through a media

_____ 7. Face-to-face interaction between a seller and a buyer

_____ 8. Anything that interferes with communication

_____ 9. An incentive, such as a coupon, rebate, or premium, offered to the consumer

_____ 10. Organizes the design of an advertisement and helps to focus communication efforts

a. advertising
b. advertising theme
c. AIDA process
d. decoding
e. encoding
f. feedback
g. integrated marketing communication
h. media
i. media schedule
j. noise
k. organizational ads
l. personal selling
m. product ads
n. product placement
o. promotion
p. publicity
q. sales commission
r. sales promotion

Circle the best answer.

11. Television and radio are examples of which type of media?
    a. electronic
    b. print
    c. broadcast
    d. outdoor

12. The most preferred method of setting promotional budgets would be
    a. matching competition
    b. percentage of sales
    c. all the company can afford
    d. based upon objectives and tasks

13. Which of the following is *not* a type of advertising theme?
    a. humor
    b. publicity
    c. sophistication
    d. comparative advertising

Think Critically

14. Choose a product. Specify the promotional mix you would use to communicate with customers. Indicate what role each part of the mix would play.

_____

_____

_____

_____

_____

_____

_____

_____

15. Describe the AIDA process. Explain why each component is important to the marketing communication process.

_____

_____

_____

_____

_____

_____

_____

_____

_____

16. Using various media, provide examples of advertisements for each of the six advertising themes discussed in Lesson 9.2.

_____

_____

_____

_____

_____

_____

_____

_____

Make Connections

17. Communication Create a drawing of the communication model. Specify how each component of the model would be used in international communication. For example, identify the sender, how the message would be encoded, what channels would be used, how you would test for decoding, who the receiver would be, how feedback would be evaluated, and what could create noise.

_____

_____

_____

_____

_____

_____

18. Marketing Math You have been asked to develop a promotional budget using the objective-and-task-based method. You have collected the following data to help in setting the budget. Determine which media you will use and your advertising budget. Explain your choice of media.

The goal is to make 90 percent of the market aware of your product benefits.

Each nationally broadcast television commercial reaches 20 percent unique market share (i.e., it does not overlap with other media in this list). Each commercial costs $300,000.

Each national magazine chosen reaches 5 percent unique market share. Each ad costs $50,000. Research shows that magazine ads have only 50 percent of the effectiveness of television ads.

New web site design costs $200,000.

_____

_____

_____

_____

_____

_____

_____

_____

19. **Research** Use the Internet and locate a company's web site. Describe how the company uses its web site to create interest and desire for its product or service. List ways to improve the web site to help generate more customer interest.

_____

_____

_____

_____

_____

_____

_____

_____

PUT MARKETING ON THE MAP

International Marketing Plan Project

Your international marketing plan must develop a communication strategy to promote your company and its products. You must take into consideration the factors that will influence your strategic design.

Work with a group and complete the following activities.

1. For your promotional campaign, specify the communication goals you will be setting for the countries you plan to target. Be specific in identifying those goals.

2. Use the Internet to research the factors that will impact the promotional strategy to be used for a country you are targeting. Research factors such as legal restrictions, cultural norms, and gender roles. Explain how these factors will impact your promotional strategy design.

3. Recommend a promotional mix. Justify how this mix will allow you to reach your communication goals.

4. Develop an advertisement based on a theme. Explain the use of this theme given the factors you have researched that influence your promotional strategy.

5. Explain how you will use the steps in the sales process. Describe how you will train salespeople to sell your product in the markets you are targeting.

6. Use the integrated marketing communication process concept to justify your entire promotional strategy. Indicate how this strategy will consistently convey your product image to customers.

Case Study

THE PERSONAL NATURE OF SELLING

Businesses actively involved in international trade realize that understanding the culture of a potential trade partner is essential for success. Greetings, personal space, religious practices, gifts, business cards, business meeting practices, and many other factors must be considered before conducting international business.

Appropriate greetings indicate a level of respect. An international trade partner may be offended by U.S. workers dressed for casual Friday in a business office. Business may be lost due to an expectation of a more formal setting.

Personal space is another issue that deserves attention when conducting international business. Americans become uncomfortable when people are too close to their personal space. But some cultures operate within much smaller personal spaces.

Religion plays a powerful role in most cultures. Different religions are frequently stereotyped, resulting in distrust and uncertainty. Business success depends on respecting religious practices. Scheduling a business meeting on a religious holiday will not win business allies.

Many cultures exchange gifts when doing business. Studying a culture in advance will help individuals avoid giving gifts that may convey unintended meaning.

Business cards are important for many cultures. Good business cards are printed in English on one side of the card and the language of the trade partner on the other side. A business card should be accepted with both hands and should be shown sincere attention.

Business meetings can make or break a business deal. Many cultures are turned off by the fast-paced, multitasking American culture. Ample time must be allowed for a business meeting. Do not try to rush through meetings.

In international business environments, it is important to understand other cultures. Individuals should not assume that what is considered polite in their culture will meet the same approval in other cultures. Different generations, genders, and cultural backgrounds result in different interpretations of thinking and communication styles. Business people must adjust strategies to meet the needs of their clients.

THINK CRITICALLY

1. Why should you take time to study a culture before conducting international business?
2. How can stereotypes affect a business deal?
3. Should international trade partners be expected to follow U.S. business practices when attending a meeting in the United States?
4. Which aspect of culture do you think is the most misunderstood? Explain why.

ADVERTISING CAMPAIGN EVENT

Participants in the Advertising Campaign Event are challenged to prepare an advertising campaign of any length for a real product, service, company, or business and present the campaign to a prospective client. The participants also must indicate an appropriate budget and select media.

This event consists of outlined fact sheets, a written comprehensive exam, and an oral presentation. One to three students will design and present their advertising campaign.

The body of the written entry must be limited to ten numbered pages, not including the title page and table of contents. Participants will bring visual aids to the event briefing. The oral presentation will consist of 15 minutes to explain the plan to the judge and 5 minutes for the judge's questions.

You have been hired by an upscale clothing store that sells professional business suits for both men and women. Prices charged for your merchandise are in the middle to upper range.

You are challenged to equate business success with dressing in professional business attire. Your advertising campaign must be aimed at changing the mindset of consumers from casual office wear to more formal attire, which is now the trend. You need to catch the attention of recent college graduates and young business professionals.

Performance Indicators Evaluated

- Understand the challenge of changing a dress code mindset.
- Define the relationship between professional dress and business success.
- Analyze the international business market and expectations for business attire.
- Demonstrate critical thinking and problem-solving skills.
- Communicate an effective advertising campaign that meets company goals.
- Prepare a budget for an effective advertising campaign.
- Create a diverse advertising campaign that reaches the target market through multiple channels of communication.

Go to the DECA web site for more detailed information.

THINK CRITICALLY

1. Why is an advertising campaign needed to persuade business people to wear suits?
2. What communication channels for the advertising campaign will be the most effective financially? Explain why.
3. Give two examples of how the business can use personal selling to work with customers to change business wardrobes.

www.deca.org

International Payment Flows

CHAPTER 10 · CHAPTER 10 · CHAPTER 10 · CHAPTER 10 · CHAPTER 10

10

10.1 International Exchange

10.2 International Pricing and Payments

10.3 Balance of Payments

© BRAND X PICTURES

Point Your Browser

▶ ▶ ▶ ▶ ▶ intlmarket.swlearning.com

The Gold Standard

Gold is soft, heavy, and relatively rare. It can be melted easily and beaten into very thin sheets. Gold does not corrode, so it keeps its luster indefinitely. It has long been considered valuable and has been used as a basis for money and trade.

In 1844, the Bank of England's notes, or paper money, became the legal standard for Britain. These notes were fully backed by gold, placing Britain's currency on a "gold standard." Around the same time, the United States adopted a "silver standard" and established a fixed amount of gold to the U.S. dollar. The value of both gold and silver was based on the supply and demand of the metals. For a country to expand the amount of money in an economy, it had to back its currency with larger amounts of silver or gold.

Gold held in a country's central bank to back currency would be used to balance international trade accounts. For example, if a country exported products and received another country's currency, the purchasing country would have to transfer gold for its paper notes. The gold reserves of a country would be depleted, reducing the money supply. Less money would reduce demand, causing economic activity and prices to drop. In theory, this situation should have decreased the demand for imports and dropped prices on that country's exports. In practice, it has led countries to raise barriers to imports in order to limit gold transfers.

The gold standard contributed to the Great Depression of the 1930s. In the 1920s, the United States Federal Reserve enacted monetary policies to restrict the money supply in order to control inflation. This action slowed the economy. Barriers to international trade were raised to protect gold supplies, further limiting the economic growth that can come from trade. Most countries around the world abandoned the gold standard in the 1930s.

Think Critically

1. Explain why countries would use gold as a basis for their currency.

2. Explain why countries abandoned the gold standard. Describe the benefits of not having currency linked to gold.

International Exchange

- Explain the law of supply and demand.
- Describe the factors that influence exchange rates.

- money
- hard currency
- soft currency

- demand
- supply
- exchange rate

Going Global

McDonald's Big Mac sandwich is basically the same around the world. It not only has the same look and taste, but it also uses the same ingredients and processes. So, in theory, all Big Macs should cost about the same in every culture. The international business journal *The Economist* has been using a *Big Mac Index* since 1986. It compares the average of Big Mac prices among countries based on the idea that each country's currency should reflect its purchasing power.

In 2005, a Big Mac's average cost in countries using the euro was €2.92. The average price in the United States was $3.06. This comparison showed that Europeans spent $1.05 more than Americans,

indicating that the euro was overvalued by 17 percent against the dollar. Price differences can come from costs other than ingredients, such as rent and labor costs. Rent and labor is much higher in Switzerland ($5.05 Big Mac) than in China ($1.27 Big Mac). Differences in prices also can exist because currencies do not reflect true exchange rates.

The Big Mac index has shown some relevance. Purchasing power indexes can give a direction to where currencies are headed over the long run. *The Economist* introduced a new *Tall Latte Index* based on a cup of Starbucks coffee. This index also showed the euro as being overvalued.

Working with a partner, explain why a Big Mac is a good product for comparing international currencies. Other than a tall latte, what else could *The Economist* use?

INTERNATIONAL CURRENCY

Money is a medium of exchange used by a society. Money can store value and act as a unit for accounting. Over time, money has made a transition from silver or gold coins that had real value to notes and coins that represent value because they are backed by gold or something else of value. Today, most money acts as a means of exchange without any real value. Money has value only because the people who use it believe in it. The U.S. dollar is legal tender for all debts, public and private, but it is not backed by gold. It has value only because it holds the faith of the world's population.

The U.S. dollar is considered to be a hard currency. A **hard currency** has the confidence of international traders. These currencies typically come from economically and politically stable countries. The British pound, the euro, and the Swiss franc are all hard currencies and often are used as payment for international trade. A **soft currency** is not acceptable for international exchange, most often due to unrealistic exchange rates or economic and political instability within a country. Understanding how currencies can fluctuate in value requires a review of demand theory.

The Law of Supply and Demand

The law of supply and demand attempts to explain how changes in the demand and quantity of goods sold in competitive markets impact a price. **Demand** is the quantity of a good or service that consumers are willing and able to buy at a given price. **Supply** is the quantity that producers are willing to offer at a given price. Graph A illustrates the intersection of the demand and supply curves.

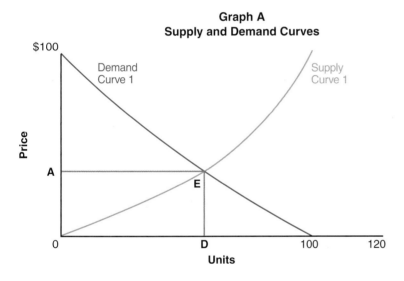

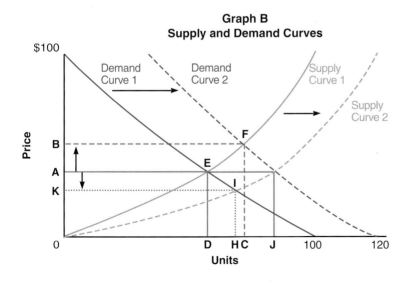

As illustrated in Graph A, if the price asked is $100, zero units will be demanded, but suppliers would be willing to supply 100 units. At a price of $0, 100 units would be demanded, but no suppliers would be willing to supply the product. Each curve is based on the nature of the product, the nature of competition, and the buyers' and sellers' needs. Where these two lines cross results in an equilibrium point E, where D number of units will be demanded and sold at price A. Shifts in the supply or demand curve to the right or left will result in changes in the equilibrium point, units sold, and sale price, as illustrated in Graph B. The following table summarizes the changes shown in Graph B.

Demand Curve	Supply Curve	Units Sold	Market Price
Shifts to the right (Demand Curve 2)	Stays the same (Supply Curve 1)	Increases (Units D to C)	Increases (Price A to B)
Stays the same (Demand Curve 1)	Shifts to the right (Supply Curve 2)	Increases (Units D to H)	Decreases (Price A to K)
Shifts to the right (Demand Curve 2)	Shifts to the right (Supply Curve 2)	Increases (Units D to J)	Remains stable (Price A to A)

Reversing the supply or demand curve directions will decrease units sold. The law of supply and demand works for most goods and services. This law also holds true for the global demand for currency. Instead of changes in price, the exchange rate between countries will shift.

Checkpoint

List the two types of international trade currencies.

Time Out

The euro (€) replaced the currencies of Austria, Belgium, Finland, France, Germany, Greece, Ireland, Italy, Luxembourg, the Netherlands, Portugal, and Spain in the Eurozone. The exchange rate for the euro started at €1 = $1.18. It has dropped as low as €1 = $0.83 and has risen as high as €1 = $1.37.

CURRENCY EXCHANGE RATES

FINANCING

When the world was on a gold standard, all exchange rates were based on a currency's relationship to gold. Today, most currency exchange rates are based on the law of supply and demand. An **exchange rate,** also known as a *foreign-exchange rate,* is the ratio of how much one currency is worth in terms of another currency. For example, in October 2005, the dollar-to-euro exchange rate was $1.21479 per euro. The euro-to-dollar exchange rate was €0.823181 per dollar, or just over 82 euro cents. These small percentages have little meaning for small exchanges, but they have a big impact when millions of currency units are exchanged.

When exchange rates are set by supply and demand considerations, a currency is said to *float.* A currency also can be *pegged,* or have a set rate to another currency. Hard currencies normally float. Some soft currencies are pegged to their largest trading partners. For example, the Chinese yuan was pegged to the U.S. dollar at a fixed rate of 8.28848 yuan to the dollar ($0.12067 to the yuan) until July 22, 2005. The yuan was then repegged by the Chinese government at a rate just over 8.076 yuan to the dollar ($0.12384 to the yuan). This change made Chinese goods 2.6 percent more expensive for Americans.

The exchange rate, or price, for a country's currency is determined by the demand for the currency and its supply. There are four major factors that influence the exchange rates between countries.

Transactional Demand   Economic activity in a country is the basis for *transactional demand.* Economic activity and growth within a country can draw in foreign investors. For example, Hyundai has seen growth in the demand for its automobiles in the United States. It decided to build a new $1 billion factory in Alabama. Hyundai needed to exchange South Korean won for U.S. dollars, increasing the foreign demand for dollars. At the same time, a growing U.S. economy provided more money for workers to purchase foreign imports, increasing the demand for foreign currency. Both of these examples shift the demand curve for currencies.

Economic Confidence   The confidence in a country's economy can have an impact on both the demand for a currency and its supply in the market. Confidence can be linked to both economic conditions as well as perceived political stability. If Hyundai did not have confidence in the U.S. economy, it would not be demanding additional U.S. dollars to expand its plant. In fact, it might consider selling its assets and converting its dollars to won. This action would decrease the demand for dollars and increase the supply of dollars available in the global financial market. A decrease in demand and increase in supply could move an exchange rate from equilibrium point F to point I in Graph B. This movement would lower the value of a currency. If international investors lose confidence in an economy, they may try to sell their currency holdings.

Money Supply   A country's central bank can control the amount of money available in an economy. Today, the money supply typically is controlled through changes in key interest rates. The lower the interest rate, the more money is created in an economy through increased bank lending. In the 1920s, the U.S. Federal Reserve set interest rates too high. This action slowed the U.S. economy and decreased demand for goods and services. A slowing economy can decrease both the currency demand by foreign investors and a country's demand for imports.

Countries often see the greatest danger as having lending rates that are too low. These low rates can place too much currency in the market and can cause inflation. This situation can shift exchange rate equilibriums from point E to point I in Graph B, lowering the value of a currency.

The United States cannot control all of the U.S. currency. *Eurodollars* are U.S. dollars held in banks outside of the United States, meaning they are outside of U.S. Federal Reserve control.

Ethics Around the World

In the late 1700s, China was willing to sell products but was not willing to purchase products from around the world. Therefore, China accumulated large amounts of wealth from foreign countries. China would only accept payment in silver for its tea and other products. The demand for Chinese goods in England was high, but the Chinese did not believe that England had any products of value to trade.

Today, it could be argued that China operates with the same philosophy. Instead of accumulating silver, China accumulates international currencies. If China's yuan floated in international currency markets instead of being pegged, its currency should become more expensive, reducing the appeal of its export products.

THINK CRITICALLY

1. Why do you think that China was able to obtain English silver?
2. Evaluate the pros and cons of China's current trade strategy.

Speculative Demand The fourth factor that influences exchange rates is speculative demand. *Speculative demand* involves the direct buying and selling of a currency based on speculated future exchange rates. The major currency exchanges are in Tokyo, London, and New York. They create a 24-hour exchange market, trading almost $2 trillion in world currencies per day.

These markets set the spot rate for currency. The *spot rate* is the exchange rate for any given time of day. They also set the *forward market rates,* or contractual promises to meet future exchange rates. Before Hyundai makes its $1 billion payment for its new U.S. factory, it would need to determine if it was better to exchange its currency on the spot market and hold U.S. dollars or to purchase a forward contract, locking in a better rate in the future when it needs the money.

Some international investors use forward markets to speculate on future currency exchange rates. An investor can purchase a forward contract at a fixed exchange rate. If rates become more favorable, the investor can sell the contract at a profit. If, however, rates become less favorable, the investor can lose all of the assets. Future markets do serve a purpose in maintaining stability in currency markets.

Exchange Controls

Many countries will set exchange controls on their currencies. Exchange controls limit the amount of a currency that can be exported or exchanged with other countries. These controls allow a country to maintain greater control over its exchange rate. International businesses may find that it is hard to send profits back to a home country from a country with exchange controls. Often the business may need to purchase export products and then resell those products to move profits out of a country. For example, businesses selling in Kazakhstan may purchase oil in Kazakhstan to sell abroad to recover their profits. Countries with floating currencies are less likely to have exchange controls.

Checkpoint

List four major factors that influence the exchange rates between countries.

Understand Marketing Concepts

Circle the best answer for each of the following questions.

1. A currency that has the confidence of international traders is called
   a. hard currency
   c. international currency
   b. soft currency
   d. gold standard

2. The quantity that producers are willing to offer at a given price is called
   a. demand
   c. industrial demand
   b. supply
   d. inventory

Think Critically

Answer the following questions as completely as possible.

3. Using Graph C, describe how the four factors that influence exchange rates impact the currency supply and demand curves.

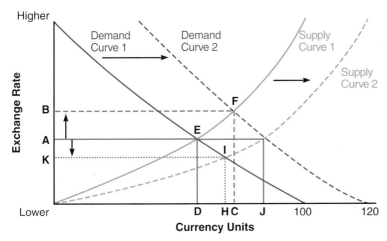

Graph C
Currency Supply and Demand Curves

_____

_____

_____

4. Recommend a strategy to move profits out of a country that has exchange controls.

_____

_____

International Pricing and Payments

Terms / Goals

Goals
- Explain each of the four global pricing strategies.
- Describe methods of international payments.

Terms
- price
- price floor
- price ceiling
- penetration pricing
- skim pricing
- market pricing
- prestige pricing
- elasticity of demand
- letter of credit

Going Global

How low can the price for music go? Music companies currently are facing that question. Prior to 1995, customers purchased CDs, cassettes, or LPs (long-play records) from local music stores. Prices were set based on the costs involved in selling the music, such as inventory and overhead costs, as well as local competitive conditions. Price differences existed not only within a country but also across national borders.

The Internet era has brought new pricing dynamics. The music industry was under considerable threat from download sites that pirated music and offered it for free. Most of these sites now have closed. Today, music download sites, such as Apple's iTunes, MP3.com, Rhapsody.com, and others, offer music for a fee to individuals around the world. Some of these sites give a limited number of songs away for free and then offer music downloads for a per-song or per-album price. In most cases, individuals can download the same music from any online site, so online stores have been forced to offer music at the same price. The music industry wants online providers to increase prices. Microsoft believes that the music industry currently is charging too much in royalty fees, which can lead to an increase in price and a decrease in demand.

Working with a partner, describe the factors that would affect individual song prices on the Internet. Explain why it would be difficult to charge different prices for different countries.

GLOBAL PRICING STRATEGIES

PRICING

A product's price is used as a strategic tool. Marketers see **price** as the amount of money, goods, or services needed to acquire a given quantity of other goods or services. The price a company sets for a product must be justified against the benefits the customer will receive. Most often the price for a product is paid in money. A more ancient form of exchange is based on *barter*. In a barter system, goods and services are directly exchanged for other goods and services. This practice was more common before the use of hard currency. Before 1990, many communist countries needed to engage in barter because they could not pay in hard currency.

Price is a strategic tool that companies can change very rapidly. If a company has too much inventory, it can lower prices to increase sales. If competitors enter a market, prices can be changed to compete. When international marketers want to expand into new markets, they must use price as a strategic tool.

Setting Prices

The price a global marketer sets for a product is based on a number of factors. The price of a product must support the overall marketing mix and the goals of the company. When setting prices, companies face some constraints. The **price floor** is the lowest price that a company can charge and still cover costs. If an international marketer sets a price lower than the cost of the product, it can be accused of dumping, and it may be penalized. A **price ceiling** is the maximum price that can be charged in a market. The price ceiling is set by the value customers see in the product and the price that the competition charges.

There are a number of pricing strategies that companies use to achieve their marketing goals.

Time Out

Tradeable currencies have allowed for the growth of international trade throughout history. Roman denari were used from around 200 B.C. to 300 A.D. Today, the standard world trade currency is the U.S. dollar.

- **Penetration pricing** sets a low price compared to competitors. This strategy helps a company capture market share. Penetration pricing often is used for a short term until market share goals are met.

- **Skim pricing** is typically a temporary strategy where a company sets a price at a high level for a short period of time. A skimming strategy requires the company to target a market that is willing to pay a high price. New, innovative products entering a marketplace could use a skim-pricing strategy because some buyers are willing to pay a high price to have the newest products.

- **Market pricing** is used when competitive products already exist in a marketplace. A careful analysis must be undertaken when entering new international markets to find a price that is justified given the benefits offered by competitive products. Market price does not imply charging the same price as competitors. Prices can be higher or lower than market averages based on the competitive advantages.

- **Prestige pricing** is a strategy where a company sets a high price throughout the life of a product. The high price is designed to signal quality. BMW sets a high price for cars, in part, to signal that they are high-quality automobiles.

Wal-Mart has used its low-price strategy to penetrate new markets and capture market share. This strategy hasn't always worked, however. It has had considerable trouble expanding into Germany. Wal-Mart ran into a competitive discount market-pricing environment and has captured only two percent of the German market. Wal-Mart has a cost advantage for a number of different products but not in food sales. Food products need to be sourced locally to meet local tastes. Wal-Mart cannot price below its floor because it will lose money and violate laws. Even when Wal-Mart is priced lower, local German discount stores often are more convenient.

Toyota found that its price floor was moving too high for it to be priced competitively in a market-price-driven environment. Toyota undertook a cost-cutting strategy throughout its supply chain to lower the price floor, allowing for a decrease in price. Using a different strategy, Honda developed the Acura line to set prestige prices.

Standard Global Pricing   Ultimately, a company will need a set price in the markets where it is selling. However, it is unlikely that an international company would adopt a standard global price even though it may have a standard pricing strategy. Wal-Mart follows a low-price strategy in all markets. BMW follows a prestige pricing strategy around the world. However, their prices will vary among markets. In the case of Wal-Mart, the price will be based on local market conditions, but it will still adhere to the low-price strategy. Online environments do allow for a single global pricing strategy. iTunes offers products at a single global price. Individuals from around the world can go online and purchase the same products for the same price.

Elasticity of Demand

International marketers want to be able to sell their products at the highest price possible. There are two basic strategies to raise the price of a product. The first strategy is to try to make a product more inelastic. The second strategy is to shift the demand curve to the right.

Elasticity of demand describes the relationship between changes in a product's price and the demand for that product. *Inelastic products* typically have few substitutes, perhaps due to patents or copyrights or because of a strong brand image. There are several good substitutes for *elastic* products. Price has less of an impact on inelastic products. Starbucks is able to charge a high price for coffee because of its brand image in the marketplace. Making the demand curve more inelastic changes the slope of the demand curve from Demand Curve 1 to Demand Curve 2 in Graph D. This change allows price to increase from price A to price K. If the product is more elastic, the slope would become shallower and the price would drop.

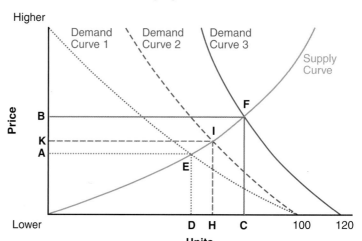

Graph D
Changing Demand Curves

Shifting the demand curve to the right allows for an increase in price as long as supply remains stable. The ideal strategy would be to both increase demand and create an impression that there are no substitutes. This would shift the demand from Demand Curve 1 to Demand Curve 3 in Graph D. This shift allows for a change in price from Price A to Price B.

In the 1980s, Japanese automobile manufacturers were able to charge a premium price for their cars. Customers in the United States viewed Japanese cars as higher quality than U.S.-made cars. In addition, there was an overall increase in the demand for high-gas-mileage cars.

If the demand curve has a steep slope, indicating an inelastic demand, a change in price will not change the quantity sold as much as when there is a shallow slope, or elastic demand. Companies with inelastic demand products often will lose revenue by lowering prices. Companies with elastic demand products often will gain revenue by lowering prices. The more competition that exists or the more substitutes for a product, the more likely it is that the demand curve will be elastic. This situation often forces companies to lower the price to increase revenue.

Other Factors Affecting Global Pricing Strategies

International marketers must consider a number of external factors when setting prices. Government regulations can affect prices. In some cases, governments will attempt to protect local industries by raising the price of imported products through the use of import tariffs. Prices also can be affected by taxes. Many countries use a *value-added tax* (VAT). A VAT is levied on the value added at each step of the supply chain. For example, a tax is paid on the sale of grain to a mill. A tax is then paid on the flour produced. This is followed by a tax on the bread baked. This is included in the price of the bread to the consumer. Because taxes are not just collected at the final sale, a VAT system helps to limit cheating and smuggling that can occur because of high sales taxes and tariffs.

The stability of exchange rates also can have an impact on prices. Often, the national currency used in international sales is negotiable. A U.S. company would prefer to negotiate sales in U.S. dollars. If there is exchange rate instability, companies may want to raise or lower prices to be sure they get the profits desired in their home currency.

Checkpoint

Name four pricing strategies.

INTERNATIONAL PAYMENTS

FINANCING

Once a price has been set and agreed upon by both the buyer and seller, a secure way of making payments and receiving products must be determined. Negotiating international payments is not the same as operating within a single country. At least two legal systems are involved when sales are made between countries. Buyers want to ensure that they will receive the product, and sellers want to ensure that they will receive the payment. Enforcing contracts can be difficult because of the distances and different legal systems. One of the strategies companies

Tech Zone

How big is the supply of money? This question has multiple answers. Economists look at different ways of measuring the money supply. Worldwide there is almost ten trillion dollars in U.S. currency. Of this amount, there are fewer than 700 billion U.S. dollars in printed currency and coins. The vast majority of U.S. currency is electronic. Electronic currency exists in checking, savings, and money market accounts as well as in certificates of deposit, Eurodollars, and repurchase agreements.

The most common way for these currencies to move internationally is through wire transfers, also called bank transfers. Bank-to-bank wire transfers are one of the safest ways of moving funds internationally. Both the sender and receiver must have a proven identity. Wire transfers can be made through secure encrypted networks. Within the United States, money moves through electronic fund transfers. This method includes transferring money from bank accounts to pay bills.

Western Union is one of the world's largest wire transfer companies. Its international wire transfers are not bank-to-bank. Many people use Western Union to transfer funds to over 225,000 locations worldwide.

THINK CRITICALLY

Describe the role that electronic transfers play in international exchange. Explain why there is more electronic currency than paper currency.

can use is to receive *cash in advance*. This strategy requires the buyer to pay in cash before receiving the product. This shifts the risks to the buyer. If the seller sells on credit, the risks are shifted to the seller.

Letters of Credit

A letter of credit system is used to limit international purchasing risk. A **letter of credit (LC)** is a financial document issued by a bank guaranteeing payment. Letters of credit are one of the most common methods used for making international payments.

Assume a U.S. business is purchasing products from China. The U.S. importer will request its bank to issue a letter of credit. This LC is sent to the exporter's Chinese bank. The Chinese bank will notify the exporter when the LC is received. The exporter will approve the terms set forth in the LC. Once the LC is approved, the exporter will ship the products. The exporter then sends shipping documents to the U.S. bank. Once the U.S. bank is satisfied that contract conditions have been met, it will make payment to the Chinese bank. This LC system limits risks for both the buyer and seller. Letters of credit may be either revocable or irrevocable.

- *Revocable letters of credit* may be revoked or modified by the issuing bank without notification until the point where the sales contract is completed. Once the proper documents have been presented to the issuing bank and conditions in the letter of credit are met, the letter of credit cannot be revoked. Revocable letters of credit are not common.

- *Irrevocable letters of credit* cannot be revoked or amended without the agreement of the importer's bank, the exporter's bank, and the exporter. Irrevocable letters of credit are the most common type of LC.

Checkpoint

Name two ways companies can handle international payments.

Understand Marketing Concepts

Circle the best answer for each of the following questions.

1. A pricing strategy that sets a price low compared to competitors, allowing a company to capture market share, is called
   a. skim pricing
   b. prestige pricing
   c. penetration pricing
   d. market share pricing

2. A financial document issued by a bank guaranteeing payment is called a(n)
   a. bill of lading
   b. letter of credit
   c. invoice
   d. letter of demand

Think Critically

Answer the following questions as completely as possible. If necessary, use a separate sheet of paper.

3. Make a list of products sold internationally. Determine the pricing strategy that would most likely be used for each product. Explain why you chose the pricing strategy for each product.

   _____

   _____

   _____

   _____

   _____

   _____

   _____

   _____

4. Choose a product sold internationally. Make a list of the factors a company would need to consider before it set a price for international markets.

   _____

   _____

   _____

   _____

   _____

   _____

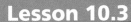

Balance of Payments

Goals

- Explain the components of the balance of payments.
- Describe the role that international banking plays in international trade.

Terms

- inflation
- balance of payments
- export-import bank
- central bank

Going Global

Argentina is the second-largest country in South America. It has a population of more than 30 million. Argentina has all the factors you would expect to see in a country with a strong economy. It has natural resources, an educated population, and a diversified industrial base. However, in the 1980s, Argentina's economy was failing. Argentina attempted to stabilize its economy by obtaining international loans. This large international debt put pressure on the government to make payments. Another problem that plagued the economy was high inflation. By the end of the 1980s, Argentina's inflation rate was over 200 percent per month, or 3,000 percent annually. International investors and the citizens of Argentina lost confidence in the economy. In 2001, Argentina faced the problem of capital flight. Individuals and businesses were withdrawing their savings from banks and sending their money overseas. Pesos were sold in the international market. The Argentinean currency lost 75 percent of its value. Unemployment reached over 18 percent.

Argentina's economy began to recover in 2003. Imports decreased, and exports increased. Inflation was lowered, and growth in the economy created jobs. Capital flight decreased, and foreign investment increased. The foreign demand for pesos was so high that it threatened Argentina's currency exchange advantage.

Working in small groups, discuss how Argentina could have reached a state of financial collapse. Describe how these financial crises affected Argentina's ability to engage in international trade.

INTERNATIONAL ACCOUNTS

International marketers must develop strategies within their economy and the economies where they do business. Inflation has a major impact on a country's economy and, in turn, on international marketing. **Inflation** is the increase in overall prices in an economy. Argentina is not the only country to have suffered from the dual evils of large national debt and inflation. In the 1990s, Brazil, Turkey, and Yugoslavia suffered from large national debts and *hyperinflation.* Hyperinflation is an extreme

FINANCING

case of inflation. Germany suffered from both of these economic problems in the 1920s. Germans burned their currency because it had little value and was cheaper to burn than firewood. Hyperinflation led to both economic and political instability and the rise of the Nazi party.

National debt and inflation can have a direct impact on international exchange rates, which then can directly impact the price of exports and imports. If a country's currency gains strength, its imported products become cheaper, but its exported products become more expensive. If the country's currency loses strength, its exported products become cheaper, and its citizens become poorer in comparison to other countries. The supply and demand for international currencies impact exchange rates. This effect is tracked through a country's balance of payments.

Balance of Payments

A large number of transactions flow in and out of a country. Some of the transactions represent flows of currency that leave the country. Others involve the flow of currency into a country. These payment flows are measured in a **balance of payments (BOP)**. A country's balance of payments can be positive or negative. If more currency flows out of a country than comes in, the country has a *negative BOP*. If more currency flows into a country than flows out, it has a *positive BOP*. A country's balance of payments is a good indicator of economic activity and global competitiveness. The BOP also has a direct impact on exchange rates. There are two major balance of payments components.

- *Current accounts* include the purchase of goods, or tangible products. These goods could include everything from cars and farm products to jet airplanes. Current accounts also include the purchase of services. These services may include intellectual property, such as software, movies, and music.

- *Financial and capital accounts* include financial transactions such as loans, stock purchases, or the buying and selling of companies.

Economists view the balance of payments as somewhat self-regulating. China has been running a positive balance of payments against most other countries. When countries around the world demand more Chinese current and financial assets, the supply of foreign currency held in China increases. This increase in foreign demand for Chinese currency should increase the value of the yuan, making Chinese goods more expensive. To minimize the increasing value of the Chinese yuan, China has a stated goal of balancing its BOP by 2010.

Marketing Myths

Prices are not always based on the cost of a product. The final price that international customers pay can vary widely. Many companies have a pricing system based on the willingness and ability to pay or market conditions.

There have been considerable complaints lodged against U.S. pharmaceutical companies. Customers can cross borders into Mexico or Canada and purchase the same products at lower prices. In the case of Canada, the government purchases vast amounts of products and receives quantity discounts. Mexican customers do not have the same ability to pay as American buyers, so Mexican customers receive a lower price.

U.S. companies argue that they need to make their profit in the United States because most foreign countries cannot afford to pay high prices for drugs.

THINK CRITICALLY

1. Explain why companies would charge different prices in different markets.
2. Explain why this pricing policy could hurt the image of a company.

Current Accounts

Current accounts track the flow of currency from trade into and out of a country within a one-year time period. The current account consists of four accounts. These accounts include goods, services, income, and transfers. *Current account income* includes returns from investments made in the past. *Current account transfers* includes the sending of funds to other countries. International aid is included in this account.

A country runs a trade deficit or trade surplus when the current account does not balance. A *trade deficit* occurs when a country imports more than it exports, which means that more money leaves a country than comes in. A *trade surplus* occurs when a country exports more than it imports, meaning that more money comes into a country than leaves it. In 2004, the United States ran a trade deficit of more than $600 billion. Many economists worry that this trade deficit is an indication of lack of U.S. competitiveness in global markets.

China, Japan, and other countries hold vast amounts of U.S. currency. If they decide to sell these holdings, they could decrease the demand for U.S. dollars, shifting the demand curve to the left and lowering the exchange rate. Some studies have shown that there is a decreased foreign interest in investing in U.S. companies. In addition, some foreign governments are limiting their investment in U.S. dollars. Investors do not want to hold a currency that will devalue.

The total values of the 2004 U.S. current account, capital and financial accounts, and balance of payments are shown below.

2004 U.S. Balance of Payments (in millions of dollars)

Current account

Exports of goods and services and income receipts		1,530,975
Goods	807,536	
Services	343,912	
Income receipts	379,527	
Imports of goods and services and income payments		−2,118,119
Goods, balance of payments basis	−1,472,926	
Services	−296,105	
Income payments	−349,088	
Unilateral current transfers, net		−80,930
Trade Deficit		−668,074

Capital account

Capital account transactions, net		−1,648

Financial account

U.S.-owned assets abroad		−855,509
Foreign-owned assets in the United States		1,440,105
Net Balance of Payments		−85,126

Checkpoint

List the components of the balance of payments.

INTERNATIONAL BANKING

FINANCING

International bankers play a significant role in the international trade process. They issue letters of credit and finance international trade. *Commercial banks* offer a variety of services, such as accepting deposits and making loans. They work with both importers and exporters around the world. Their willingness to work with clients will depend upon the creditworthiness of the individual or business. International marketers need to assess their bank to be sure it is able to operate in a global marketplace.

A country needs to have healthy banks to support economic growth. Japan and China have both suffered from banking problems. In the late 1990s, Japanese bankers were worried that they could be prevented from trading internationally because their reserve capital—the money needed to pay current demands—was dropping too low. Chinese banks have been directed to support non-profitable Chinese government projects, so there is more of a risk that these banks could go bankrupt.

Export-Import Banks

To support exports, many countries set up export-import (ex-im) banks. **Export-import banks** are independent banks established by governments to finance or insure the export sales of a country's products. This reduces the risk for exporters. For example, if the exporter loses sales due to political actions in another country, such as war, the ex-im bank will reimburse the exporter.

In 2005, the Ex-Im Bank of the United States supported the sale of $277 million in U.S. grain to Iraq. The grain was sold to the Iraqi government on a 180-day credit term under the Ex-Im Bank's short-term insurance program. Letters of credit were issued by the Trade Bank of Iraq and confirmed by Chase Bank in the United States. The transaction was insured by the Ex-Im Bank for the exporters.

Central Banks

Central banks play an important role in international economic competition. A **central bank** serves as the government's bank and is responsible for a country's monetary policy. In the United States, the Federal Reserve is the central bank. Its duties include maintaining the stability of the national currency and money supply. The central bank sets interest rates and lends money to a country's banks. By setting interest rates, central banks have some control over inflation.

Central banks finance government debt by selling bonds. Government debt, or *national debt*, is money owed by a government at the federal, state, and local level. Governments must pay principal and interest on these bonds. To motivate international investors, a country's central bank may be forced to set a higher interest rate if it needs to cover a nation's debt.

Countries with hyperinflation must print currencies with extremely large denominations. In the 1990s, Turkey printed one-million-lira bank notes. Brazil printed 500,000-cruzeiro bank notes. Yugoslavia printed 500-billion-dinar bank notes.

Part of the national debt is owed to lenders outside of a country. This part of a national debt can have an impact on exchange rates. An economically and politically stable country can become a safe haven for international investors. They feel they can loan money to a strong country at low risk. If there is a stable supply of a country's currency and investors demand more of that currency, a favorable exchange rate is created. If it appears that a country could suffer from economic or political instability, investors no longer will purchase government bonds. This action forces a central bank to increase interest rates on its bonds.

Central banks actively attempt to control interest rates by purchasing foreign currency. Japan has purchased U.S. dollars to strengthen the dollar and weaken the yen, making its export prices lower. Japan holds about 16 percent of U.S. Treasury bonds. As the Japanese economy has strengthened, it has been buying fewer U.S. bonds. Foreign countries hold more than $1.4 trillion of U.S. Treasury securities, or U.S. government bonds. The largest purchaser has been Japan, followed by China and Hong Kong. These large holders of U.S. currency do not want to see it devalued because it would lower the value of their invested assets.

Checkpoint

List three types of banks.

_____

_____

World Stars   ANNE MULCAHY

In the 1990s, Xerox Corporation was facing a number of crises. It faced strong price competition from international competitors. The total number of copier and printer products on the market drove prices down. Xerox copiers were not much different from a large number of its competitors' copiers. In addition, a number of Xerox's top managers were under indictment for accounting fraud.

To help turn the company around, Xerox turned to Anne Mulcahy. Mulcahy began her career with Xerox in 1976 as a sales representative. Mulcahy gained international experience as Vice President for Customer Operations for South and Central America, Europe, Asia, Africa, and China. She then took a lead role as Vice President for Human Relations. In 2001, Xerox appointed Mulcahy as CEO. Her first steps were to cut costs so the price floor could be lowered. She cut the workforce from 79,000 to 58,000. At the same time, she worked hard to be sure key personnel did not leave the company. She also brought in new products to move away from competing on price. Since Mulcahy became CEO, Xerox's stock price has gone up 65 percent.

THINK CRITICALLY

Explain the crises that Xerox was facing. Identify the factors that would have made Mulcahy a good choice for CEO. Explain why international experience would be a benefit to Mulcahy's career.

Understand Marketing Concepts

Circle the best answer for each of the following questions.

1. A measurement of the inflows and outflows of international transactions is called
   a. current account
   b. deficit
   c. balance of payments
   d. financial accounts

2. Which of the following is an independent bank established by governments to finance or insure foreign purchases of a country's products?
   a. commercial bank
   b. federal bank
   c. central bank
   d. export-import bank

Think Critically

Answer the following questions as completely as possible. If necessary, use a separate sheet of paper.

3. Describe each component of the balance of payments. Recommend how your country could improve its BOP.

_____

_____

_____

_____

_____

_____

_____

4. **Research** Visit the web site for the Export-Import Bank of the United States. Identify at least two examples of how it has helped companies export. (*Hint:* Try www.exim.gov.)

_____

_____

_____

_____

_____

_____

Chapter 10 Assessment

Review Marketing Concepts

Write the letter of the term that matches each definition. Some terms will not be used.

_____ 1. A currency that has the confidence of international traders

_____ 2. The quantity of a good or service that consumers are willing and able to buy at a given price

_____ 3. A strategy where a company sets a high price throughout the life of a product

_____ 4. A bank responsible for a country's monetary policy

_____ 5. The maximum price that can be charged in a market

_____ 6. A strategy where a company sets a low price compared to competitors to capture market share

_____ 7. The lowest price that a company can charge and still cover costs

_____ 8. The increase in overall prices in an economy

_____ 9. A temporary strategy where a company is able to set a price at a high level for a short period of time

_____ 10. The quantity that producers are willing to offer at a given price

_____ 11. A financial document issued by a bank guaranteeing payment

_____ 12. The ratio of how much one currency is worth in terms of another currency

a. balance of payments
b. central bank
c. demand
d. elasticity of demand
e. exchange rate
f. export-import banks
g. hard currency
h. inflation
i. letter of credit
j. market pricing
k. money
l. penetration pricing
m. prestige pricing
n. price
o. price ceiling
p. price floor
q. skim pricing
r. soft currency
s. supply

Circle the best answer.

13. Which of the following currencies are most likely to float?
    a. legal currencies
    b. soft currencies
    c. hard currencies
    d. international currencies

14. When a company sets a price based on the competitive advantages of its product, it is using a _____ strategy.
    a. penetration
    b. skimming
    c. market pricing
    d. prestige pricing

Think Critically

15. Identify three products. Specify whether they have inelastic or elastic demand curves. Explain your answer.

_____

_____

_____

_____

_____

_____

16. Draw a graph to illustrate how prices and quantities sold would change when supply and demand curves shift.

_____

_____

_____

_____

_____

_____

17. Refer to the BOP financial statement on p. 246. Specify how both the current account and the total BOP could be made positive.

_____

_____

_____

_____

_____

_____

18. Assume Europe has stated that it wants to lower the value of the euro. Explain why it would make this choice. How could it lower the exchange rate?

_____

_____

_____

_____

_____

_____

_____

19. **Research** Using the Internet, research the exchange rates for four international currencies. Specify how many U.S. dollars it would take to purchase 100 units of each currency.

_____

_____

_____

_____

_____

_____

_____

20. **Problem Solving** Describe how government strategies could affect both the supply of currency and the demand for currency in an economy. Indicate how this would affect exchange rates.

_____

_____

_____

_____

_____

_____

_____

21. **Marketing Math** Your company has signed a contract to purchase a company in Europe for $1,000,000 one year from now. Assume the spot exchange rate for the euro is $1.27 to €1. You have checked the one-year future rate. It shows €0.81 to $1. Should your company obtain euros now or purchase the future (forward) contract? Explain your answer.

_____

_____

_____

_____

_____

_____

_____

_____

22. **Communication** Assume your boss has asked you to create a strategy to ensure that your company is paid for its export products. Write a memo outlining how ex-im banks and letters of credit will aid in this process.

_____

_____

_____

_____

_____

_____

_____

_____

PUT MARKETING ON THE MAP

International Marketing Plan Project

Your international marketing plan must develop a pricing strategy. This strategy must also ensure that payments will be received.

Work with a group and complete the following activities.

1. Specify the countries you have targeted where you will sell your products. Identify whether they have hard or soft currencies. If they have hard currencies, specify the exchange rates. If they have soft currencies, specify how you will move profits out of the country.

2. List the four factors that can affect exchange rates. Identify how each of these factors will impact the countries you are targeting. Speculate how these factors will affect future exchange rates. Use the Internet to look at future contracts for these currencies.

3. Determine if your products have elastic or inelastic demand curves. Develop a strategy that will allow you to raise your price.

4. Specify a pricing strategy for your product or service. Indicate how this supports your overall company goals and the marketing mix.

5. List the global pricing strategy factors that could affect your price. Indicate how these pricing factors can be addressed to allow you to reach your company's goals.

6. Specify how you will use banks to help sell your products. Indicate how you plan to use letters of credit.

Case Study

THE CHECK IS IN THE MAIL

Business transactions between companies can be challenging. Producers or manufacturers sell products and services to retailers with the expectation of payment. Methods of payment may include cash, check, credit, money orders, and other arrangements. Individuals involved in business transactions soon learn that some trade partners are more dependable than others. Excuses for not sending payments in a timely fashion can become extremely frustrating. Once a producer or manufacturer establishes a positive long-term relationship with a retailer, the producer is more likely to offer flexible payment plans.

Although there is a risk involved when conducting business with another company, that risk is magnified when conducting international business. International business transactions will probably involve more than one currency, so close attention must be given to the latest currency exchange rates. Businesses shipping products overseas want to be guaranteed that they will receive payment. A letter of credit from the international business partner's bank guarantees that the producer will receive the money it is owed.

Individuals participating in international business transactions should establish a close relationship with international bankers who understand trade laws and currency exchange rates. Insurance also can be purchased to cover losses suffered when international transactions go bad.

Pricing merchandise for international markets is affected by more than the cost of manufacturing a product. Modifications to meet cultural and legal expectations will cause the cost of merchandise to rise. Tariffs and other export fees also contribute to the increasing price of imports. Preparing export documentation costs money. Those fees will be included in the selling price of the products shipped abroad.

Collecting payments from customers within your own country sometimes can be difficult. The challenge greatly intensifies when conducting international business. International business transactions give a whole new meaning to "the check is in the mail."

THINK CRITICALLY

1. Why does a business involved in international trade need special banking services?
2. Why is it even more important to check the credit standing of an international customer?
3. How will cash flow for an international business be different from cash flow for a domestic business?
4. What influences the price charged for popular imported products such as cars?

FINANCIAL ANALYSIS MANAGEMENT TEAM DECISION-MAKING EVENT

For this event, participants will analyze activities at banks and other financial institutions and then recommend ways to improve the marketing and management functions.

Each team must be composed of two members. Each team member will be given an exam that tests knowledge of e-commerce. Teams also will be given a decision-making case study involving a management problem.

The team will have 30 minutes to organize its analysis using a management decision-making format. During preparation, team members may consult only with one another. They may use notes taken during preparation for the presentation. Teams will have ten minutes to present their strategy to the judge. Judges will have five minutes to ask questions.

American Bank just located in your community. Two or three competing banks are located nearby. Most of the banks have focused their marketing on personalized customer service, low-fee banking, and better rates on loans and savings.

American Bank wants to emphasize its international banking services and attract customers involved in international trade. You must create an effective strategy to determine which businesses conduct international trade in your community and the most effective way to persuade those businesses to bank at American Bank. You must explain your marketing strategy and create effective advertising to attract customers from the business community. Make sure you describe special personalized services not offered by competitors.

Performance Indicators Evaluated

- Explain the importance of international banking.
- Understand the challenges faced by businesses conducting international trade.
- Describe a plan for increasing the number of bank customers.
- Communicate financial concepts effectively.
- Highlight international services offered by the bank.
- Display strong listening and team management skills.

Go to the DECA web site for more detailed information.

THINK CRITICALLY

1. Why should banks be involved in international business transactions?
2. List two services that businesses involved in international trade want from banks.
3. What promotional item could the bank offer that prospective international business customers would find useful?

www.deca.org

Strategic Planning for International Business

CHAPTER 11 · CHAPTER 11 · CHAPTER 11 · CHAPTER 11 · CHAPTER 11

11

11.1 **Developing Global Strategic Plans**

11.2 **International Market-Entry Strategies**

11.3 **Global Entrepreneurship**

© GETTY IMAGES/PHOTODISC

Point Your Browser

▶ ▶ ▶ ▶ **intlmarket.swlearning.com**

An International Mission

Colleges and universities around the world compete globally. They develop strategies to attract students from both local and international markets. Training students for careers is not the only mission of universities. Turning students into educated citizens is also part of their mission.

Most colleges and universities in the United States are accredited. The Council for Higher Education Accreditation (CHEA) or the United States Department of Education (USDE) authorizes accrediting organizations to evaluate the quality of colleges and universities. CHEA has required that colleges and universities develop strategies to attract students from both local and international markets.

Missouri Southern State University in Joplin, Missouri, has set a mission to foster the total education of each student with a strong commitment to international education. Missouri Southern's goals include educating students to understand world affairs, international issues, and other cultures as seen through these countries' history, geography, language, literature, philosophy, economics, and politics. These philosophies guide the development of programs and the design of classes. In pursuit of its mission, Missouri Southern organizes international travel opportunities for students and sets up international internships.

Missouri Southern has received national recognition for how well its strategy has fulfilled its international mission. Awards include the Andrew Heiskell Award for Innovation in International Education. The American Council on Education selected Missouri Southern as one of eight institutions in the United States that is a Promising Practices Model for Comprehensive Internationalization.

Think Critically

1. Explain why Missouri Southern would choose an international mission.

2. Describe the strategy that Missouri Southern is using to fulfill its mission.

Developing Global Strategic Plans

- Explain the role of strategic planning in international marketing.
- Discuss the strategic planning process.
- Describe the role of a strategic business unit.

- strategic planning
- tactical planning
- mission statement

- SWOT analysis
- strategic business unit

Going Global

In 1891, Frederik Philips and his son had a great idea. They decided to start a light bulb company with the goal of creating reliable light for everyone. For over a century, Royal Philips Electronics of the Netherlands has continued to produce technology products. Today, Philips is one of the world's largest electronic companies.

Philips has clearly expressed its mission. It wants to improve the quality of people's lives through the timely introduction of meaningful technological innovations. Its vision is to create technology solutions for healthcare, lifestyle, and enabling technology. Philips believes it can reach this goal by taking advantage of core competencies in key areas. It wants to build key partnerships with both customers and other businesses. It also wants to invest in world-class innovation.

Andrea Ragnetti joined Philips as chief marketing officer. Ragnetti has helped Philips develop a new brand positioning strategy based on three factors. First, products should be designed with the consumer in mind. Second, products should be easy to use. And third, products should be technologically advanced. This strategy fits Philips' mission.

Working with a partner, describe Philips' mission. Explain how Philips is fulfilling that mission through its strategies.

STRATEGIC PLANNING

MARKETING–INFORMATION MANAGEMENT

Businesses are complex entities. They consist of many individuals, departments, policies, and procedures. Individuals and departments within a business often have conflicting goals. Businesses engage in strategic planning to ensure that all factors within an organization are heading in the same direction. **Strategic planning** is the process of determining how to move to a desired future state. For businesses, strategic planning requires evaluating the environment, identifying long-term objectives, and developing the plans to reach those objectives.

Strategic planning typically takes a wide view while **tactical planning** is more narrowly focused and more short-term.

When done properly, strategic planning forces a business to analyze the whole organization and the environment in which it operates. Planning can help map the future and can develop a common understanding and agreement within an organization. It helps focus energy toward common goals. Strategic planning allows a business to respond better to problems and change direction in response to a changing environment.

International businesses operate in an environment that is more complex than a business operating within a single culture. Cultural differences can lead to conflicts inside an organization. An international company's size and physical distance between divisions adds to the complexity.

Approaches to Planning

Management must have a strategic view in order to allocate its resources. Developing an international marketing strategy allows a business to be *proactive,* or willing to take action before environmental pressure forces a strategy. Proactive international marketers realize that there are profits to be gained in global trade. They may have evaluated their products and found they have unique advantages for markets around the world. Many businesses find it important to gain economies of scale to be able to compete, especially when international competitors are ready to enter global markets.

A business also can have a *reactive* strategic approach when it is forced to react to environmental pressure. Many companies without an international focus find themselves facing competitive pressure from international companies. They are forced to conduct business internationally to maintain market share and customers. Companies also may find that they have excess inventories that they are unable to sell in their home market. They may be forced to look overseas for new market opportunities. Sometimes companies actually lose their home market. Perhaps new technology has replaced the need for their existing products, or other pressures have forced them to move existing product lines into new international markets. Foreign customers can also initiate change by placing orders, which opens up international business opportunities.

© GETTY IMAGES/PHOTODISC

List the two types of planning approaches.

Checkpoint

STRATEGIC PLANNING PROCESS

MARKETING–
INFORMATION
MANAGEMENT

Strategic planning helps a company lower risks. The strategic planning process considers those factors that allow a business plan to succeed as well as those that can keep a plan from succeeding. When businesses use strategic planning, they must balance opportunities and risk. There are two types of risks related to planning. There is risk involved in taking action, and there is risk involved in taking no action. Many businesses do not get involved in international marketing. This inaction can increase long-term risks, forcing a business to be reactive to global competitors. Strategic planning follows a six-step process:

1. Develop a mission statement
2. Conduct a situation analysis (SWOT analysis)
3. Develop alternative goals and strategies
4. Develop the strategic plan
5. Specify action plans
6. Evaluate and control the plans

Mission Statements

A **mission statement** defines the purpose of an organization. A mission statement provides direction, commits resources, inspires individuals, and focuses activities. Missouri Southern has a mission of fostering the total education of the student. Philips Electronics set its original goal as creating reliable light for everyone. Mission statements guide the development of a company's strategy. Once a company has developed a mission statement, it develops *vision statements,* which are more specific in terms of setting objectives and time frames.

SWOT Analysis

MARKETING–
INFORMATION
MANAGEMENT

A **SWOT analysis** is an environmental assessment of the strengths, weaknesses, opportunities, and threats that a business faces. A SWOT analysis provides the information necessary for developing strategic plans. Most strategic planners use *environmental scanning* to assess changes in the business environment. Environmental scanning involves collecting information from a variety of sources to aid in the analysis process. The analysis of strengths and weaknesses has an internal focus. Evaluating opportunities and threats has an external focus.

Marketing Myths

A number of business fads have come and gone. A study in the *Harvard Business Review* evaluated the use of 200 different management practices. The study's findings showed that it did not matter which management practice companies used. The most important thing was that the companies executed the practice perfectly.

Researchers have noted that the largest barrier to executing practices perfectly is the lack of strategic planning. Many managers assume that the future will be like the past, and they develop plans accordingly. Business researchers have found that the most successful companies are headed by bosses that set high standards and hire managers who understand and are willing to follow the company's mission.

THINK CRITICALLY

1. Explain why executing a strategy perfectly is more important than the strategy itself.
2. Describe how a business can execute a strategy well.

- **Strengths** A core part of the strength of an international business comes from its competitive advantages. But there are other areas of strength. A business's entire value chain can add strength. The value chain can include such things as how the business produces and distributes products or how it provides customer service. A business can also gain strength by working with strong international partners. A business's strengths allow it to be proactive when pursuing opportunities.

- **Weaknesses** Weaknesses are typically the result of changing environmental factors. These weaknesses can result in a shift in market power. For example, a business that may have been able to compete in its home market may suddenly find itself competing against larger, more powerful businesses. Many small retailers in the United States found themselves in competitively weak positions when Wal-Mart entered into their markets. Many manufacturers around the world found themselves in competitively weak positions when Chinese firms started competing in their markets.

- **Opportunitites** Opportunities are areas that businesses decide to pursue. Businesses find opportunities through environmental scanning. Once an opportunity is spotted, a business must carefully develop plans to determine whether the opportunity can be profitable. Currently, many international businesses are evaluating fast-growing markets to determine if they can find opportunities in India, China, Mexico, and many other countries.

- **Threats** Most threats come from the external environment, including competitors and other social forces. In many global markets, changes in government can create threats. These threats could be due to government instability or shifting government alliances. For example, the political actions of a country can have a negative country-of-origin effect, reducing sales for all products from that country. Changing social factors and social pressures within a country can create very strong threats, such as a demand for changes in products.

Plan Development

Once the business has developed its mission and conducted a SWOT analysis, it must develop a set of alternative goals and strategies. Focusing on just one alternative can increase risks. Creating the strategic plan requires the business to set specific action plans. The action plans should designate who is responsible for specific actions. They also should set due dates and establish criteria to be met. Assigning responsibility and deadlines helps to ensure that the plan is actionable and will be followed. Finally, the plan needs to be evaluated and controlled to monitor its progress.

List the six steps of the strategic planning process.

Checkpoint

STRATEGIC BUSINESS UNITS

MARKETING-INFORMATION MANAGEMENT

A **strategic business unit (SBU)** is the smallest unit around which a business develops a strategy. Each SBU must follow the six steps of the strategic planning process. The SBU's mission should fit within the parent organization's mission. Each SBU should conduct its own environmental scanning to identify factors that will influence its strategy. Parent companies often control the larger strategic planning process and allow the SBU to control the smaller tactical planning process.

An international parent company must determine how to structure its SBUs. Businesses without an international presence may design SBUs based on product lines or target markets. At one time, Procter & Gamble designed its strategies around product line SBUs. Internationally focused companies may design SBUs based on global markets. For example, a company could have a European division, North American division, and Asian division. SBUs also could be country-specific.

Evaluating Alternatives

Parent companies and SBUs often face a number of alternative strategies. The strategies may involve pursuing a variety of products or alternative markets. Other alternative strategies could involve products or markets the company might want to abandon. In 2005, General Motors announced that it would close 12 plants and lay off 30,000 employees. GM was forced to apply this cost-cutting strategy to maintain its competitiveness in the face of global pressure.

Each alternative must be evaluated by looking at the advantages and disadvantages. GM evaluated a number of alternatives before it settled on its strategy. Cisco, a large U.S. networking company, has spotted opportunity in India. It looked at the advantages and disadvantages of the environment both in China and India. India has an unregulated economy while China's economy is centrally planned. India has a large human capital base for software engineering while China favors its home software industry. In India, there is high product potential while in China, intellectual property is not well protected. India also offers a less competitive industry for Cisco.

Once a company decides on a strategy, it should assign responsibility, measurable goals, and a timeline. Without these three criteria, it is difficult to move strategies to action.

Checkpoint

Describe the role of a strategic business unit.

_____

_____

_____

Understand Marketing Concepts

Circle the best answer for each of the following questions.

1. A _____ statement defines the purpose of an organization.
   a. vision
   b. mission
   c. strategy
   d. positioning

2. Which of the following is *not* part of a SWOT analysis?
   a. strategy
   b. weaknesses
   c. opportunities
   d. threats

Think Critically

Answer the following questions as completely as possible. If necessary, use a separate sheet of paper.

3. Describe the difference between strategic planning and tactical planning.

_____

_____

_____

_____

_____

_____

_____

_____

4. Make a list of information sources that an international business can use for environmental scanning. List the advantages and disadvantages of each source.

_____

_____

_____

_____

_____

_____

_____

_____

International Market-Entry Strategies

Terms | Goals

- Explain the concept of environment-strategy fit.
- Describe different international entry strategies.

- placid environment
- turbulent environment
- macroenvironment

- environmental shocks
- joint venture

- foreign direct investment
- wholly-owned subsidiary

Going Global

With over 20,000 pharmaceutical firms, the country of India is a highly competitive drug market. Most of these businesses produce low-priced copycat drugs based on expired patents. This practice allows these businesses to sell drugs in India and other less-developed countries. Before Indian firms can capture part of the world's $40 billion market for generic drugs, they have some competitive disadvantages to overcome. One disadvantage is that "made in India" is not viewed as high quality. To sell in the United States, Indian firms must have FDA approval. Indian companies also must develop distribution networks.

One Indian entrepreneur, Dr. Kallam Anji Reddy, is looking to developed countries for opportunities. Dr. Reddy believes that Indian firms can develop new drugs. Indian firms are evaluating market-entry strategies for developed countries. Some Indian firms act as suppliers or revenue-sharing partners to American companies. One of Dr. Reddy's companies, Cheminor, has formed a series of alliances with American generic drug firms. Wockhardt, another Indian firm, has formed a joint venture with a New Jersey-based laboratory to split profits evenly. The Indian firm Ranbaxy has used all of these strategies, and, in addition, it has bought an American company.

Working with a partner, describe the factors that would allow India to capture part of the generic drug market. Explain the strategies that Indian firms are using to enter new markets.

ENVIRONMENT-STRATEGY FIT

MARKETING – INFORMATION MANAGEMENT

One of the basic principles of strategy development is that there must be a fit between environmental conditions and a business's strategy. Managers often assume that the business will continue to operate as it has in the past. They assume there will be a **placid environment** where there is very little change. But most international businesses operate in a **turbulent environment** where environmental change often is rapid and unpredictable. Businesses operating in placid environments can develop strategic plans for longer time periods.

Businesses operating in turbulent environments must develop strategic plans for shorter time periods. For example, businesses in technology industries operate where there is rapid change in both products and competitors. High-technology industries have planning cycles of about 18 months.

Businesses operate in a **macroenvironment**, which includes environmental factors that influence the economy, governments, legal environment, technology, ecology, social cultural factors, and competition. Businesses can experience **environmental shocks**, which are rapid changes in the macroenvironment. The fall of the Iron Curtain and communism in Europe in the 1990s and the terrorist attacks on September 11, 2001 in the United States were environmental shocks. There are a number of factors that influence the strength of the current international environment. These factors include rapid changes in technology, competition, consumer demand, and political and legal environments.

Environmental Planning

Most companies around the world operate in a turbulent environment. This kind of environment forces companies and governments to extend their environmental scanning outside of the country and shorten the scope of their strategic planning. Governments can help to ensure stability by strengthening their resource base and relationships with other countries.

It is difficult to plan for every macroenvironmental change. When businesses or governments see trends or an increased chance of a threat, they should be proactive. In 2005, there were a number of threats to U.S. business, which called for plans of action. One was the threat of Asian bird flu. To be prepared for a widespread outbreak, it was suggested that businesses develop plans to pull employees from infected countries. Businesses needed to devise strategies in case a high percentage of workers became ill. For example, inventory levels might need to be increased in case foreign suppliers could not send products.

The U.S. National Association of Manufacturers released a report in 2005 stating that the United States had a serious shortage of qualified employees for manufacturing jobs. This shortage was affecting the ability of the United States to compete in the global economy. Modern manufacturing requires higher technical skills. Over 90 percent of U.S. manufacturers reported a moderate to severe shortage of qualified skilled production employees, such as machinists, operators, craft workers, distributors, and technicians. The report also found that there were not enough engineers and scientists to support manufacturing.

The United States government has set forth proposals to help ensure continued U.S. leadership in science and technology. Federal funds will be directed to the National Science Foundation to create regional "centers of excellence" for basic research. The U.S. goal is to graduate 100,000 new scientists, engineers, and mathematicians over four years. In 2005, President George W. Bush also went to China to attempt to help U.S. businesses. The Chinese government promised to purchase 70 Boeing 737 airplanes. China also promised to protect intellectual property and move to more market-based exchange rates.

Time Out

The U.S. Current Account tracks the flow of currency from trade. Its balance has changed since 1960 as follows (in millions):

1960: $2,854
1970: $2,330
1980: $2,317
1990: −$78,969
2000: −$413,443
2005: −$700,000

© DIGITAL VISION

Checkpoint

List seven factors that are included in the macroenvironment.

INTERNATIONAL ENTRY STRATEGIES

MARKETING–INFORMATION MANAGEMENT

Businesses can enter into international markets using a variety of strategies. The lowest level of commitment to international marketing is indirect exporting. The highest level of commitment is to use the company's resources and set up a wholly-owned subsidiary. Before a company pursues any strategy, it must carefully evaluate its missions, alternative strategies, and the environmental factors that create opportunities or pose threats.

Strategies businesses can pursue to enter international markets include:

- **Exporting** A business can enter international markets through both direct and indirect exporting. These approaches represent the lowest level of international commitment and pose the lowest risk. Exporting can create a market for a product in the importing country and provide additional profits to the business. However, by establishing a new market, local producers or other exporters may come to realize there is a potential for sales in the country. Also, if a business does not want to commit to having a local presence, it risks losing market share to companies that set up businesses to serve the local market.

- **Contracting** Contractual agreements enable a business to work with partners in foreign markets. Contractual agreements may involve manufacturing, sales, licensing, and franchising. Contractual agreements

Tech Zone

Who owns Internet assigned names and numbers? The Internet Corporation for Assigned Names and Numbers (ICANN) is a private-sector company that operates under a contract with the U.S. government. ICANN coordinates the Internet's domain-name system (such as .com and .org), national addresses (such as China's .cn), and routing numbers. Some countries believe this gives too much power to the United States and U.S. companies.

Some countries have proposed that the assigning of Internet names and numbers be controlled by the United Nations. The United States has argued that putting the Internet control system into a political environment could hinder the development of technology. However, the countries opposing U.S. control believe that a U.S. role could have the same effect. This argument reflects two different philosophies of how governments control business.

THINK CRITICALLY

Why do you think countries are concerned about who has control in assigning Internet names and numbers?

are a higher level of commitment. They create a presence for an international company in a foreign market by bringing in local partners who understand local market needs. By monitoring local environmental conditions, local partners can provide information that supports proactive planning.

- **Joint Venture** In a **joint venture,** two or more businesses create a new business to pursue a strategic goal. The parent businesses agree to share ownership, capital, and revenue of the new business. Like contract relationships, joint ventures can bring in local partners. But joint ventures increase risk because businesses commit resources and can be at the mercy of the local environment. Rupert Murdoch (owner of Fox Broadcasting Company) formed a joint venture between his News Corporation's Star TV and Chinese company Qinghai Satellite. Murdoch made statements about how broadcasting is a threat to one-party state governments. The Chinese government closed down the joint venture, accusing Star TV of illegally selling decoders to forbidden News Corporation channels.

- **Direct Investments** There are two types of direct investments. A **foreign direct investment (FDI)** is the purchase of assets in a foreign country by a business. Foreign direct investments could include the purchase of land, property, or ownership in a foreign company. The purchase of land in Kentucky by Japan for its Toyota manufacturing plant is an example of an FDI. The highest level of commitment is when an international business purchases a company as a **wholly-owned subsidiary,** which is an independent company owned by a parent company. The China National Offshore Oil Corporation attempted to purchase the U.S. company Unocal for $18.5 billion as a wholly-owned subsidiary. This proposal caused a large uproar in Washington, D.C. There was considerable criticism that a Chinese company would buy a U.S. company as large as Unocal. Eventually the Chinese company dropped its offer. Even though a wholly-owned subsidiary is owned by a parent company, it must still operate within the legal, political, and cultural environment of the host country.

The United States has received more foreign investment than it has invested. Foreign investment is seen as a positive evaluation of the U.S. economy. Foreigners invest because they believe in the U.S. economy.

Name four international market-entry strategies.

Checkpoint

Understand Marketing Concepts

Circle the best answer for each of the following questions.

1. An environment characterized by rapid and unpredictable change is called
   a. changeable
   b. turbulent
   c. placid
   d. hazardous

2. When two or more businesses create a new business to pursue a strategic goal, they have formed a(n)
   a. export company
   b. joint venture
   c. parent company
   d. wholly-owned subsidiary

Think Critically

Answer the following questions as completely as possible. If necessary, use a separate sheet of paper.

3. Describe the differences in environmental conditions between a turbulent environment and a placid environment. Identify how these differences affect planning.

_____

_____

_____

_____

_____

_____

4. Describe the advantages and disadvantages of each of the foreign market-entry strategies.

_____

_____

_____

_____

_____

_____

_____

Global Entrepreneurship

- Discuss the factors that encourage an entrepreneurial culture.
- Describe the strategies countries use to plan for their economies.

- entrepreneur
- business incubator
- five-year plans
- industrial policy
- deregulating

Going Global

Stephan Schambach is from Jena in the former East Germany. In 1994, after the fall of the Iron Curtain, he began writing software programs for local firms. His business evolved into Intershop, one of the world's top three software companies for online shopping. Today, the company is worth nearly more than $8 billion. Schambach is a legend in Europe where there are few modern-day examples of high-tech entrepreneurs.

In Europe, high-tech companies account for only 25 percent of the total value of the stock market. In the United States, high-tech companies account for around 30 percent. Europe does little to encourage entrepreneurship and builds too many barriers, including high financial risk. If entrepreneurs go bankrupt, they can be pursued for payment for up to 20 years. Labor contracts can be difficult to break. Once employees are hired, it can be difficult to fire them. There also is a weak link between universities and companies, making it difficult to get innovative ideas to market.

Working in small groups, discuss why entrepreneurs would have a harder time pursuing opportunities in Germany. Recommend a strategy that Germany could follow to allow for more entrepreneurial activity.

INTERNATIONAL ENTREPRENEURSHIP

An **entrepreneur** is someone who undertakes a new venture. Entrepreneurs are typically seen as individuals who are willing to take on the risk of starting a business. In fact, most entrepreneurs are good at spotting *windows of opportunity,* or areas of opportunity that others don't see. What others perceive as risky, entrepreneurs may perceive as a good opportunity. Entrepreneurs play an important role in developing new products, markets, and employment. In the United States, *small- and medium-sized enterprises (SME),* often defined as businesses with fewer than 250 employees, account for more than 99 percent of all employers. They employ more than half of all private-sector employees. They pay 44.5 percent of total U.S. private payroll and annually generate 60 to 80 percent of new jobs. They also create more than 50 percent of nonfarm,

Ethics Around the World

Did Russia adopt a market economy too quickly? In 1991, the Soviet Union collapsed into Russia and 15 independent republics. During this transition, Russia returned state ownership of companies to Russian citizens by issuing stock shares. Many Russian entrepreneurs were able to purchase this stock at very low prices. Russia's entire oil industry sold for $600 million. Russian citizens did not understand the value of their ownership of companies.

These new entrepreneurs were seen as oligarchs, or business magnates (wealthy people who influence the Russian state government). Dissatisfaction with the new free market system led to widespread anger from Russian citizens. In 2000, Vladimir Putin was elected president. Putin pulled back economic reform and political freedoms. Russia's current challenge is to find ways to grow its economy by encouraging SMEs. It will require Russia to develop a business climate that is supportive of entrepreneurs.

THINK CRITICALLY

1. Why do you think the oligarchs were able to obtain ownership of businesses?

2. Explain how Russia could encourage the development of entrepreneurship.

---

private gross domestic product (GDP). Statistics are similar in Europe. A number of factors affect the development of entrepreneurship.

- **Personal Property Ownership** The ability to own personal property is key for the development of entrepreneurship. While this may seem natural in the United States, before the 1990s, many communist countries did not permit the ownership of personal property. Personal property ownership allows entrepreneurs to keep the rewards of their ventures.

- **Investment Capital** Entrepreneurs must be able to obtain financial capital to support business development. Capital is likely to come from individual investors called *venture capitalists,* the sale of stock, and banks. Most U.S. banks see small businesses as their primary customers. In other parts of the world, banks may view small businesses as a higher risk, or they may have exclusive relationships with larger businesses.

- **Government Regulations** The development of small businesses is often hindered by government regulations. Compared to most other countries in the world, starting a business in the United States is relatively easy. Some countries impose high regulations or fees on small businesses. These regulations can affect the startup time as well as how the business is run. Regulations related to job protection are also tougher in other countries, making it difficult for entrepreneurs who have employees.

- **Entrepreneurial Culture** Countries can have an entrepreneurial culture. Individuals within these countries may view business startup and ownership as a primary means of reaching their personal goals. Countries with strong traditional cultures may not have an entrepreneurial culture. They may believe entrepreneurship does not provide social status, wealth, or security.

Supporting Business Development

Most countries consider innovation and entrepreneurship vital for economic development and GDP growth. Europe and Asia have supported the development of colleges and universities that specialize in entrepreneurship training. The United States has a number of programs to support small business development. The U.S. Small Business Administration (SBA) offers online and print support material for business startup and small business management. The SBA supports *Small Business Development Centers* (SBDC), which offer free consulting services for small businesses. The SBA also will guarantee small business loans. This lowers the risks for banks that make loans to support small businesses. The United States also supports exporting through U.S. Export Assistance Centers, which provide SMEs with export assistance.

Business Incubators

Many governments support business development through business incubators. A **business incubator** is usually a physical facility set up to offer office or factory space at a reduced price. Business incubators also offer staff support and consulting services. Businesses in incubators typically have one to two years to grow before they must move into their own facility.

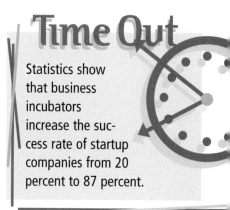

Statistics show that business incubators increase the success rate of startup companies from 20 percent to 87 percent.

List four factors that affect the development of entrepreneurship.

Checkpoint

PLANNING ECONOMIES

MARKETING– INFORMATION MANAGEMENT

One of the challenges of globalization is that it opens markets to international competition. Businesses are forced to become more efficient in order to compete. Governments are forced to create conditions that allow businesses to change in response to a changing environment. The dropping of trade barriers and lowering of tariffs has improved living standards for millions of people around the world. But this has created considerable turbulence in the economies of many countries. While some countries have called for more tariffs and trade barriers, most countries want to make their economies more competitive.

Countries can use three different strategies to plan for their economies. Countries may use a central planning strategy to develop long-term plans. Communist countries used to set **five-year plans,** which were defined plans with specific economic goals for the country. This type of planning did not work well because it was not flexible enough for changing conditions. Countries that follow free-market practices, such as the United States, do not develop long-term plans for the economy. Instead, they follow a free-market strategy that applies a general philosophy, such as "keep inflation low."

Between these two extremes is the concept of industrial policy. An **industrial policy** is a strategy that a country adopts to support competitiveness. China has set an industrial policy to become a manufacturing center for the world. India has set an industrial policy to become a world center for knowledge industries such as programming, services, and medicine. The United States has set industrial policies in the past. The U.S. government was instrumental in setting up the Radio Corporation of America (RCA) to gain dominance in radio technology. The U.S. government also fostered the development and growth of the Internet.

Deregulation

Most countries want to encourage innovation and growth but do not want to create turbulence in their economies. Many countries have moved toward deregulating parts of their economy. **Deregulating** removes government controls and restrictions on the way businesses operate. In the 1990s, many countries deregulated their telecommunication industries, which opened these industries to competition. The results were lower prices, more product alternatives, and more innovation.

Checkpoint

List three types of planning strategies that countries use to develop a competitive economy.

_____

_____

_____

World Stars ANGELA MERKEL

In November 2005, Angela Merkel became Germany's first female chancellor (head of state). Only 15 years earlier, she was a professor of physics in communist-controlled East Berlin. When the Berlin Wall fell, Merkel became spokesperson for the East German Christian Democratic Union (CDU). When Germany united, she became the environment minister. In 2002, she was chosen to be head of the CDU's parliamentary group.

Merkel has a gift for long-term thinking. She has proposed a long list of reform plans to help the German economy. She wants to simplify German taxes, change pension policies, reduce job protection, and weaken the trade unions. Merkel is looking to change Germany the way that Margaret Thatcher changed Great Britain in the 1980s. She wants to move Germany from a labor-friendly country to a business-friendly country.

Merkel's job involves holding together a coalition of parties and enacting an agenda for change. She began her chancellorship by presenting a mission statement for her government. Merkel intends to clearly communicate the steps necessary to reform the German economy. She sees this as the first step in getting the government to focus on the country's problems.

THINK CRITICALLY

Explain the problems that Germany is facing. Explain the strategy that Merkel is following to move Germany toward reform.

Understand Marketing Concepts

Circle the best answer for each of the following questions.

1. Someone who undertakes a new venture is called a(n)
   a. adventurer
   b. venture seeker
   c. entrepreneur
   d. industrialist

2. A strategy that a country adopts to support competitiveness is called a(n)
   a. five-year plan
   b. industrial policy
   c. free-market strategy
   d. deregulated strategy

Think Critically

Answer the following questions as completely as possible. If necessary, use a separate sheet of paper.

3. Describe the role that an entrepreneur plays in an economy.

_____

_____

_____

_____

_____

_____

_____

_____

_____

4. Explain the advantages and disadvantages of each of the three strategies that countries use to plan for their economies.

_____

_____

_____

_____

_____

_____

_____

_____

Review Marketing Concepts

Write the letter of the term that matches each definition. Some terms will not be used.

_____ 1. A physical facility set up to offer office or factory space at a reduced price

_____ 2. An environment where there is very little change

_____ 3. Rapid changes in the macroenvironment

_____ 4. An independent company owned by a parent company

_____ 5. The purchase of assets in a foreign country by a business

_____ 6. Environmental factors that influence the economy, governments, legal environment, technology, ecology, social culture, and competition

_____ 7. Process of determining how to move to a desired future state

_____ 8. Defined plans with specific economic goals for a country

_____ 9. Removing government controls and restrictions on the way businesses operate

_____ 10. Smallest unit around which a business develops a strategy

_____ 11. An environmental assessment of the strengths, weaknesses, opportunities, and threats that a business faces

_____ 12. Defines the purpose of an organization

a. business incubator
b. deregulating
c. entrepreneur
d. environmental shocks
e. five-year plans
f. foreign direct investment
g. industrial policy
h. joint venture
i. macroenvironment
j. mission statement
k. placid environment
l. strategic business unit (SBU)
m. strategic planning
n. SWOT analysis
o. tactical planning
p. turbulent environment
q. wholly-owned subsidiary

Circle the best answer.

13. The highest level of commitment to international marketing for a business is to set up a
    a. strategic business unit
    b. joint venture
    c. foreign direct investment
    d. wholly-owned subsidiary

14. Planning that is more narrowly focused and more short-term is called
    a. strategic planning
    b. proactive planning
    c. tactical planning
    d. reactive planning

Think Critically

15. Make a list of the reasons why planning for an international business is more complex than planning for a business that operates in just one culture.

_____

_____

_____

_____

_____

_____

16. Identify at least three factors that could result in environmental shocks. Specify the type of business planning that would be needed to minimize the effect of these shocks.

_____

_____

_____

_____

_____

_____

17. Make a list of the factors that affect entrepreneurship. Specify how the United States has advantages in these areas. Explain what other countries would need to do to aid in new venture creation.

_____

_____

_____

_____

_____

_____

18. Visit the Small Business Administration's (SBA) web site. Outline how the SBA supports the development and growth of SMEs.

_____

_____

_____

_____

_____

_____

Make Connections

19. **Communication** Develop a presentation outlining the differences between proactive and reactive planning. Specify the advantages and disadvantages of each approach.

_____

_____

_____

_____

_____

_____

20. **Problem Solving** Choose a large international business. Go to its web site and locate its mission statement. Make a list of goals the company might set to accomplish its mission.

_____

_____

_____

_____

_____

_____

_____

21. **Marketing Math** Your company has evaluated two alternative international opportunities. Each alternative has a risk profile. Which alternative should be pursued?

Alternative A has a 90 percent chance of revenue totaling $1.5 million. Costs would be $1 million.

Alternative B has a 75 percent chance of revenue totaling $2 million. Costs would be $1.25 million.

_____

_____

_____

_____

_____

_____

_____

22. Research Choose a product. Use the Internet to identify two countries where this product could be sold. Outline the advantages and disadvantages of selling the product in each country. Then explain which country represents the best marketing opportunity.

_____

_____

_____

_____

_____

_____

_____

_____

_____

_____

_____

PUT MARKETING ON THE MAP

International Marketing Plan Project

Your international marketing plan must include a strategic plan, starting with a mission statement. As you build your plan, you must evaluate and justify your strategic choices.

Work with a group and complete the following activities.

1. Develop a mission statement and vision statements for your business. Explain how this mission statement will guide your strategic planning process.

2. Conduct a SWOT analysis for your business. Evaluate this list and develop a plan for taking advantage of strengths and opportunities and how to deal with weaknesses and threats. Explain whether your competitive environment is turbulent or placid.

3. Evaluate each product alternative and country alternative you have previously proposed. Specify the advantages and disadvantages of each alternative.

4. Evaluate each of the alternative market-entry strategies. Outline the advantages and disadvantages of each of these strategies for your business. Make and justify a market-entry recommendation.

5. Consider what long-term threats your business will face. Identify any industrial policies your country should adopt that will help ensure the long-term survival of your business.

PIRACY AND COUNTERFEIT GOODS

The growth of pirated and counterfeit goods threatens America's economy. Bogus products throughout the world include CDs, DVDs, watches, software, processed foods, automobile parts, pharmaceuticals, and other consumer products. Counterfeit goods account for up to seven percent of global trade and cost honest businesses around the world billions of dollars each year. Consumers ultimately become the victims of counterfeit goods, especially in the case of pharmaceuticals that do not meet government standards.

Operation Bullpen has recovered $15 million of counterfeit autographed sports and entertainment merchandise and has successfully brought forth 15 court indictments. Strategy Targeting Organized Piracy (STOP!) is an initiative to end criminal networks that distribute fake merchandise and stop trade of pirated and counterfeit goods at America's borders. It also blocks bogus goods around the world and helps small businesses enforce their rights in overseas markets.

The United States has established a hotline (1-866-HALT) to help businesses protect their intellectual property at home and abroad. It provides information to businesses on how to use government resources to protect their trademarks, patents, and copyrights overseas.

Tighter restrictions at the U.S. border will help stop counterfeit and pirated goods. The Bureau of Customs and Border Protection (CBP) has implemented new procedures and risk assessments to better identify businesses that routinely traffic counterfeit goods.

The stakes for international pirates and counterfeiters have risen with the publication of the names of overseas firms that produce and trade fake products in the United States. Companies can rely on the Lanham Act, which allows them to conduct private seizures of fakes when accompanied by federal marshals armed with seizure orders and injunction notices.

International trading partners must work together to eliminate the sale of counterfeit goods. Law enforcement must be aggressive in stopping illegal activities that result in lost sales for authentic producers of goods.

THINK CRITICALLY

1. Why have piracy and counterfeit goods become so popular with international trade?
2. What artistic works are frequently copied illegally and sold to the public? Who loses when these transactions occur?
3. Why is the pharmaceutical industry a prime target for fake goods and piracy?
4. Why should the government pay special attention to international transactions that take place online?

RESTAURANT AND FOOD SERVICE MANAGEMENT EVENT

The Restaurant and Food Service Management Event consists of two major parts: a written comprehensive exam and a role-playing event. Participants are given a written scenario to review and present to the judge. Participants must develop a professional approach to solving the problem. During the presentation, participants may use notes made during the preparation time, but no note cards may be used.

The students are allowed ten minutes to present their plan of action to the judges. The judges have five additional minutes to ask questions about the proposal.

A major restaurant located in a Chinese business district of a large U.S. city relies heavily on customers from the business community and surrounding neighborhoods. The restaurant takes great pride in the authenticity of its food, but it needs tips on improving customer service. During the busy lunch hour, customers may have to wait 50 minutes to be seated even though the host has told them that the wait is only 10 minutes.

Some customers overlook the long waits due to the high-quality food and fair prices. Other customers are not as forgiving when they have to spend their entire lunchtime waiting to be seated.

Another issue for the restaurant is limited parking spaces for customers. Upon leaving the restaurant, some customers find that their cars have been towed.

You have been hired by the restaurant to develop ideas for better customer service. Your plan should serve the largest number of customers by providing high-quality food with no hassles.

Performance Indicators Evaluated

- Understand the importance of quality products and service.
- Define the problems and offer relevant solutions.
- Demonstrate critical thinking and problem-solving skills.
- Prioritize customer expectations and design strategies to meet their desires.
- Communicate a plan to assure repeat customers.

Go to the DECA web site for more detailed information.

THINK CRITICALLY

1. What does this restaurant do effectively? What are the areas of concern?
2. How is the marketing concept of location relevant?
3. Give at least one solution to each of the customer service problems listed in this case.
4. Why is it important for the restaurant to understand the U.S. business culture?

www.deca.org

International Marketing Management and Careers

CHAPTER 12

© GETTY IMAGES/PHOTODISC

Point Your Browser

▶ ▶ ▶ ▶ intlmarket.swlearning.com

As GM Goes, So Goes the Nation

More than 100 years ago, the automotive industry consisted of a number of small startup companies. Three of these companies were Olds Motor Vehicle Co. (formed in 1897), Cadillac Automobile Co. (formed in 1902), and Buick Motor Co. (formed in 1903). In 1908, Buick incorporated as the General Motors Company (GM). It was quickly joined by Oldsmobile and Cadillac. In 1909, GM purchased the Pontiac car line. This new corporation was built around divisional lines in a time period when management was strong and labor was weak.

In 1943, a young scholar named Peter Drucker studied GM and wrote a groundbreaking book on management called *Concept of the Corporation*. GM ignored Drucker's advice on decentralized management, which would have moved the responsibility for decision making down to those people closer to the source of the problem. GM was the world's largest car manufacturer. It believed that it could continue operating as it had in the past. By 2005, GM was in a different world. In the face of global competition, GM had to close or cut production at 12 U.S. plants and cut 30,000 jobs. Most of these jobs had to come from retiring union laborers who wanted additional incentives to retire.

But GM does have some bright spots. GM's European and Brazilian operations are recovering. GM's South Korea division, Daewoo, is doing well. GM's Chinese operations are growing rapidly, with the Buick brand projected to sell more cars in Asia than in the United States.

GM has structured itself for global expansion. Under GM's chairman, there are a number of global leaders, including a Global Manufacturing and Labor Relations Chairman, a GM Europe President, and a President of GM Asia Pacific & GM Latin America.

Think Critically

1. Explain why GM has faced decline in the United States and may have more opportunities in foreign countries.

2. Explain why GM now has international executive positions.

International Marketing Management

Goals

- Explain how management styles relate to cultures.
- Describe the relationship of labor and management across cultures.
- Discuss the role of organizational culture.

Terms

- autocratic managers
- participative managers
- labor mobility
- labor union
- organizational culture
- bureaucratic culture

Going Global

China has a long history of conducting business. Throughout its history, the Chinese were traders, manufacturers, exporters, and importers. A series of trails and sea routes called the Silk Road linked China to markets in the West for thousands of years. China was in turmoil after World War II. Chinese communists took over the mainland in 1949 by forcing its leader Chiang Kai-shek to flee to Taiwan. The Chinese economy did not do well under Mao Tse-tung's communist government. In the early 1960s, Mao was forced from power. In 1966, he regained control by motivating young people between the ages of 15 and 25 to engage in a Cultural Revolution. Jonathan Chu is an ordinary Chinese citizen who was part of the Cultural Revolution generation. Chu's father was banished to a remote area in China for harboring "Rightist" thoughts. Chu's grandfather had been a powerful rice merchant from Shanghai. He spent 24 years in prison because he was in a photo with Chiang Kai-shek.

Mao eventually lost control, but China lost a generation of educated and trained managers. Individuals like Jonathan Chu are referred to as the "lost generation." This generation now must work in a free market Chinese economy with no management training or experience. Many Chinese businesses have a Communist Party member who has veto control of management practices. These individuals have no management training and are likely to have political goals instead of management goals.

Working with a partner, explain why China's loss of a generation of managers has delayed China's progress. Explain how Communist Party members could hinder China's business development.

INTERNATIONAL MANAGEMENT

MARKETING-INFORMATION MANAGEMENT

Management is a science. Companies study the process of management in order to maximize the chances that organizations will operate effectively. Managers perform four functions—planning, leading, organizing, and controlling. Managers of international businesses face the challenge of planning, organizing, leading, and controlling across national, cultural, and legal borders.

Prior to the 1980s, many international businesses from developed countries staffed their foreign offices with *expatriates,* usually managers from the business's home country. The general belief was that there was not enough trained management talent in developing countries. Perhaps a larger part of the problem was that many businesses tried to manage in foreign markets the same way they managed in their home country. They did not consider the historical and cultural differences in these new markets that would require a change in management style.

Management Styles

There needs to be a fit between the competitive environment and a business's strategy. There also needs to be a fit between a business's strategy and the management style, the organizational culture, and the business's employees. Management styles range from autocratic to participative. **Autocratic managers** make decisions with little or no input from employees. **Participative managers** work with employees to set goals and give employees freedom in deciding how to reach goals.

Managers may have a preferred personal style of management. This preferred style can come from a manager's cultural background or experience. Effective managers will use a management style that best fits the situation. For example, most younger employees in the United States prefer to work under participative managers. Geert Hofstede, an expert on interactions between cultures, developed measures of cultural differences that can provide insight into preferred manager-and-employee interactions within various cultures.

- **Power/Distance**   There is a large amount of inequity between superiors and subordinates in high power/distance cultures. Mexico, India, and Arab countries are high in power/distance. Management in these cultures is likely to be more autocratic. In low power/distance countries, such as the United States, Germany, the Netherlands, and Great Britain, there is less distance between superiors and subordinates. Management in these cultures is likely to be more participative.

- **Individualism/Collectivism**   The concept of "I" versus "we" is evident in individualism/collectivism cultures. Collectivist countries include China, Japan, and countries in West Africa and South America. Businesses in these cultures may include employees in some decision making. Japanese management style often is seen as bottom up. Consensus is gained from workers at the bottom of an organization before actions are taken. In high individualistic countries, such as the United States, the Netherlands, and Great Britain, workers believe that they can take care of themselves. They prefer not to work for an authoritarian manager.

- **Uncertainty Avoidance**   Another management style seen in various cultures is uncertainty avoidance, which refers to the level of threat people feel from uncertainty. Countries with high uncertainty avoidance include Japan, Greece, and France. These cultures are likely to have management processes that are less adaptable to change. This resistance to change has led to problems for Japanese and French firms. They have not always been

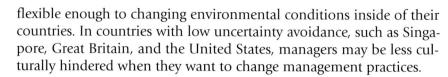
flexible enough to changing environmental conditions inside of their countries. In countries with low uncertainty avoidance, such as Singapore, Great Britain, and the United States, managers may be less culturally hindered when they want to change management practices.

- **Masculinity**   The value a culture places on success versus caring for others and quality of life is referred to as the masculinity element of a culture. Japan scores high in masculinity. Achievement on the job is very important to Japanese workers. The Netherlands has a low masculinity rating. Individual achievement by managers and employees may be less important than maintaining a quality of life.

It can be very difficult for managers to cross cultural lines. Japanese employees often see their identity tied to their company. This identity has led to the term *company man.* Japanese employees value the company's rules and practices and lifetime employment (uncertainty avoidance). Japanese workers look for internal promotion and have loyalty to the company (high collectivism). They also have many layers of management, highly structured organizations, patriarchal societies governed by men, and paternalism (high power/distance).

Checkpoint

List and define the two management styles.

_____

_____

_____

LABOR RELATIONSHIPS

MARKETING– INFORMATION MANAGEMENT

Relationships between management and labor vary considerably around the world. Differences are related to the power of labor and its legal rights. In countries with few labor rights, employees can be fired at will. If employees are injured on a job, they may have few legal options. But some countries have very strong labor rights. France has enacted a number of laws that are designed to protect workers. Once a worker is hired in France, the employer must prove to the government that the employee should be fired. After the employee is fired, the employer must pay unemployment for months. Other benefits can go on for years. These laws result in very little incentive for French firms to hire employees. In addition, once individuals are hired in France, they may not want to leave their jobs because they fear not finding another job. Unemployment rates in France are close to ten percent. Young people often will leave France to find employment elsewhere.

Labor Mobility

The United States has a factor-of-product advantage in labor. This advantage comes not only from the high quality of U.S. labor but also from labor flexibility and labor mobility. **Labor mobility** refers to the ability of workers to pursue jobs that make the best use of their skills. A U.S. employee can lose a job, get retrained, and move anywhere in the country to seek new employment.

The flexibility of U.S. labor is considered to be one of the United States' factor-of-production advantages. When employees can easily move to maximize their income, they are likely to retrain for better jobs and maximize their skills. Many countries and regions do not have labor mobility. Even though it is legal for labor to move across borders in Europe, language differences and regional preferences often lock workers into local areas, even within their own country.

Trade and Labor Unions

The relationships between management and labor have changed over the last century. In the beginning of the 1900s, labor had little power over management. In the early part of the last century, there were a number of labor strikes around the world. Some were violent. The labor movement led to the development of labor unions around the world. A **labor union** is an organization that has the legal right to represent workers in negotiation with management.

Labor unions peaked in the United States in the 1950s with about 36 percent of the workforce in unions. Since that time, the number of workers in labor unions in the United States has dropped to about 13 percent. The situation is different in many other countries. Labor unions in many developed countries have much more power than in the United States. Political parties in England, Ireland, Australia, and Israel are called Labor Parties because of their strong ties to labor concerns. Labor unions have the highest representation in Scandinavian countries. Unions in these countries represent workers across the entire country.

Labor unions and management may have close or hostile relationships. Labor unions in Germany are strong. They negotiate with management and often have a seat on the company's board of directors. Unions and management in Japan work very closely together to reach goals.

Marketing Myths

There is no perfect management design. For many decades, management was seen as a process of developing the "perfect" design, incentives, and assessment method. It was believed that once this process was developed, individuals would fit themselves into this management design.

In 2002, Daniel Kahneman received a Nobel Prize in Economics for integrating psychological research into economic science. His work focused on how human judgment and decisions are made under uncertain conditions. In today's competitive environment, understanding people is more important than a "perfect" management design.

THINK CRITICALLY

1. Explain why companies would think that there could be a "perfect" design.
2. Explain why understanding how people make decisions would be more important than management design.

Define labor mobility.

Checkpoint

ORGANIZATIONAL CULTURE

MARKETING-INFORMATION MANAGEMENT

Businesses develop their own cultures. **Organizational culture** is defined as a shared basic assumption about how a business should operate internally and interact with customers externally. Organizational cultures often reflect a business's larger social culture and the management style of the business's leaders.

There are a number of different corporate cultures with differing philosophies relating to employee motivation, management and employee relationships, communication flows, and management control. Two extremes of organizational culture are bureaucratic and participative. A **bureaucratic culture** would be characterized as having a strong set of rules and regulations for the way a business operates. Individual roles would be highly structured. Communication would flow strictly along predetermined lines. A *participative culture* would have more open flows of communication and fewer formal rules and regulations. Studies have shown that U.S. corporate cultures have a tendency to be more participative. Many other countries have cultures that are more bureaucratic.

For a business to be successful, its organizational culture must fit the competitive environment. Businesses that are in the same industry often will have the same cultures. For example, businesses operating in high-tech industries typically have young, well-educated workers. These workers are in high demand and can move easily from business to business. The industry is highly competitive and fast-paced. Decisions must be made quickly, often with the support of the workers who must implement the decisions. Organizational cultures in high-tech industries are more likely to have a participative culture even across national borders.

Leadership Style

International businesses must have global leaders. These leaders must have the ability to work and interact with individuals from multiple cultural backgrounds. They have to be able to communicate internationally. Ideally they should know at least one other language. They must be able to operate comfortably in a foreign cultural setting. Global leaders must be capable of managing across cultures. They also need to understand how to motivate individuals from a variety of cultures in order to achieve the organization's goals.

One of the hardest tasks for a global business leader is to take over a business with a pre-existing organizational culture. For example, a U.S. manager could be put in charge of a foreign business with a bureaucratic culture. If the manager tried to use a U.S. participative management style in this culture, chances are it would not be very effective.

Checkpoint

Name two types of organizational cultures.

_____

_____

Understand Marketing Concepts

Circle the best answer for each of the following questions.

1. A(n) _____ manager uses little or no input from employees.
   a. bureaucratic
   b. participative
   c. autocratic
   d. foreign

2. The ability of workers to pursue jobs that make the best use of their skills is called
   a. union-supported
   b. labor mobility
   c. labor freedom
   d. workers' rights

Think Critically

Answer the following questions as completely as possible. If necessary, use a separate sheet of paper.

3. Describe the differences between autocratic managers and participative managers.

_____
_____
_____
_____
_____
_____
_____

4. Explain how U.S. labor can be considered a factor-of-production advantage.

_____
_____
_____
_____
_____
_____
_____
_____
_____

International Organizational Design and Control

Goals

- Describe the role of organizational design.
- Explain how organizations design control systems.
- Describe the transnational-network structure.

Terms

- organizational design
- line-and-staff structures
- multinational matrix structure
- time orientation
- motivation
- work centrality
- transnational-network structure

Going Global

Global companies have been struggling with how they should design their organizations. Companies have adopted a number of different strategies. Procter & Gamble (P&G) traditionally used a matrix of product lines and regions. P&G learned that it needed to be more flexible in its organizational design.

P&G's new organizational design incorporates flexibility. When customers worldwide react to a product in the same way, P&G uses a Global Business Unit (GBU).

When customers' preferences for a product line differ around the world or when there is a lot of competition, P&G creates Market Development Organizations (MDOs). These MDOs are organized by product line within an individual country. P&G uses Global Business Services (GBS) to provide business technology and services. It also uses Corporate Functions (CFs) to maintain quality. P&G believes that this new structure will help it "Think Globally" (with GBUs) but "Act Locally" (with MDOs).

Working with a partner, describe why P&G needed to restructure organizational design. Explain why P&G would need to design a flexible system.

ORGANIZATIONAL DESIGN

MARKETING–INFORMATION MANAGEMENT

Businesses must structure their management systems to coordinate activities and maintain control. Businesses develop an **organizational design** to structure the flow of communication and authority within a business to achieve strategic goals. This organizational design is illustrated in an *organizational chart*. There are a number of different ways to structure organizational designs.

Line-and-Staff Structures

One type of organizational design is the line-and-staff structure. **Line-and-staff structures** show lines of communication and flows of authority. These organizational structures typically are shaped like a pyramid.

Line-and-staff structures can be organized by job function, product, or geography. A line-and-staff organizational structure organized by geography is shown below.

A business organized by geography has the advantage of having regional experts in key positions. But this structure does have disadvantages. These separate divisions may compete for organizational resources, such as funding, human resources, equipment, or management time. Separate divisions can also make it more difficult to develop a global corporation that wants to design global products for the entire world.

Line-and-Staff Organizational Structure Organized by Geography

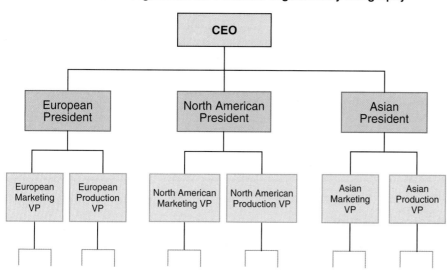

Businesses can have a tall or flat organizational structure. *Tall organizational structures* have many management layers. These structures often exist in bureaucratic businesses or in businesses that operate with formal rules and regulations. Although they often exist in large complex companies, they also may be found in cultures with high power/distance measures. *Flat organizational structures* have fewer layers of management. These structures may be found in cultures that have lower levels of power/distance measures.

Matrix Structure

Matrix structures show areas of responsibility, but they do not show individual lines of communication and authority like line-and-staff structures do. A **multinational matrix structure** places a functional area on the left of the matrix and regions across the top. A multinational matrix structure is shown on the next page. A matrix structure allows a functional area, such as product development, to design a product for a single region or for all global markets.

Most businesses will adapt organizational structures to best fit their business operations. Accenture, a global consulting firm, had a traditional matrix structure with financial services and an industrial area across five global divisions, each with its own regional organization. Accenture restructured around 12 regions, which lessened communication and control problems.

Multinational Matrix Structure

	Europe	North America	Asia
Product Development VP	European Product Development Manager	North America Product Development Manager	Asia Product Development Manager
Marketing VP	European Marketing Manager	North America Marketing Manager	Asia Marketing Manager
Product VP	European Production Manager	North America Production Manager	Asia Production Manager

Checkpoint

List two types of organizational design.

Tech Zone

Thanks primarily to the Internet, global communication is rapidly becoming instantaneous and free. Two technologies are helping businesses communicate internally across borders. The first is the use of *intranets*, which are internal Internets. Businesses set up internal web sites for internal communication, locking out users outside of the company. Employees from business divisions around the world can go to a single point to find information.

The second technology being used is Internet telephony. This technology connects telephones to the Internet. Because the Internet allows information to be sent for free, global telephone calls can be made at no cost.

THINK CRITICALLY

Describe how Internet-based technology affects internal communication within global businesses. Describe how it could impact management practices.

ORGANIZATIONAL CONTROL

MARKETING– INFORMATION MANAGEMENT

One of management's key functions is to maintain control within an organization. This process can be fairly simple in small businesses with few employees at one location. Maintaining control in global companies with multiple divisions across countries and cultures is much more difficult.

Organizational design sets a framework for coordination and control. Businesses also must select and control methods of measurement to enable managers to monitor the company's progress. Worldwide computer systems that allow managers to coordinate workflows and share information aid the control process.

A business's financial statements are a major means of control. Modern computer systems make financial information from individual business units readily available to local managers and corporate headquarters. Monitoring this information allows a business to look for positive and negative trends. This information also can be used as a motivational tool for managers. For example, Oracle Corporation, a software company, gives its country managers a daily ranking on their country revenue and expenses. Oracle encourages its country managers to compete against each other to maximize performance.

Time Orientation

There are some general trends in how U.S.-based multinational corporations differ from foreign-based multinationals in organizational control. U.S.-based companies often look at more short-term financial information. European multinational companies may be more flexible and look at regional differences in performance. Japanese firms often have more of a long-term view when evaluating financial returns. These differences can be due to different time orientations. A **time orientation** is the short-term versus long-term view that managers take. American managers often have a short-term orientation. They expect results quickly. This expectation is driven, in part, by U.S. financial markets, where quarterly reports can have an impact on stock price. Japanese firms do not need to react to the stock market as quickly, so they view things over the long term.

Motivation

A business can have an organizational design and control system in place, but they will not be effective unless employees are motivated to comply with the work process. Businesses view **motivation** as a process that results in goal-directed behavior. Businesses must design a motivational system to move employees toward desired goals.

Setting up motivational systems in an international business requires an understanding of how individuals in the country relate to work. There are cultural differences in **work centrality,** which is the importance of work in an individual's life. Japan is very high in work centrality. Japanese workers view work as the most important activity in their lives. British workers rank low in work centrality. They view work as less important than other activities in their lives, such as family and leisure. The United States ranks in the middle between Great Britain and Japan.

To create a motivational system, a business must understand the reasons why people work. People work because they need income. They also work because they want to interact with other people. Some people work for the sense of accomplishment. In many developing countries, the major reasons people work are because they need income and they desire a secure job. In more developed countries with plenty of job opportunities, contact with people and feelings of accomplishment can be more important. In countries where income is a primary concern, a motivational strategy should revolve around wages. In countries where feelings of accomplishment rank high, recognition and awards could be a motivator.

Motivational systems also must fit within the larger cultural factors of the society. For example, in high-power/distance cultures, motivation might be tied to the workers' obligations to their managers. In high-uncertainty-avoidance cultures, job security could be a motivator. In high-individualism cultures, feelings of accomplishment could be a motivator. In high-masculinity cultures, achievement could be a motivator.

Time Out

A study conducted by the International Society of Performance Improvement found that properly designed incentive programs can increase employee performance between 25 and 44 percent.

List two factors that influence organizational control.

NETWORKED ORGANIZATIONS

A new organizational design is being used to control widely diversified businesses around the world. The **transnational-network structure** connects a series of *nodes,* or organizational centers. As shown in the figure below, a transnational-network structure allows each country or division to develop the organizational structure that best meets local conditions. In this example, the United States and the United Kingdom have matrix structures. Japan, Mexico, and South Africa have line-and-staff (L&S) structures. Network structures are very flexible in allowing control to be designed for local conditions.

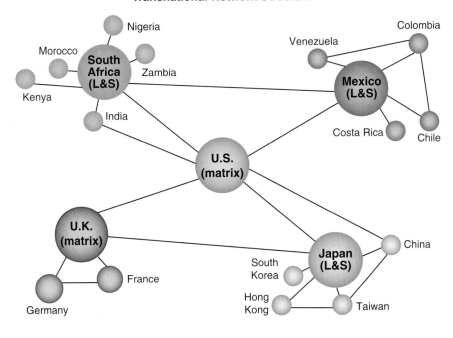

Transnational-Network Structure

Identify the benefits of a transnational-network structure.

Understand Marketing Concepts

Circle the best answer for each of the following questions.

1. An organizational structure that has lines showing flows of communication and authority is called a
    a. tall organization
    b. line-and-staff structure
    c. multinational matrix
    d. bureaucratic structure

2. The amount of importance given to work in an individual's life is called
    a. work centrality
    b. work/leisure orientation
    c. time orientation
    d. work motivation

Think Critically

Answer the following questions as completely as possible. If necessary, use a separate sheet of paper.

3. Describe the difference between a line-and-staff organizational structure and a multinational matrix structure.

    _____

    _____

    _____

    _____

    _____

    _____

    _____

    _____

4. Make a list of the factors that could influence motivation in an international business.

    _____

    _____

    _____

    _____

    _____

    _____

    _____

    _____

International Careers

Goals

- List the skills needed for an international career.
- Identify the issues facing expatriates.
- Explain how an individual can start developing an international career.

Terms

- culture shock
- foreign enclaves
- repatriation culture shock

Going Global

Teri grew up in a small midwestern town. She became interested in international business when she was in high school. She studied Spanish in high school. When she went to college, she majored in international business and minored in Spanish. Her first international trip was a tour of Mexico through the college's Spanish department.

During her junior year in college, she spent a semester in Madrid, Spain, as a business intern with the U.S. consul. When she returned to college, she interned with a local trucking firm, CFI, that specializes in transferring cargo between Mexico and the United States. Teri's language skills allowed her to act as a marketing support representative with Mexican firms. After working for CFI for a year after graduation, she spent a year in Japan teaching English. Through this job, she learned to speak Japanese.

Teri now is planning to work in Austin, Texas, for Toyota. The plant will have Hispanic workers and Japanese managers. Teri has all of the skills needed to move forward with an international marketing career.

Working in small groups, discuss how Teri has gained experience in international marketing. Describe skills that Teri has gained that will allow her to pursue her international marketing career.

INTERNATIONAL STAFFING

MARKETING– INFORMATION MANAGEMENT

To be competitive, businesses operating in an international marketplace must be able to staff, or hire, the most qualified employees for their competitive conditions. Over time, staffing philosophies for international businesses have changed. At one time, multinational companies used *expatriates,* or individuals from the home country, to staff management positions. The general belief was that there were not enough trained managers in foreign markets. Over the last 20 years, there has been a shift toward using host country nationals to staff businesses. Staffing decisions need to be made based on strategic considerations and the goals of the business. If a business wants to set up a new division in a foreign market, an important strategic consideration is how to get the new division to work well with the parent company. In this case, the parent company may want to use expatriates in the new market. These individuals could set up a new division and begin training managers to operate in the host country. Once the division is fully established, management can be taken over by host country nationals.

International businesses do not always set up divisions in other countries. In these cases, international marketers may be involved in developing or supporting marketing efforts in multiple countries. The skills required for international marketers can be considerably different from the skills required for a manufacturing manager setting up a division.

Certain factors contribute to success in international business. The importance of these factors will depend upon the countries served and the nature of the business. In general, these factors, listed in order of importance, are:

1. ability to adapt

2. technical competence

3. spouse and family adaptability

4. human relations skills

5. desire to serve overseas

6. previous overseas experience

7. understanding of host country's culture

8. academic qualifications

9. knowledge of host country's language

International marketers must be able to adapt to new cultures and new situations. They will have to interact with foreign customers in both formal and informal settings. Factors such as technical skills and academic qualifications can be easily evaluated, but other factors, such as family adaptability and human relations skills, must be closely examined by the parent company.

Ethics Around the World

Females do not have full employment rights in Japan. Japan is a patriarchal society, which is a society governed by men. Female employees in Japan do not have the same career opportunities as male employees. One female marketing representative in Japan found that male buyers would not take her seriously. When she hired a man to go with her, her overall sales increased.

Japan's economy faces a number of problems. Its workforce is getting older, and there are not enough young males to fill all the open jobs. About 40 percent of Japanese women work, but only 9 percent hold management positions, compared to 45 percent of U.S. women. Japan's economic recovery may be hindered because of Japan's social biases.

THINK CRITICALLY

1. Why do you think Japanese businesses do not offer equal opportunities to women?
2. Speculate on the loss to the Japanese economy caused by not fully utilizing its labor force.

In the past, why were expatriates used to staff management positions in multinational companies?

Checkpoint

A cost-of-living index measures the cost of a group of goods and services. Cost-of-living indexes for major cities around the world, using New York City as the base city (100), are

Tokyo	134.7
London	120.3
Moscow	119.0
Geneva	113.5
Budapest	93.3
Los Angeles	86.7
Chicago	84.6
San Juan	77.7
Asuncion, Paraguay	40.3

EXPATRIATE ISSUES

There are advantages and disadvantages to being an expatriate. Living abroad can greatly enhance a marketing career with an internationally focused company. At the same time, foreign assignments can remove an executive from the day-to-day activity at a parent company. Executives must carefully consider what will best serve their long-term career goals.

Because the cost of living can vary widely around the world, compensation packages for expatriates are typically much larger than they would be for a host country manager. In addition, expatriates incur higher costs when they need to move families, place children in school, or attempt to minimize cultural differences in their new living area. Expatriates often will receive not only their base salary but also additional benefits and compensation to cover taxes, housing costs, and cost-of-living adjustments. Expatriates' salaries can be two to three times higher than they would be in their own country. These large differences in pay can be an issue between expatriate managers and local managers. Many international companies attempt to minimize these payments by hiring managers from their host country as soon as possible.

Culture Shock

A study of managers from the United States, Europe, and Japan found that the major reasons that expatriates fail in foreign markets is because they suffer from **culture shock,** the trauma experienced when one moves into a foreign culture. Culture shock may be felt not only by the expatriate but also by the expatriate's spouse and family. Often expatriates and family members start out well because the situation can be exciting and new. After a period of a few months, the need to adjust to the differences in the host country's culture can be very stressful.

Some countries have **foreign enclaves,** or special areas where foreigners reside. These enclaves can be set up by international corporations or by host country governments. Enclaves are designed to limit culture shock by providing a culture similar to that of the host country.

Female expatriates may face considerable work-related culture shock. Female executives who come from countries without gender discrimination may find that they get little respect in patriarchal countries where society is governed by men. This discrimination can make it difficult for women to engage in international negotiations or sales.

Repatriation

Expatriates can also suffer from **repatriation culture shock,** which is the culture shock experienced when returning to their home country. They may actually find it hard to readjust to their home culture. In addition, there are almost always changes that have occurred at the parent company. Relationships that once existed may be gone.

Expatriates' families also have to readjust to their home culture and reestablish networks and friends. Companies attempt to limit repatriation problems by providing support and counseling for returning executives and their families.

List two types of shock expatriates may face.

STARTING A CAREER IN INTERNATIONAL MARKETING

International marketing is the future of marketing not just because of the increased interest in global marketing from U.S.-based firms but also because of the growth of international competition. The combined populations of India and China are almost ten times larger than that of the United States. These two countries alone offer large new marketing opportunities. At the same time, they are potential competitors in global markets.

When considering an international marketing career, the first step that individuals should take is to determine their own personal goals. An international marketing career has advantages and disadvantages. International marketing can be a highly exciting, interesting, and lucrative career path. At the same time, it may seem very daunting to leave your home country, family, friends, and the other parts of your life that are tied to your culture.

Examining the factors needed for success (discussed earlier in this lesson) is a good starting point for developing an international career. Adaptability is the most important factor to success, and many opportunities exist to help you learn this skill. Working with teams in school, working on special projects, and working with a wide variety of people, especially international students, can help individuals learn to adapt to situations. Technical competency is also something that should be mastered at the school level. Global corporations can hire globally. They can hire employees from many countries around the world who are bilingual and have a high competency in science, math, and writing. There is intense competition for all jobs, not just international jobs.

A business education is based on the foundation of a general education. At one time, the United States was one of the dominant leaders in business education. Today, schools and universities around the world are offering strong business educations to their students. Individuals need to expand their business education background to compete against other students.

Language Skills

English is the world's business language. It is not unusual to find non-native English speakers who have mastered the English language better than many native speakers. Communication skills are one of the most important skills that employees and managers possess. Mastering both verbal and written English skills is vital for international communication.

Learning at least one other language is important for a number of reasons. Learning a second language can help you communicate in foreign cultures. In addition to improving your communication skills, learning a second language increases your understanding of foreign cultures. Even if an executive does not speak the host country's language, he or she should learn a few fundamental words to show respect.

Checkpoint

Explain why language skills are important to an international career.

_____

_____

World Stars | PETER DRUCKER

Peter Drucker has been called the man who invented management. Drucker was born in Vienna in 1909. He studied law in Hamburg, Germany. Drucker wrote two pamphlets that offended the Nazis. He left Germany and came to the United States in 1937 where he began a writing career. He wrote *Concept of the Corporation, The Practice of Management, The Effective Executive,* and 35 other books. *The Practice of Management,* written in 1954, was the first book on professional management.

Drucker was one of the first people to identify that corporations need to select the best people for the job. He also believed managers should focus on opportunities, not on problems. He stressed that all businesses should focus on the customer, understand competitive advantages, and continually reassess. Drucker recognized the importance of competing in a knowledge economy where educated workers are a key to global competitive advantages.

Drucker is seen as someone who changed the course of thousands of businesses around the world. He influenced General Electric to decentralize (move decision making down to those closer to the source) in the 1950s. In the 1980s, he convinced General Electric to focus on areas where it could be first or second in its field. In 2002, Drucker was awarded the Presidential Medal of Freedom, the nation's highest award for distinguished civilian service. Drucker died in 2005 at the age of 95.

THINK CRITICALLY

Explain how Peter Drucker has influenced management practice. Briefly describe Drucker's management ideas. Explain why Drucker would be given the Presidential Medal of Freedom.

Understand Marketing Concepts

Circle the best answer for each of the following questions.

1. The trauma experienced when one moves into a foreign culture is
   a. culture shock
   b. repatriation culture shock
   c. stress
   d. work motivation

2. A special area set up by companies or governments for foreign workers is called a(n)
   a. foreign trade zone
   b. foreign enclave
   c. housing area
   d. international living zone

Think Critically

Answer the following questions as completely as possible. If necessary, use a separate sheet of paper.

3. Describe the factors that contribute to an individual's success in an international career.

_____

_____

_____

_____

_____

_____

_____

4. **Communication** Develop an ideal resume that you would like to have in five years. Include those events that would make you a good candidate for an international marketing career.

_____

_____

_____

_____

_____

_____

_____

_____

Review Marketing Concepts

Write the letter of the term that matches each definition. Some terms will not be used.

_____ 1. An organizational culture that has a strong set of rules and regulations for the way a business operates

_____ 2. A process that results in goal-directed behavior

_____ 3. Structures the flow of communication and authority within a business to achieve strategic goals

_____ 4. An organizational design that places a functional area on the left and regions across the top

_____ 5. An organization that has the legal right to represent workers in negotiation with management

_____ 6. A structure that connects a series of nodes, or organizational centers

_____ 7. Managers that work with employees to set goals

_____ 8. The short-term versus long-term view that managers take

_____ 9. Trauma experienced when expatriates return to their home country

_____ 10. Organizational design that shows lines of communication and flows of authority

_____ 11. Managers that make decisions with no input from employees

_____ 12. The ability of workers to pursue jobs that make the best use of their skills

a. autocratic managers
b. bureaucratic culture
c. culture shock
d. foreign enclaves
e. labor mobility
f. labor union
g. line-and-staff structures
h. motivation
i. multinational matrix structure
j. organizational culture
k. organizational design
l. participative managers
m. repatriation culture shock
n. time orientation
o. transnational-network structure
p. work centrality

Circle the best answer.

13. A basic assumption about how a business should operate internally and interact with customers externally is called a(n)
    a. organizational structure
    b. organizational culture
    c. national culture
    d. system design

14. Line-and-staff structures can be organized by
    a. job function
    b. product
    c. geography
    d. all of the above

Think Critically

15. List each of Hofstede's cultural measures and indicate how these cultural measures can affect management styles.

_____

_____

_____

_____

_____

_____

16. Use Hofstede's cultural measures to explain why union membership is high in some countries.

_____

_____

_____

_____

_____

_____

17. Design two organizational charts using the line-and-staff structure. One chart should be organized by job function. The other chart should be organized by product lines.

_____

_____

_____

_____

_____

_____

18. Make a list of the skills and traits that an individual would need to become a successful international manager. Explain why each of these skills and traits is important.

_____

_____

_____

_____

_____

_____

_____

Make Connections

19. Communication Write a paper about labor unions in the United States. Discuss the history of labor unions, significant events, and the present-day status of labor unions.

_____

_____

_____

_____

_____

_____

_____

20. Research Use the Internet to research labor relationships in another country. Describe whether the country is more labor-friendly or business-friendly. Explain why.

_____

_____

_____

_____

_____

_____

_____

_____

21. Marketing Math Your company has one CEO who supervises four vice presidents. Each vice president has three divisional managers. Each divisional manager has five managers. Each manager has ten employees. How many people work for your company?

_____

_____

_____

_____

_____

_____

22. Problem Solving Develop a plan for how you can gain the skills necessary to pursue an international marketing career. Compare your plan to other students' plans.

_____

_____

_____

_____

_____

_____

_____

_____

_____

PUT MARKETING ON THE MAP

International Marketing Plan Project

Your business must be designed in a way that will allow for management communication and control. You will need to justify a design system that will allow you to reach your goals.

Work with a group and complete the following activities.

1. Describe the culture of the countries where you will do business. Describe the employees you will need to hire. Explain the management style you think would work best with the employees in this country. Be sure to consider Hofstede's cultural measures.

2. Describe the type of organizational culture you will need to have in order to fit the conditions outlined in Question 1 above.

3. Design an organizational structure that will allow you to reach your goals today and in the future. Justify this design by relating it to Hofstede's cultural measures.

4. Specify how you will maintain control over the different parts of your organization. Indicate if you will have to work with unions in the countries where you will do business. Specify how your management process will be affected if you have to work with unions.

5. Assume that you will be using expatriates. Devise a training program to minimize culture shock for the expatriate and his or her family.

Case Study

MARKETING REQUIRES A GAME PLAN

An international marketing plan requires more effort than a domestic marketing plan. The plan must consider how geography, culture, and politics will influence international marketing activities. Can the product be marketed successfully in its current form, or will it need adjustments to meet the needs of international markets?

Another major consideration for marketing products in other countries is whether the citizens can afford the product or service. Does the target market perceive a need for the product or service? Are they willing to pay the price?

When a major automobile manufacturer develops a new vehicle, it must consider whether the product can be successfully marketed in other countries. A new energy-efficient automobile will definitely grab international attention since rising fuel prices are a major concern. However, citizens in many countries will not be able to afford the price. Pollution standards and other government restrictions will vary among countries. Large oil corporations may block the car from ever being available to the public. Climate and geography may influence the success of the automobile in another country. Some countries have a large number of automobiles without air conditioning. Modifications may be necessary to make the vehicle more appealing in another country.

Politics will also enter into the marketing plan. Tariffs and other trade barriers must be considered when doing business with other countries. Countries in conflict will not produce an environment conducive to international trade.

Advertising can vary greatly from one country to another. Advertising techniques in one country may be offensive in another country. Humor and other advertising strategies vary greatly even in neighboring countries.

The marketing plan also must consider the cost of distribution in other countries. Some countries have highly sophisticated delivery systems while others are fairly crude. Distribution methods can have a major impact on the price charged for the product.

All marketing plans involve risk. There are numerous factors to consider for an international marketing plan, but decisions must be made because indecision can be a bigger risk.

THINK CRITICALLY

1. What makes an international marketing plan more complicated than a domestic plan?
2. Why is culture so important for the marketing plan?
3. How might advertising in Middle Eastern countries be different from advertising in the United States?
4. Why do you have to take risks when developing marketing plans?

INTERNATIONAL BUSINESS PLAN EVENT

Students who complete the International Business Plan Event must apply marketing skills by preparing a written proposal for a new international business venture. The venture can be a new business or a new product or service for an existing business. This project consists of a written document and the oral presentation. The written document accounts for 70 points, and the oral presentation accounts for the remaining 30 points.

The International Business Plan can be completed by teams consisting of one to three members. The body of the written entry is limited to 30 numbered pages, including the appendix but excluding the title page and the table of contents.

The oral presentation will consist of ten minutes for participants to explain and describe their project and five minutes for the judge's questions.

Major sections of the written plan include the Executive Summary, Introduction, Analysis of the International Business Situation, Planned Operation of the Proposed Business/Product/Service, Planned Financing, Bibliography, and Appendix.

After your study of international marketing, you now have the opportunity to choose a new international business proposal. Your business venture choice must demonstrate an understanding of economic need, cultural differences, and appropriate strategies for marketing the product/service in another part of the world. You must follow the DECA guidelines for this project.

Performance Indicators Evaluated

* Understand the challenge and opportunity for an international business venture.
* Explain the need to expand business internationally.
* Demonstrate sensitivity to another culture.
* Detail a financial plan for an international business venture.
* Conduct research to support the probability of success for the international business venture.
* Outline an international marketing strategy for success.

Go to the DECA web site for more detailed information.

THINK CRITICALLY

1. Why must a person conduct intense research before proposing an international business venture?
2. Why is it important to have a thorough understanding of the culture where you plan to locate a business?
3. What role does international politics play in the success or failure of an international business proposal?

www.deca.org

Glossary

A

Absolute advantage   a country can produce more units of a product at a lower cost using fewer resources than other countries (p. 26)

Advertising   any form of paid, non-personal communication (p. 213)

Advertising theme   organizes the design of an advertisement and helps to focus communication efforts (p. 215)

Agent   brings together buyers and sellers but typically does not take title, or ownership, of the product and usually takes a percentage of sales (p. 184)

AIDA process   process of making an audience *aware* of a company's advantages and product benefits. It then moves to create *interest* and then *desire*. Finally, it calls for *action*. (p. 206)

Approach   method that a salesperson uses to start the sales process (p. 219)

Autocratic managers   managers who make decisions with little or no input from employees (p. 283)

B

Back translation   process by which a native speaker translates material to his or her own language. This translation is then translated by another native speaker back to the original language. This process helps to ensure that words and meanings are translated correctly. (p. 57)

Balance of payments (BOP)   a country's balance of payments can be positive or negative. If more currency flows out of a country than comes in, the country has a *negative BOP.* If more currency flows into a country than flows out, it has a *positive BOP.* (p. 245)

Balance of trade   the difference between the dollar value of exports sold and the dollar value of imports purchased (p. 38)

Barter   involves the exchange of one product or service for another product or service (p. 162)

Belief system   allows individuals to understand their place in the larger universe; sets rules of conduct and ethics that indicate how people should interact with others and how they should live their lives (p. 55)

Bill of lading   document issued by a carrier (transporter) to a shipper (exporter) acknowledging that the carrier has received the goods (p. 187)

Birdyback   system of transportation that requires the transfer of containers between truck and air cargo (p. 190)

Boycott   the ban of commerce and trade that occurs when the participants think the organization or country in question has done something wrong (p. 35)

Brand   name, word, or design that identifies a product, service, or company that creates a certain expectation in the minds of customers (p. 157)

Brand equity   the additional value that a brand name brings to a product or company (p. 158)

Brand recognition   how well a product's name is recognized in a market (p. 139)

Bribe   money or something of value that is given in order to persuade someone else to violate ethics or laws (p. 65)

Buildup method   method of estimating sales, which starts with an estimate of individual behavior and then extends it to the entire market (p. 114)

Bureaucratic culture   culture characterized as having a strong set of rules and regulations for the way a business operates (p. 286)

Business incubator   usually a physical facility set up to offer office or factory space at a reduced price (p. 271)

C

Capital equipment   land, buildings, and expensive pieces of equipment (p. 163)

Capital resources   manmade items such as buildings, machinery, and funds (p. 29)

Case law   based upon British common law, it allows for the interpretation of statutes to specific situations (p. 92)

Central America Free Trade Agreement (CAFTA)   trade agreement passed in July 2005 that links the United States with Costa Rica, El Salvador, Guatemala, Honduras, Nicaragua, and the Dominican Republic (p. 87)

Central bank   bank that serves as the government's bank and is responsible for a country's monetary policy (p. 247)

Certificate of origin   document that indicates the country in which goods being exported are obtained, produced, manufactured, or processed (p. 187)

Channel captain   assumes the leadership role in organizing a distribution system, which lessens the chances for conflict (p. 184)

Channel of distribution   the path used to move products from their source to the customer (p. 180)

Class mobility   the ability of an individual to change social classes (p. 82)

Collectivism   characterizes a culture that views individuals as belonging to a strong cohesive group for their entire lifetime (p. 60)

Commercial banks   banks that offer a variety of services, such as accepting deposits and making loans (p. 247)

Commercial policies   regulations and restrictions that countries use to control international trade (p. 33)

Commodity   raw material or agricultural product (p. 28)

Commodity products   goods that cannot be easily differentiated such as grains, minerals, and petroleum (p. 165)

Common market   customs union that allows for labor, capital, and technology to move between members (p. 86)

Communism   one-party political system in which all property belongs to the state (p. 90)

Company characteristics   financial resources the company has to create a global brand. The international orientation of management and the ability of the company to find and take advantage of international opportunities are other company characteristics. (p. 157)

Comparative advantage   a country specializes in the production of a product that it can produce relatively better, or more efficiently, than other countries (p. 27)

Comparative advertising   directly comparing one product to another (p. 215)

Competitive advantage   exists when a product has greater value in benefits or price than competitive products (p. 130)

Component parts   parts that are partially completed by one manufacturer to be used by another manufacturer (p. 163)

Concentrated segmentation strategy   marketing strategy used when a business focuses on one clearly defined market segment (p. 105)

Conceptual equivalence   question asked in one culture may not have the same meaning in another culture (p. 119)

Consulates   government-appointed officials from one country that reside in another country to represent the business interests of the appointing country's citizens (p. 36)

Consumers   end users for products (p. 192)

Context   the background or surrounding circumstances of an event; can be interpreted through the communication process (p. 53)

Contract   any legally enforceable promise or set of promises made by one party to another (p. 93)

Convenience stores   have a limited inventory offering width but little depth (p. 194)

Corruption   misuse of an official position for one's own benefit (p. 93)

Cost-plus method   pricing method in which all export costs are included in the price of the product (p. 165)

Cross-cultural equivalence   explains how similar research results are achieved across cultures (p. 118)

Cultural hegemony   the idea that a culture can be dominated by another group's culture (p. 62)

Culture   system of shared beliefs, values, customs, and behaviors that define how a group of people lives (p. 52)

Culture shock   trauma experienced when one moves into a foreign culture (p. 296)

Customs   acts as immigration control for products entering the country (p. 187); common practices among a group of people passed from one generation to the next (p. 65)

Customs broker   an intermediary that helps products move through customs (p. 187)

Customs union   free trade area with a common trade policy to non-members (p. 86)

D

Data collection equivalence   exists when researchers are not able to collect data in similar ways across cultures (p. 119)

Decoding   process of interpreting a message (p. 207)

Demand   quantity of a good or service that consumers are willing and able to buy at a given price (p. 233)

Democracy   allows for direct elections by a country's citizens (p. 90)

Demographics   population characteristics such as age, gender, race, income, and education (p. 106)

Department stores   consist of a number of individual departments that specialize in specific products (p. 193)

Deregulating   removes government controls and restrictions on the way businesses operate (p. 272)

Derived demand   demand that comes from the end purchaser (p. 164)

Developed countries or *first world countries*   have a high per capita, or per person, income; a high standard of living; and a strong diversified economy (p. 78)

Developing countries or *third world countries*   have low personal incomes, low levels of industrialization, and poor infrastructure (p. 79)

Differentiated segmentation strategy   marketing strategy used when a company targets two or more segments with unique strategies (p. 105)

Diffusion of innovations   theory that explains what influences cultural change (p. 61)

Direct competition   refers to competitors working within the same industry (p. 135)

Direct exporting   a company actively controls finding markets and exporting products (p. 187)

Distribution   involves determining the best methods and procedures to allow customers to locate, obtain, and use the products and services of an organization (p. 6)

Distribution channel   consists of the companies and individuals who participate in the exchange of good and services (p. 134)

Dumping   countries sell products for less than the cost of production (p. 35)

E

E-commerce   using the Internet to aid in the sales process (p. 194)

Economic system   governs how a country controls the production, distribution, and consumption of goods and services (p. 85)

Economies of scale   exist when a large amount of product is produced, which in turn lowers the cost of each individual product (p. 132)

Elasticity of demand   describes the relationship between changes in a product's price and the demand for that product (p. 240)

Embargo   the ban of commerce and trade with a certain country (p. 34)

Emigration   leaving one's home country (p. 143)

Encoding   process of using language and symbols to design a message (p. 207)

Enculturation   process that helps people learn about their culture (p. 53)

Entrepreneur   someone who is willing to take on the risk of starting a business (p. 269)

Environmental scanning   process of collecting information from various sources that may include international business journals, news programs, the Internet, and industry trade magazines (p. 117)

Environmental shocks   rapid changes in a business or company's macroenvironment (p. 265)

Ethnocentrism   the belief that one group is better than another group (p. 59)

Exchange rate or *foreign-exchange rate*   the ratio of how much one currency is worth in terms of another currency (p. 234)

Expatriate   individual who lives or works in a foreign culture (p. 59); someone from one country who works in another country (p. 143); individual from a company's home country sent abroad to staff a management position (p. 294)

Export Assistance Centers (EACs)   U.S. Department of Commerce program that helps businesses with all aspects of exporting (p. 39)

Export-import banks   independent banks established by governments to finance or insure the export sales of a country's products (p. 247)

Exporting   the process of shipping a product to another part of the world for trade or sale (p. 186)

Export management companies (EMCs)   specialize in helping businesses distribute products. EMCs typically specialize in specific products and markets and can act as an agent, or broker, for a company. (p. 184)

Export subsidies   direct or indirect payments made by governments to support the export of products (p. 36)

Export tariffs   taxes placed on goods going out of a country (p. 34)

F

Face   related to self-image (p. 64)

Factors of production   items that are used to produce products, including natural resources, human resources, and capital resources (p. 29)

Fair trade   commitment to buy products at a fair price and with labeling that identifies the source of the products (p. 12)

Family brand   typically the brand name of a company named after the original founder (p. 159)

Feedback   receiver's reaction to a message that should be collected by the sender. The sender must then determine if the message has been decoded in the intended way. (p. 207)

Financing   budgeting for marketing activities, obtaining the necessary funds needed for operations, and helping customers purchase the business's products and services (p. 7)

Fishyback   term used for the containerized shipping of goods between trucks and ships (p. 190)

Five-year plans   defined plans with specific economic goals for a country, usually one with a communist government (p. 271)

Flat organizational structures   organizational structures that have fewer layers of management and are found in cultures that have lower levels of power/distance measures (p. 289)

Foreign direct investment (FDI)   the purchase of assets in a foreign country by a business (p. 267)

Foreign enclaves   special areas where foreigners reside. They can be set up by international corporations or by host country governments and are designed to limit culture shock by providing a culture similar to that of the host country. (p. 296)

Foreign trade zone (FTZ)   area designated by a country as a specialized zone where products may be exempt from duties (p. 188)

Franchise   contractual right to licenses, trademarks, and methods of doing business in exchange for royalties and fees (p. 196)

Free trade   allows for unhindered trade of legal goods and services between countries (p. 10)

Free trade area   area in which all barriers to free trade are removed (p. 86)

G

General Agreement on Tariffs and Trade (GATT)   treaty agreement that developed a set of rules allowing countries to grant a *Most Favored Nation* status and lowered tariffs between member countries (p. 40)

Geographic segmentation   markets are segmented based on where consumers are located (p. 107)

Geography   the study of the differences that exist in physical, biological, and cultural features of the earth (p. 54)

Glass ceiling   barrier that prevents individuals from moving into top management positions (p. 143)

Global marketing strategy   highest level of commitment in international marketing in which a company treats the entire world, including its home country, as potential markets (p. 15)

Grey market   exists when products are sold outside of an established authorized distribution system (p. 158)

Gross domestic product (GDP)   the total value of all goods and services produced in an economic region (p. 9)

H

Hard currency   currency that typically comes from economically and politically stable countries (p. 233)

Heterogeneity   indicates that services can vary from provider to provider (p. 168)

High-context culture   culture in which interpersonal relationships are important (p. 53)

Human resources or *labor*   workers, management and entrepreneurs (p. 29)

I

Immigrant   someone who leaves his or her home country and goes to another country to live (p. 143)

Importing   receiving exported products (p. 186)

Import quotas   restrictions on the amount of a product that can be imported into a country (p. 34)

Import tariffs   taxes placed on goods coming into a country (p. 34)

Indirect competition   comes from the sale of products that provide similar benefits (p. 135)

Indirect exporting   a business uses brokers or agents to help find customers and export products (p. 186)

Individualism   characterizes a culture which believes people should look out for themselves (p. 60)

Industrial policy   strategy that a country adopts to support competitiveness (p. 271)

Industry   includes businesses that produce similar products (p. 10)

Infant industry argument   argument for setting trade barriers based on the idea that a developing industry in a country needs time to become globally competitive (p. 32)

Inflation   increase in overall prices in an economy (p. 244)

Innovation   new product or process (p. 139)

Inseparability   service businesses cannot be separated from their providers (p. 168)

Intangibility   a service cannot be physically possessed (p. 168)

Integrated marketing communication   planning process that attempts to ensure that all marketing communication efforts send a consistent message to customers (p. 221)

Intermodal transport   exporters using a combination of transportation modes, most often including containerized shipping linked to truck transport (p. 190)

International marketing   series of activities that creates an exchange that satisfies the individual customer across national borders (p. 4)

International marketing strategy   a company commits and plans to sell to international markets (p. 14)

International Monetary Fund (IMF)   an organization of 184 countries that supports global monetary cooperation and secures financial stability. It also helps in regulating international currency exchange rates and works to promote high employment and sustain economic growth. (p. 40)

ISO standards   global quality standards set by the International Organization for Standardization (p. 168)

J

Joint venture   two or more businesses create a new business to pursue a strategic goal (p. 267)

L

Labor mobility   the ability of workers to pursue jobs that make the best use of their skills (p. 285)

Labor union   organization that has the legal right to represent workers in negotiations with management (p. 285)

Law of supply and demand   explains how changes in the demand and quantity of goods sold in competitive markets impact a price (p. 233)

Lead time   amount of time a company is ahead of its competition in pursuing a strategy (p. 139)

Legal system   creates, interprets, and enforces the laws of a country (p. 92)

Letter of credit (LC)   financial document issued by a bank guaranteeing payment (p. 242)

Line-and-staff structures   show lines of communication and flow of authority and are typically shaped like a pyramid (p. 288)

Logistics   activities that create an orderly and timely acquisition and transportation of products through the channel of distribution (p. 180)

Lorenz curve diagram that charts the distribution of income in a population by *quintiles* or fifths (p. 79)

Low-context culture culture in which people value individualism (p. 53)

M

Macroenvironment environmental factors that influence the economy, governments, legal environment, technology, ecology, social cultural factors, and competition (p. 265)

Malls or *shopping centers* buildings that host a variety of stores and can be totally enclosed or open air. The mall or shopping center leases space to individual stores. (p. 194)

Manufacturing consists of a set of processes that use raw materials to produce final goods (p. 133)

Marginal-cost method pricing method in which firms look at the price they need to set to be competitive in foreign markets. Then, they must look at their costs to be sure that they are meeting a minimum profit. (p. 165)

Market characteristics include political and legal regulations, customer characteristics and preferences, purchasing patterns, and distribution systems. They also include the country's stage of economic development, the climate and geography, and the nature of competition. (p. 157)

Market economy economic system in which the free market determines which products are produced, marketed, and priced. Characteristics of a market economy include private property and entrepreneurship. (p. 85)

Marketing intermediary independent business that assists the flow of goods and services from producers to customers (p. 181)

Marketing research systematic process of gathering information to help make marketing decisions (p. 116)

Marketing-information management obtaining, managing, and using market information to improve business decision making and the performance of marketing activities (p. 7)

Market power exists when a firm can control pricing in an industry (p. 135)

Market pricing used when competitive products already exist in a marketplace. A careful analysis must be undertaken when entering new international markets to find a price that is justified given the benefits offered by competitive products. (p. 239)

Market segment group of individuals or organizations that share similar characteristics (p. 104)

Market share percentage of industry sales a company is able to capture from competitors (p. 114)

Masculinity measure of the dominant values in a society that relate to material success versus caring for others and the quality of life (p. 60)

Measurement equivalence occurs when survey results differ because individuals in a culture respond differently to survey questions (p. 119)

Media vehicles used to carry a message to an audience (p. 209)

Media schedule calendar that lays out when ads will play and in which media (p. 214)

Mercantilism strategy in which a nation promotes exports but limits imports (p. 10)

Micro-loans very small loans, typically around $100, which allow entrepreneurs to start businesses and make money. Micro-loans have a high repayment rate and allow many low-income people, especially women, in developing countries to make money for their families. (p. 133)

Mission statement defines the purpose of an organization, and provides direction, commits resources, inspires individuals, and focuses activities (p. 260)

Mixed economy economic system which combines market economy characteristics with varying levels of government control. In most cases, government control is used to protect consumers and laborers. It also ensures that businesses compete fairly. (p. 85)

Money medium of exchange used by a society; it can store value and act as a unit for accounting (p. 232)

Motivation process that results in goal-directed behavior (p. 291)

Multinational matrix structure organizational structure that places a functional area on the left of the matrix and regions across the top (p. 289)

N

National debt money owed by a government at the federal, state, and local level (p. 247)

National security argument argument for setting trade barriers based on the idea that a country does not want to become dependent upon other countries for products (p. 33)

Natural resources land, forests, minerals, oil, and bodies of water (p. 29)

Newly industrialized countries or *second world countries* countries that have high levels of industrialization, but may not have the high personal incomes or the infrastructure of developed countries (p. 79)

No active international marketing strategy strategy in which a company responds to international orders but does not actively seek them (p. 14)

Noise anything that interferes with the intended communication (p. 207)

Non-tariff barriers barriers often based on legislative rules and regulations related to a certain product (p. 35)

Non-verbal communication what people communicate with their bodies; can include facial expressions, eye contact, hand gestures, bowing, and showing emotions (p. 57)

North American Free Trade Agreement (NAFTA) trade treaty that created a free trade zone linking Canada, the United States, and Mexico. NAFTA eliminated duties on half of all U.S. goods shipped to Mexico, and set agreements to phase out other tariffs over the next 14 years. Treaty also protects patents, copyrights, and trademarks. (p. 87)

O

Offshoring outsourcing of jobs to other countries (p. 144)

One-party state allows for only one political party (p. 90)

Operating equipment smaller, less expensive equipment, such as personal computers (p. 163)

Opportunity cost value of what is given up in producing one product when another product is produced (p. 27)

Organizational ads promote a company or an entity and its brand image (p. 215)

Organizational culture shared basic assumption about how a business should operate internally and interact with customers externally (p. 286)

Organizational design structures the flow of communication and authority within a business to achieve strategic goals (p. 288)

Organization for Standardization (ISO) sets the global standards for quality (p. 168)

Outsourcing involves finding an outside source to perform a job function (p. 144)

P

Participative managers managers who work with employees to set goals and give employees freedom in deciding how to reach them (p. 283)

Penetration pricing sets a low price compared to competitors. This strategy helps a company capture market share. Penetration pricing often is used for a short term until market share goals are met. (p. 239)

Perishability services cannot be stored (p. 168)

Personal selling involves face-to-face interaction between a seller and a buyer (p. 219)

Piggyback system of transportation requires the transfer of containers between truck and rail (p. 190)

Placid environment environment where there is very little change (p. 264)

Planned economy economic system in which the government acts as the central planner in a planned or *command* economy. This system plans the types of products produced, determines where they can be sold and the prices to be charged. (p. 85)

Political economy the idea that international business is influenced by the economic and political/legal environments of countries (p. 84)

Political risk occurs when there is uncertainty about the stability of a political or legal system (p. 90)

Political system sets the laws under which businesses operate (p. 89)

Population pyramid diagram that shows the number of males and females in different age groups in a population (p. 81)

Portfolio of markets collection of different products in different market locations (p. 112)

Power distance measure of power inequity between superiors and subordinates (p. 60)

Pre-approach process where the salesperson conducts background research to understand the customer's needs. This research helps in crafting the sales presentation. (p. 219)

Predatory pricing the lowering of a price to gain market share (p. 35)

Prestige pricing strategy where a company sets a high price throughout the life of a product (p. 239)

Price amount of money, goods, or services needed to acquire a given quantity of other goods or services (p. 238); represents what a customer forfeits in exchange for receiving a product or service (p. 162)

Price ceiling maximum price that can be charged in a market (p. 239)

Price floor lowest price that a company can charge and still cover costs (p. 239)

Pricing establishing the price of the products and services (p. 7)

Primary data data not previously collected (p. 117)

Product something offered to a market that satisfies a want or a need (p. 156)

Product ads promote a single product (p. 215)

Product characteristics nature of a product and the purpose for which a product is used; also include the perception of product quality and product's country of origin, and the required after-sale service (p. 157)

Production possibility curve shows the tradeoff in production between two products (p. 27)

Productivity amount of a product that can be produced with a given set of resources (p. 132)

Product-market name given to a single product in a single market (p. 137)

Product placement companies pay to have their products placed into some other media outlet (p. 214)

Product positioning using a brand to create an image (p. 158)

Product/service management designing, developing, maintaining, improving, and acquiring products and services to meet consumer needs (p. 7)

Profile picture of a market segment (p. 105)

Promotion communicating to potential customers about a company's products and services (p. 7); any form of communication that is designed to inform, remind, or persuade customers about a company, its goods, or services (p. 206)

Protectorate county under partial control of a larger country (p. 89)

Publicity free communication through the media (p. 214)

Purchasing power parity (PPP) measures how much of a product a currency can buy in a country and takes into account the average price of identical products in different countries (p. 162)

Q

Qualified market characteristics include a *need* or desire for the product, the *ability to pay,* and the *authority to purchase* (p. 105)

R

Raw materials unprocessed products that are used to produce other products (p. 163)

Religion belief system that answers spiritual questions (p. 55)

Repatriation culture shock culture shock experienced when expatriates return to their home country (p. 296)

Republic form of government in which citizens elect representatives who, in turn, vote on laws (p. 90)

Research and development (R&D) process of using funds to create new products and processes (p. 134)

Retailer member of a channel of distribution that sells to the end user (p. 192)

S

Sales commission compensates the salesperson based on a percentage of sales (p. 220)

Sales presentation major communication component in the sales process (p. 219)

Sales promotion incentive, such as a coupon, rebate, or premium in addition to the product sold (p. 220)

Sample smaller number of people who have the same profile as the larger population (p. 117)

Sample equivalence occurs when the people chosen to answer a survey may have the same demographic profile but they might not share the same needs and desires or have the same authority to purchase (p. 119)

Screening process of identifying potential market opportunities to pursue (p. 113)

Secondary data data that has been previously collected (p. 117)

Self-reference criteria occurs when people view the world solely through their own cultural beliefs (p. 60)

Selling communicating directly with prospective customers to assess and satisfy their needs (p. 7)

Skim pricing temporary strategy where a company sets a price at a high level for a short period of time (p. 239)

Social class group that is distinguished from others in a society based on criteria such as income, net worth,

education, family history, political power, or lifestyles (p. 82)

Socialism strong form of a mixed economy which sets strong rules and regulations to control business practices and aims to protect all citizens equally (p. 85)

Soft currency currency that is not acceptable for international exchange, most often due to unrealistic exchange rates or economic and political instability within a country (p. 233)

Sovereign state country free from external control (p. 89)

Specialty store smaller store that specializes in a product category and has narrow width but product depth (p. 193)

Statutory law legal systems that attempt to put every possible legal issue into a specific law (p. 92)

Strategic business unit (SBU) the smallest unit around which a business develops a strategy (p. 262)

Strategic planning process of determining how to move to a desired future state (p. 258)

Supplies products and materials that are consumed in the operation of the business (p. 163)

Supply quantity that producers are willing to offer at a given price (p. 233)

Surplus driven international marketing selling inventory internationally when it cannot be sold in home markets (p. 14)

Survey common quantitative marketing research data collection method that typically has a number of questions that ask respondents to choose between answers, such as "strongly agree" and "strongly disagree" (p. 118)

Sustainability worldwide movement to allow for economic development while minimizing negative impacts on the environment (p. 93)

SWOT analysis an environmental assessment of the strengths, weaknesses, opportunities, and threats that a business faces (p. 260)

T

Tactical planning short-term, narrowly focused business planning (p. 259)

Tall organizational structures organizational structures that have many management layers and often exist in bureaucratic businesses or in businesses that operate with formal rules and regulations (p. 289)

Tariff or *custom's duty* a tax placed on imported or exported products (p. 34)

Test market small segments of customers who share the same profile as a larger market (p. 118)

Theocracy special form of government where religion or faith plays a dominant role (p. 90)

Time orientation short-term versus long-term view that managers take (p. 291)

Total cost concept the idea that all costs must be taken into consideration when designing a channel of distribution (p. 183)

Traditional economy economic system in which customs, religious beliefs, and historical patterns determine how economic questions are answered (p. 85)

Translation equivalence problem that occurs when using multiple languages in research (p. 119)

Transnational-network structure connects a series of *nodes,* or organizational centers, and allows each country or division to develop the organizational structure that best meets local conditions (p. 292)

Turbulent environment environment where environmental change often is rapid and unpredictable (p. 264)

U

Uncertainty avoidance measures how threatened people feel by uncertain circumstances; it also measures how much they have developed cultural barriers to uncertainty (p. 60)

Undifferentiated segmentation strategy marketing strategy in which a company looks at all customers as one market (p. 105)

V

Value chain breaks a business into functional areas (p. 144)

Value relationship the amount of benefits received given the price paid for a product (p. 130)

Values the shared beliefs held by members of a culture that help define what is right and wrong or good and bad (p. 65)

W

Wholly-owned subsidiary an independent company owned by a parent company (p. 267)

Work centrality the importance of work in an individual's life (p. 291)

World Bank provides loans to low- and middle-income countries. It also provides policy advice, technical help, and knowledge-sharing services; and promotes economic growth to create jobs and to allow the poorest countries to take advantage of economic opportunities. (p. 41)

World Trade Organization (WTO) governs international trade rules and trade agreements and also allows for a means to settle trade disputes (p. 40)

X

Xenophobia the fear of anything foreign (p. 59)

Index

China (continued)
    anti-dumping complaints against, 35
    automobile import quota, 34
    as automobile manufacturer, 34
    Avon in, 218, 219
    balance of trade deficit with the United
        States, 9
    banking industry, 133, 247
    ban on advertising of medicine, 208
    Big Mac Index, 232
    bribes in, 65
    business card exchange, 67
    business gift giving in, 65
    business meals, 67
    chemical plants in, 140
    collectivist culture of, 60, 283
    competitive advantage, 132, 133
    consumer income, 162
    contract law in, 92
    corruption score, 93
    counterfeiting problem, 16, 159, 163
    credit card ownership in, 111
    delayed progress of, 282
    differentiated segmentation strategy
        in, 105
    early adopter theory, 62
    economic growth of, 26
    economic reform in, 91
    economic relationship with Taiwan, 11
    economic systems in, 85
    economic weaknesses, 85–86
    education in, 80
    electrical plug sizes, 161
    employees in services businesses, 168
    express delivery opportunities in, 111
    female infanticide in, 81
    flowering plant imports, 22
    future of banking services in, 169
    General Motors (GM) in, 281
    as global manufacturing power, 134
    gross domestic product (GDP), 9, 26, 162
    growth opportunities in, 142
    as high-context culture, 53
    holdings of U.S. currency, 246, 248
    industrial policy of, 271
    intellectual property problems, 140, 152
    Jeep brand image in, 104, 106
    joint venture with Fox Broadcasting
        Company, 267
    labor demand and increased wages, 145
    local Chinese brand development, 161
    Louis Vuitton expansion in, 163
    low-cost producer, 132
    male/female ratio, 81
    managers in, 133
    manufacturing moving to, 140
    as market for products, 140
    McDonald's in, 51, 169
    as mix of developing countries
        categories, 79
    movie piracy in, 5
    as new market for automobile
        makers, 129
    oil needs, 165
    one-child policy, 81
    online purchases in, 111
    opening of, for trade, 4, 5, 84, 131
    outsourcing and, 145
    percentage of national income of
        wealthiest, 79
    piracy of movies in, 5
    political economy, 84
    political system, 90, 91
    population, 81, 297
    positive balance of payments
        account, 245
    potential market size, 167
    price of Big Mac, 162
    as producer of Wal-Mart products, 11
    promises to the United States, 265
    radio stations, 214
    research and development (R&D)
        spending, 134
    retailing development, 193
    retail sales, 84
    services as percentage of GDP, 167
    7-Eleven in, 179
    tariffs and, 87
    Tesco in, 192
    textile industry, 32
    time and, 66
    trade barrier elimination, 87
    unfair barriers for U.S. exports, 152
    voluntary export restraints, 35
    Wal-Mart in, 84, 195
    weak intellectual property laws, 135
    yuan pegged to U.S. dollar, 234–235
    Yum! Brands in, 167
China National Offshore Oil
    Corporation, 267
Chinese language, 53
Cho, Fujio, 133
Chopsticks, 67
Christianity, 55
Chu, Jonathan, 282
Cisco, 262
Classification, in industrial markets, 164
Class mobility, 82
Clean technologies, 30
Clinique, 74
Closing the sale, 219
Coach, 163
Coca-Cola, 134
    brand equity, 158
    channel captain in distribution
        system, 184
    channel of distribution, 181
    franchising of distribution
        systems, 196
    in Germany, 180, 182–184, 196
    global expertise of, 51
    global marketing strategy of, 15
    marketing research surprise, 117
    place in distribution channel, 182
    reverse channel recycling law and
        (Germany), 180
    in top ten world brands, 157
    undifferentiated segmentation
        strategy, 105
    as worldwide culture, 176
Cohen, Jack, 192
Collectivism. See Individualism/collectivism
Colombia
    cut-flower imports, 22

National Federation of Coffee Growers of
    Colombia, 206–210, 213
non-verbal communication in, 57
Command economy, 85
Commercial banks, 247
Commercial policies
    boycotts, 35
    defined, 33
    dumping, 35
    embargoes, 34–35
    import quotas, 34
    non-tariff barriers, 35
    tariffs, 34
    See also Tariffs
Commitment, in marketing strategies, 14–15
Commodity, 28
Commodity products, 165
Common market, 86
Common Market for East and Southern
    Africa (COMESA), 86–87
Communication
    about innovations, 62
    in high-context cultures, 53
    learning local language, 56
    in low-context cultures, 53
    non-verbal, 57
    process of, 207
    verbal, 56–57
Communication model, 207
Communications, promotion as, 7
Communication skills, as career asset,
    297–298
Communication superhighway, 216
Communication technology, 5
Communism
    advertising forbidden under, 208
    barter under, 238–239
    in China, 282
    defined, 90
    fall of, as environmental shock, 265
    five-year plans in, 271
Company characteristics, 157
Company resources
    financial, 133
    human, 132–133
    manufacturing, 133–134
    marketing, 134
Comparative advantage
    about, 26–28
    defined, 25, 27
    of digital content, 40
    in the workforce, 29
Comparative advertising, 215
Compensation packages, for expatriates, 296
Competition
    analysis of, 135
    barriers to, 135, 161
    cut-flower market, 22
    direct, 135
    free trade and, 12
    indirect, 135
Competitive advantages
    defined, 130
    differentiation, 131–132
    focus, 131
    history of, 130–131
    human resources, 133

316   Index

Demographics *(continued)*
　　defined, 106
　　development categories of countries,
　　　　78–79
　　education, 80
　　importance of, 78–80
　　income distribution, 79–80
　　as influence on Coke consumption, 52
　　value of studying, 106
Denmark, 77, 179
Department of Commerce. *See* U.S.
　　Department of Commerce
Department stores, 193–194
Deregulation, 272
Derived demand, 164
Design, 159
Desire, in the AIDA process, 206
Detroit, Michigan, dollar-volume of port, 190
Developed (first world) countries
　　comparative advantage in workforce, 29
　　demographics of, 78–79
　　population in, 81
　　restaurant spending in, 169
Developing (third world) countries
　　demographics of, 79
　　grocery entry, 192
　　percentage of national income of
　　　　wealthiest, 79
　　population in, 81
Development categories of countries
　　developed (first world), 78–79
　　developing (third world), 79
　　mixed, 79
　　newly industrialized (second world), 79
DHL, 5, 111
DHL-Sinotrans, 111
Diamonds
　　brand image for, 155
　　conflict (blood) diamonds, 169
"Diamonds are Forever" campaign, 155
Differentiated segmentation strategy, 105
Differentiation, 131–132
Diffusion of innovations, 61–62
Digital television recorders, 214
Direct channel, 181
Direct competition, 135
Direct exporting, 187
Direct export subsidy, 36
Direct investments, 267
Direct mail advertising, to children, 113
Direct-sales approach, 218
Direct-selling method, 219
Direct theme, in advertising, 215
Discount department stores, 194
Disintermediation, 183
Disney Corporation, 30, 157, 162
Distribution
　　centralized, 179
　　defined, 6
　　direct and indirect, 181
　　short and long channels, 181
　　See also Channels of distribution
Distribution channel, 134
Documentation, in exporting, 187–188
Dollar-to-euro exchange rate, 234
Domain-name system, 266
Domestic intercultural markets, 109

Dominican Republic, 87
Door-to-door selling, 219
Drucker, Peter, 281, 298
Dual-pricing system, 165
Dumping, 35

E
Early adopters, 62
East Asia, Tesco in, 192
Eastern Europe, 131
　　after communist control, 42
　　Avon in, 218
　　collapse of planned economy, 85
　　opportunities in, 112
eBay Inc., 68
E-commerce, 194
Economic analysis, in international marketing
　　plan, 16
Economic confidence, 235
Economic environment
　　economic integration, 86–87
　　economic systems, 85–86
　　political economy, 84–86
Economic espionage, 66
Economic integration, 86–87
Economic systems, 85–86
Economic union, 86
Economies, planning, 271–272
Economies of scale
　　cost advantages of, 139
　　defined, 132
　　for standardized global products, 157
　　Yum! Brands and, 167
Economist, The, 232
Ecuador, 22
Education
　　as career asset, 297
　　in China, 26
　　college graduates (China, India, United
　　　　States), 29
　　in India, 80, 131
　　as intangible service, 168
　　international, 257
　　for international careers, 6
　　as link to higher income, 80
　　necessary for competitiveness, 34
Effective Executive, The (Drucker), 298
E-government, 93
Egypt, 162
Elasticity of demand, 240–241
Electronic commerce (e-commerce), tariffs
　　and, 40
Electronic currency, 242
Electronic fund transfers, 242
Electronic media, 209
　　as sales support, 221
　　types of, 216
El Salvador, 87, 126
Embargo, 34, 35
Emotional appeals, in advertising, 215
Emotions, showing, 57
Employee motivation, 291
Encoding, in communication, 207
Enculturation, 53
English, as official language, 56
Enterprise resource planning (ERP), 131
Entertainment industry, 30

Entrepreneurship
　　business development support, 270–271
　　business incubators, 271
　　culture and, 270
　　deregulation and, 272
　　entrepreneur, 269
　　factors influencing, 270
　　government regulations and, 270
　　investment capital and, 270
　　market economy and, 85
　　personal property ownership and, 270
　　planning economies and, 271–272
　　small- and medium-sized enterprises,
　　　　269–270
　　windows of opportunity, 269
Entry strategies. *See* Market-entry strategies
Environmental planning, 265
Environmental scanning, 117, 260
Environmental shocks, 265
Environmental standards, 168
Equipment, 163
Equivalence data collection problems,
　　118–119
Estèe Lauder, 74, 189
Ethics Around the World feature
　　advertising, 208
　　advertising to children, 113
　　China's accumulation of international
　　　　currencies, 236
　　conflict (blood) diamonds, 169
　　female employment in Japan, 295
　　global warming, 30
　　movie piracy, 5
　　national religion, 61
　　one-child policy, in China, 81
　　outsourcing, 145
　　reverse logistics, 189
　　Russian entrepreneurs, 270
Ethnocentrism, 59
Euro, 77
　　Big Mac and, 232
　　exchange rate for, 234
　　in international trade, 233
Eurodollars, 235, 242
Euromonitor International, 114
Europe
　　airline competition, 3
　　Big Mac Index, 232
　　business meals, 67
　　consumer information, ownership
　　　　of, 106
　　economic and political unity in, 77
　　economic union in, 11
　　electrical plug sizes, 161
　　entrepreneurship training, 270–271
　　gender empowerment in, 143
　　General Motors (GM) in, 281
　　high-tech companies in, 269
　　ideal society desires, 131
　　Jeep brand image in, 104, 106
　　land transportation in, 190
　　MTV in, 205
　　percentage of national income of
　　　　wealthiest top 10 percent of a
　　　　population, 79
　　population in, 81
　　reverse logistics, 189

in top ten world brands, 157
    in the United States, 169
    worldwide sales as risk reduction, 15
    Yao Ming promotions, 162
McLean, Malcolm, 186
Meals, cultural aspects of, 67
Measurement equivalence, in data collection
    process, 119
Media, 209
Media characteristics, 214
Media schedule, 214
Media strategies, 209, 214
Medical services, 169
Medical tourism, 169
Meetings, culture and, 228
    business card exchange, 67
    greetings, 67
    language used in, 66–67
    meals, 67
    time, 66
    women and men, 67
Mercantilism
    arguments against, 11
    defined, 10
    free trade and, 10
Merkel, Angela, 272
Mexico
    autocratic management style, 283
    average hourly wages in manufacturing
        industry, 132
    cut-flower imports, 22
    export costs, 22
    fashion exports, 202
    as high power/distance culture, 60, 283
    illegal aliens from, 100
    line-and-staff structures, 292
    as newly developed (second world)
        country, 79
    North American Free Trade Agreement
        (NAFTA), 87
    pharmaceutical prices, 245
    political system in, 90
    production jobs from the United States, 41
    7-Eleven in, 179
    sugar trade, 38
    unfair barriers for U.S. exports, 152
    Wal-Mart in, 5, 84
Micro-loans, 133
Microsoft, 157, 238
Middle Eastern countries, gender
    empowerment in, 143
Ming, Yao, 162
Minuteman organization, against illegal
    aliens, 100
Mission, 257, 258
Mission statement, 260
Missouri, export goods to Korea, 10
Missouri Southern State University, 257
Mitsubishi (export trading company), 187
Mixed economy
    defined, 84, 85
    democratic, 91
    trend toward, 86
Money, 232. See also International currency
Money market accounts, 242
Money supply, 235, 242
Moscow, cost-of-living index, 296

Most Favored Nation status, 40
Motivation, 291
Movie piracy, 5
MP3.com, 238
MTV generation, 62, 205. See also Music
    Television (MTV)
Mulcahy, Anne, 248
Multinational corporations
    expatriates as staff, 294
    time orientation and, 291
    See also Expatriates
Multinational matrix structure, 289–290
Multi-party democracies, 90, 91
Multiple media platforms, 205
Multiple products/segments, 105, 112
Multiplier-effect, of Coke, in Sudan, 176
Murdoch, Rupert, 205, 267
Music, pricing for, 238
Music Television (MTV)
    background, 205
    localizing content for cultural needs, 213
    multiple media platform, 205, 214
    popular culture and, 216
Muslims
    Beurger King Muslim (Paris), 109
    "funky but respectful" call to prayer
        (MTV), 205
    soft drink market and, 52

N

NAFTA. See North American Free Trade
    Agreement (NAFTA)
Naming firms, 159
National debt, 244–245, 247–248
National Federation of Coffee Growers of
    Colombia advertising campaign,
    206–210, 213
National income, 79
National Science Foundation, 265
National security argument, for trade
    barriers, 33
National Standards for Marketing
    Management, Entrepreneurship, and
    Business Administration, 6
Natural resources, 29
Nazi party, 245
Needs, 105, 156
Negative balance of payments, 245
Negotiations, culture as influence on, 67
Nestlé, 35
Netherlands, The, 234
    European Community (EC) member, 77
    flowering plant imports, 22
    high individualism in, 60
    individualistic culture of, 283
    as low power distance culture, 60, 283
    masculinity measure, 60, 284
    mathematical achievement ranking, 145
    participative management style of, 283
    Royal Philips Electronics, 258
    vote against European constitution, 77
Networked organizations, 292
Newly industrialized (second world)
    countries, 79
New markets
    communication about innovations, 62
    cost of finding, 112

domestic or international decision, 138
    as driver of international marketing, 5
    existing channel of distribution, 182–183
    influences on, 5
    new channel of distribution, 182–183
    opportunities for, 4
    research for identifying, 112
    standardized versus adapted products
        for, 157
    third parties as locators of, 112
    through channels of distribution, 182
    Toyota considerations, 129
New Mexico, Minuteman organization, 100
New products, Toyota's introduction of, 129
News Corporation/Channel V, 205
Newspapers, as advertising medium, 214
New York
    cost-of-living index, 296
    as currency exchange, 236
New Zealand
    corruption score, 93
    as developed (first world) country, 79
    kiwi fruits and trademarks, 194
Nicaragua, 87
Nigeria, 93
Nike, 16, 126, 134
Nissan, market share in North America, 112
No active international marketing strategy
    (commitment level), 14
Nodes, 292
Noise, in communication, 207
Nokia, 112, 157
Nominal GDP, 162
Non-PPP-adjusted GDP per capita, 162
Non-religious belief systems, 55
Non-tariff barriers, 35
Non-verbal communication, 57
North America, 190
North American Free Trade Agreement
    (NAFTA), 38, 108
    defined, 87
    exports of horticultural crops to the U.S.
        and, 22
North Korea, 85, 90
Norway, 113, 179

O

Objections, answering, in sales
    process, 219
Objective-and-task-based budgeting, 209
Ocean-going water transportation, 190
Offshore endeavors, of research and
    development, 34
Ohno, Taiichi, 129 .
Oil, as commodity, 165
Oil embargo of 1973, 35
Olds Motor Vehicle Co., 281
O'Neal, Joseph Reynold (J.R.), 94
1-866-HALT (intellectual property protection
    hotline), 278
One-party dictatorships, 90
One-party state, 90, 91, 119
Online selling. See Internet
OPEC. See Organization of Arab Petroleum
    Exporting Countries (OPEC)
Open-ended questions, 118
Open markets, 12